BEYOND FAST

BEYOND FAST

*How a Renegade Coach and His Unlikely
High School Team Revolutionized Distance Running*

SEAN BROSNAN
with CHRIS LEAR and ANDREW GREIF

ATRIA BOOKS
New York   Amsterdam/Antwerp   London
Toronto   Sydney/Melbourne   New Delhi

An Imprint of Simon & Schuster, LLC
1230 Avenue of the Americas
New York, NY 10020

For more than 100 years, Simon & Schuster has championed authors and the stories they create. By respecting the copyright of an author's intellectual property, you enable Simon & Schuster and the author to continue publishing exceptional books for years to come. We thank you for supporting the author's copyright by purchasing an authorized edition of this book.

No amount of this book may be reproduced or stored in any format, nor may it be uploaded to any website, database, language-learning model, or other repository, retrieval, or artificial intelligence system without express permission. All rights reserved. Inquiries may be directed to Simon & Schuster, 1230 Avenue of the Americas, New York, NY 10020 or permissions@simonandschuster.com.

Copyright © 2025 by Sean Brosnan

All rights reserved, including the right to reproduce this book or portions thereof in any form whatsoever. For information, address Atria Books Subsidiary Rights Department, 1230 Avenue of the Americas, New York, NY 10020.

First Atria Books hardcover edition September 2025

ATRIA BOOKS and colophon are trademarks of Simon & Schuster, LLC

Simon & Schuster strongly believes in freedom of expression and stands against censorship in all its forms. For more information, visit BooksBelong.com.

For information about special discounts for bulk purchases, please contact Simon & Schuster Special Sales at 1-866-506-1949 or business@simonandschuster.com.

The Simon & Schuster Speakers Bureau can bring authors to your live event. For more information or to book an event, contact the Simon & Schuster Speakers Bureau at 1-866-248-3049 or visit our website at www.simonspeakers.com.

Some dialogue has been recreated.

Interior design by Kyoko Watanabe

Manufactured in the United States of America

1 3 5 7 9 10 8 6 4 2

Library of Congress Cataloging-in-Publication Data

ISBN 978-1-6682-0438-2
ISBN 978-1-6682-0440-5 (ebook)

BEYOND FAST

PROLOGUE

ON THE NIGHT BEFORE the national championship our team had been building toward for five years, there was only one thing left to do.

Buy a tent.

It was December 3, 2021. The boys of California's Newbury Park High School cross country squad, the top-ranked high school cross country team in the United States, were eating a carb-loading dinner at an Airbnb in Huntsville, Alabama. The next morning, at a park in the city, was the RunningLane Cross Country Championships. Months earlier, when a meet in Oregon that had long determined the best team of distance runners in the United States had been canceled over COVID-19 concerns, coaches such as me had scrambled to find another race to settle who was the nation's best. The best teams agreed that RunningLane would be this season's new de facto title stage.

The runners, their parents, and I arrived in Huntsville two days before the race, and since we'd left Newbury Park, our Los Angeles suburb, I'd gone through a mental checklist to make sure we had everything we'd need on race day.

We had experience.

This national meet would not be our first.

We had speed.

Any one of our top four runners—senior Colin Sahlman, who had a laid-back surfer personality and an explosive closing kick; his younger brother Aaron, a junior with huge potential but inconsistent; and twin juniors Lex and Leo Young, the younger brothers of a national champion, who had become stars on and off the track because of their speed and social media presence—could have been the best runner on any other team in the country.

We had the attention of the running world.

Our state titles, national records, and unprecedented times had been written about by every track and field magazine and website. Our accomplishments were celebrated and argued over. Judging by what you read in online running forums, I was either the greatest or worst thing to happen to high school running. Our runners' social media accounts were followed by thousands because our runners ran times so fast that they changed expectations for how fast teenagers could be. Only a few weeks earlier, in November, while running in the most competitive division in the most competitive state in the country, we had achieved statistical perfection. Even people who had no idea about running were taking notice.

I went down my checklist again. We had everything we needed—with one exception. And so, as the boys ate dinner at the house with their parents, I left with my wife, Tanya, to shop for a pair of pop-up tents.

When Newbury Park's cross country teams showed up to meets during my first year at the school, in 2016, we might as well have been anonymous. And for good reason. Five decades after our school opened its doors just off Highway 101 northwest of LA, it had produced almost zero success in distance running.

Over the next five years, things changed. A lot.

When our runners arrived at meets, fans mobbed them for selfies. Even their competitors asked them for autographs—before races. The need for a tent, then, was partly practical. Our athletes not only needed a dry place to store their gear but also a space in which to retreat and focus before the starting gun, away from the autograph- and selfie-seekers and the spotlight their success had created.

But never before had we faced the kind of attention we would the next morning, December 4, in Huntsville's John Hunt Park.

The day before, the boys began the warm-up that was our custom before every race. We started with the rope-assisted stretching I'd learned from my unorthodox journey observing top coaches. Then the boys ran the course—the first mile very slowly, the second mile a little faster, and the last mile not at true race pace, but at a good tempo. They finished drills to practice running form, then ran 800-meter strides, their legs turning over with the speed they would need to burst off the starting line and beat hundreds of other runners to the front of the pack.

Conditions were perfect—blue skies, temperatures approaching the seventies, the brown grass under our feet feeling firm and fast. I ran half of the 5,000-meter, or 3.1-mile, course with them and they did the rest. When the season began earlier in the fall, I thought our top five runners could average a time of 14 minutes, 30 seconds, a pace of 4:40 per mile. But as the season went on and Newbury Park broke records left and right, I realized that wasn't fast enough. In the history of high school cross country, the 5K record was 14:10. It had stood for twenty years. If things played out like I believed they could, I thought our top four could all break that national record, and the times of our top five could average under 14:20. Our strategy had two parts, because we weren't only racing the other hundreds of runners in the race but the runners whose records were still on the books from decades earlier. I wanted our team to run the first mile in 4:30 and keep pushing in the second mile to drop as many competitors as possible. Then they needed to go all out over the last mile to chase down records.

Over the years, I have been asked many times about the secrets behind Newbury Park's success, how we'd gone from being just another high school team to pulling off accomplishments no other school had. Running fast is not just about knowing when to program a workout of seven repeats of one kilometer. Anyone can figure out how to schedule an easy day, a long run, and an interval. But no one believed they could run fast quite like Newbury Park's runners. This success wasn't just the result of two fast families, as many coaches and critics claimed. Our speed went deep down the roster because, slowly but eventually, our runners had bought into the philosophy that our fastest could always be fast*er*. It wouldn't have happened without the right environment. During our months of training, that meant creating an atmosphere around our team in which we believed anything was possible. So it didn't matter what was being said about us by outside voices, because inside our literal and figurative tent, we believed.

It was why one of the first things I did that Friday morning, one day before the RunningLane championships, was stake out a good location within John Hunt Park for our tent. This was a relatively new meet and didn't have an area roped off for competitors only; if we wanted to pull off the kind of performance I thought we could, we would need our own space, where the boys could focus beforehand, away from distractions.

At a big-box store in town, Tanya and I found a pair of tents that were each eight by ten feet. We'd push them together the next morning to create a mini-compound. The tents were brown, not the black and gold that everyone had come to know Newbury Park by. But the tents had what was most important to me—zippered-on walls that would keep our biggest fans, biggest critics, and selfie-seekers out. We didn't need anyone from the outside interrupting plans that were years in the making.

I knew something big was going to happen on race day. We'd gotten this far because of the extreme belief that we could always run faster—and harder. Why stop now? The question wasn't whether we could win a national championship. It was whether we could do something no one had ever seen.

CHAPTER ONE

MY MIND WAS RUNNING.

I had always been a better daydreamer than a student. It wasn't because I was incapable, more that I was uninterested. Books had never held my attention like thoughts of riding my bike. As early as elementary school, I would stare out classroom windows thinking about where I would ride that afternoon, how fast I would go. Things hadn't changed much as my junior year of high school began. The kid who didn't know what was going on when the teacher called on him? That was me, a lot of times.

For as long as I can remember, I've been a racer, whether against someone or toward something. This was passed down. I grew up hearing about my uncles who ran in college and watching my dad and my mom's father coach my older brother into becoming a good runner while I waited for my turn to join the local youth team. Some kids are pushed into a sport, but I rushed into it by myself. When I was five, I begged my parents to let me run a 5K in my hometown, on New York's Long Island. For some reason they agreed to let a child not yet in kindergarten run 3.1 miles. I must have been persuasive.

Lacrosse, soccer, and baseball seasons came and went, but running brought out a different level of passion from me. When my family watched TV specials about the Olympics, the stories that caught my attention were about gymnasts who had given up their childhood to travel away from home and train in grueling conditions to make the Olympics. It's not like I took it that far. I wasn't ready to give up days at Jones Beach, passing the water tower on the way to the sand. But the stories planted an idea. I wanted to become the best at something. What would it take to realize my true potential? How much could I withstand to reach it? Questions like that were always on my mind, even at school.

I ran and I ran. But as I got a little older, it became clear that running wasn't seen as the cool sport. Not like BMX, anyway, with its helmets and gear and ability to reach even faster speeds. When I was nine, I took all of the energy I'd put into running and moved to racing bikes. I did it the only way I knew how: full throttle.

I would get to the top because I always thought that if I could do more than everybody else, I would be better—that I would be the best. BMX bikes are powered by a rider, not an engine, but I saw myself as that engine, each day on my bike a chance to fine-tune something. I set my alarm for 5:00 a.m. to practice sprints and gate starts before class. Being a bad student didn't matter to me, not when there seemed to be a life ahead of me as a professional BMX racer.

That's why I was staring out those windows. A few weeks into my junior year, I got my chance to prove it.

The National Bicycle League held its 1993 Grand Nationals in Memphis, Tennessee. It was essentially the national championships of the sport. My parents couldn't come, not with my mom, Patricia, running her own real-estate firm and my dad, Bill, working as a Nassau County homicide detective, so I traveled with friends from the circuit and sponsors to race in my age division, 16-expert. Each round started with the racers perched atop a platform in the track's center, a metal gate propped in front of the front wheels of about eight racers. Only four would advance to the next round. When the gate fell, the race was on. We leaned over our handlebars as we exploded down a ramp, over a small hill, up a bigger one, then into a banked right turn. The course bent back on itself, with more hills sending us and our bikes flying, and banked corners allowing riders to maintain speed through the turns. Each round lasted only 40 seconds.

After finishing fourth in my semifinal, the last guy to make the final, I found a pay phone and dug out my calling card. I dialed my mom to tell her my news. Then I called my dad. I don't know if either of them heard it in my voice, but the realization that I was among the final eight racers in one of the toughest divisions at Grand Nationals left me with a deep sense of pride. My school daydreams had become reality. Maybe racing bikes around a half-empty arena in Memphis didn't look like it, but setting a huge goal and reaching it felt like my Olympic moment. I wanted to chase that feeling.

The 16-expert championship final was next.

Bright white helmet. Neon-yellow shirt. I was easy to spot in the middle of the starting line. We were about to find out who was the best in the country in my age group. Four seconds in, I knew it wouldn't be me.

The closest rider on my left had gone out fast to the front through the first rise. Then he started wobbling. He crashed in the opening straightaway, right in the path of me and a few others. I'd worked seven years to get here, and I was already done. I got up and kept going but finished seventh.

When I got home to New York, something in the back of my head just knew that I'd probably competed in my last big BMX race. Setting a huge goal and reaching it again and again felt addictive, and setting a hard training regimen felt like the only test I wanted to ace. The more I thought about it, the more it felt right to chase that feeling in my first love, running.

The idea had actually come to me a year earlier, as a sophomore. Injuries are part of BMX racing, but breaking an arm twice in the same year frustrated me, put my arm in a full cast, and kept me off my bike. When my cast was cut down to cover just my forearm, I went out for MacArthur High School's indoor track team to stay in shape for BMX riding. Just for fun, I entered the mile and within a few months I was running in the 4:40s and competing in the county championships. The season ended, my cast came off, and I went back to dreaming about Grand Nationals.

But change was coming.

I had always lived in Wantagh, near Long Island's southern shore. Before my junior year of high school my mom, whom I lived with after my parents divorced when I was in grade school, bought a house in a different area of town that was part of a different school district. That meant I was going to a new school. Luckily, I recognized a few faces there. A few people I'd run with on the area's youth track team also ran for the Wantagh High cross country team. As a kid, I enjoyed running long distances on the track or on the roads. I'd never run cross country, though, where packs of runners fought for position on courses from 3 to 3.1 miles (or 5 kilometers), which often wound through parks or golf courses. That total inexperience, combined with it already being late September when I returned from Grand Nationals, well after the high school season started, made me question my new classmates' invitation to me to join Wantagh's cross country team. But they were persuasive, and it was good to be around people I knew.

I joined the team carrying zero expectations.

By my second race, I was the fastest runner on the boys varsity team. By season's end, I qualified individually for the New York State high school championships. To be perfectly honest, I was surprised I did so well with no real training, and the speed with which I found success brought back the tug I'd felt as a kid. I still wasn't dedicated to academics, but I was all in on exploring how good I could be as a runner.

Indoor track is a big deal in New York, as in most cold-weather states, and at Wantagh, I took it far more seriously than I had at

MacArthur. Outdoor tracks are a 400-meter oval, while most indoor tracks are half that size, meaning a mile indoors is usually eight laps. But the track at my first indoor county championship for Wantagh was ridiculous: eleven and a half laps of constant turning on a hard rubber-mat surface. I missed advancing to the state meet by one spot. It crushed me. I skipped school the next day, playing the race over and over in my head, searching for my mistake.

That spring, I didn't need coaxing from my teammates to go out for outdoor track. My weekly running mileage rose. I was even monitoring how much sleep I was getting every night. Running the 2 mile in the 9:30s qualified me for the New York State meet in the 3,200 meters, which is just short of two miles. At the state meet I also represented my county by running a 1,200-meter leg on the distance-medley relay.

When I didn't place high enough to earn all-state recognition, a familiar cycle resumed. I felt crushed by disappointment, then poured my energy into figuring out how to change things. Twin Lakes Preserve was my local park, and in the summer before my senior year its four-mile dirt-trail loop became my proving ground, as I developed my mental and physical endurance. A group of local college stars including the St. John's University foursome of Brian Quinn, John Honerkamp, Chris Graff, and Chris Fogarazzo, and Iona's Dave Frazer trained there; I hung on for dear life during our weekly fartlek workouts, where we alternated between faster and slower paces. Being able to stick with them on those summer runs increased my strength and confidence in tandem. Afterward, we'd shoot the shit at a pizza joint in Bellmore and roll our eyes every time Dave would play "Brandy" on the jukebox. I was in heaven. Running was no longer just a passion; I was becoming a Runner.

Riding my bike had been at the core of all of my imagined future plans, but the longer I was in it, the more the sport and its lifestyle no longer felt like a perfect match. I'd built my life around it, but I wasn't sure how to build a future within it. BMX wasn't an Olympic sport, and it was hard to figure out the blueprint for how to go from being a good amateur rider to a professional. Riding BMX was the first time I'd trained with real discipline in a sport, but I also often believed that blinders-on focus made me an outlier. Running fascinated me because you could be part of an amazing team, but success still came down to the individual. The uniqueness of training could be the difference between being great or simply good. I still daydreamed, but now it was about training. What made you fast? Why did coaches call for certain workouts? I knew just whom to ask.

Nobody was more excited about my return to running than my grandfather, who lived only a five-minute drive away. I was a seeker of information without a driver's license, and he possessed both. He took me to all the big meets—the Millrose Games in Madison Square Garden, and meets at Mitchel Field on Long Island and on Randalls Island—and made me pay attention to the small details, like what the ease of a runner's stride, or the way they carried their arms, could tell you about their potential.

And what about my own? My grandfather went to great lengths to help me find out. Once, years later when I was in college, a snowstorm on Long Island a few days before Christmas closed all the tracks and kept me on a treadmill. That wasn't good enough for my grandfather. We looked at forecasts and figured out the closest place where there was no snow—Virginia. We drove to Virginia Beach and did the workout. In high school, we didn't need to go quite that far. He believed soft surfaces limited the pounding on my legs, so he'd drive me to local tracks, or routes at Bethpage State Park, with miles of crisscrossing dirt trails. After my workout, he'd pick a restaurant. Nothing fancy—often Italian, because this was Long Island. Around the table, we talked training for hours. Movies like *Rudy* had made me wonder, "If I train right, can I really do this—do work and effort really outweigh talent?" It doesn't always, but if you put them together, it's magic. I had the effort. My talent was unclear. So we would spend hours discussing the final variable: the work. He wanted me to understand that everything about training was individualized and should be placed in a bigger context. That there was more than one way to reach a goal. That there was always room to fine-tune the plan, to get better.

Sometimes, his lessons seemed paradoxical: "In order to move forward, you're going to have to move back," he'd caution.

A runner's 4:15 mile might be more impressive than their previous 4:10 because they closed with a stronger, faster final 400 meters. Did it matter more if a runner's fastest race for a season was 4:20, or that their workouts put them in the 4:10 range but they couldn't find the right race to put it all together? My grandfather would draw graphs and explain the why behind a workout. Since I'd gotten back into running, I was all in. Qualifying for the state track meet as a junior, in my first year of taking the sport seriously, left me hungry for more improvement—and impatient for it, too. My grandfather sensed that and told me to keep a big-picture perspective: There would be peaks and valleys on the path to success.

Oddly enough, the lesson that resonated most had nothing to do with running. One of my uncles had become successful as a stockbroker in New York, and my grandfather thought I should get into business and the stock market, too. It wasn't my thing. But his larger point still stood: He didn't like self-limiting talk.

"The only reason you're not going to be a successful stockbroker, the only reason you're not going to be successful in whatever you do, is because you tell yourself that," he said.

Soon, I had even more time to think about running.

Because I couldn't run.

A few weeks into my senior year, just as my first full season of cross country was beginning, it was over. I was messing around with my friends playing football in PE when I jumped to catch a pass and heard a pop when I landed. Within a couple of hours, my knee ballooned and I could barely walk. I thought I'd dislocated it. After pleading with the school nurse for me to go home, and making a panicked phone call to my mom, I got the diagnosis from a doctor: a torn ACL. I didn't have great grades to show colleges, great times to show college coaches, nor much time in the year to produce faster ones. This wasn't the 1970s, when a torn ligament in your knee meant the death knell for an athlete's career, but undergoing surgery in November still meant that being healthy enough to run my final season of outdoor track in the spring wasn't guaranteed. What was that my grandfather had said about limits?

The silver lining was that because I'd injured myself on school grounds, the district paid for teachers to come to my house, and I finished classes halfway through the day. With my afternoons free, I drove a half hour to an indoor pool, where I'd swim for two or three hours, a high school kid sharing lanes with retirees. Days not in the pool were spent working out on a handbike. I read *Track & Field News* cover to cover, memorizing the top runners from all the eras, obsessing over Roger Bannister and the day in May 1954 when he became the first to run a sub-four-minute mile.

I was so determined to cross-train my way back that I'd convinced myself there was no way I wasn't going to run fast again before I graduated. It was easy to be negative about other aspects of my life, but when it came to my recovery, and running, I didn't want any negative thoughts, any seed of doubt. *Don't tell me it's not possible.*

I was back running by April. A few weeks later, I ran 4:18 to finish fifth in the mile at the state meet, high enough to earn the all-state recognition I had long sought.

In June of 1995, a few weeks after graduation, I was back at a national championship. But this wasn't Memphis, and this wasn't on a bike. The National Scholastic Track and Field Championships were on the campus of North Carolina State University, and the boys mile drew runners from Junction City, Oregon, to Duluth, Minnesota, to Long Island. Only ten months after tearing my ACL and thinking my world was over, I finished twelfth in 4:23.84. In the previous two years, I'd proven I had some natural talent, and I loved pushing myself in training. But while talking with the legendary coach of my dream school, I realized there was still so much to learn.

A few coaches from local colleges had called to recruit me, but I wanted to hear from the University of Arkansas. By my senior year, Arkansas had won eight national championships in cross country, four in outdoor track, and eleven consecutive indoor national titles under its coach, John McDonnell. Because I'd started late and gotten hurt, I, of course, had a paper-thin résumé. They weren't going to call me. So I called the Arkansas athletic department and was transferred to McDonnell's answering machine. I was shocked when the legendary coach returned my call. I told him my mile and 2-mile times, but he wanted answers to questions that none of the other coaches had asked.

"How fast do you run the 400 meters?" McDonnell asked. "What kind of tempo work do you do?"

I didn't know what a "tempo" was. Wantagh High practices consisted of either speed workouts or easy days, and I didn't know any better. McDonnell's questions intrigued me. Arkansas's titles were proof he knew the secret to speed. I needed to know how coaching could unlock my own. I had a million questions. I never wanted to be without an answer again.

CHAPTER TWO

I WOKE UP IN my Nissan Maxima.

It was the summer of 1997, and my road trip from California to see an old running buddy in Raleigh, North Carolina, had hit the trip's literal high point, seven thousand feet above sea level in Flagstaff, Arizona.

My arrival there wasn't by mistake. Endurance athletes had figured out that training at high elevation could help them run stronger, for longer, because the body adapted to become more efficient at delivering oxygen as less of it became available. It was my first time in "Flag," as the locals called it, but not my first time training at altitude.

McDonnell's questions during our brief call taught me that there was more to identifying and uncovering talent than looking at the basics of race times and personal bests. That was the most I would learn from him, though, because Arkansas wasn't in my plans. I'd scrambled during my senior year of high school and found tiny Brevard College, which was tucked two thousand feet up in North Carolina's Blue Ridge Mountains. The most notable moment of my one year there came after a run, when I was icing my legs in the creek that ran through campus and looked down to see a copperhead snake in the water, swimming between my legs. I froze in fear.

My development as a runner seemed frozen in place at year end as well. I fell prey to a mistake many young collegiate runners make. In an effort to prove to myself that I could train with the best, I dramatically increased my mileage while simultaneously ratcheting up the intensity of my runs. The trial by fire proved too hot, and a cycle of injury and frustration culminated with a stress fracture in my right tibia. In need of a change of scenery, I looked West.

I had always envisioned moving out West and figured California's palm trees and beaches would offer a great training environment. I landed in Pasadena. There, I connected with Jesse Gomez, the coach at Pasadena City College, and spent the year taking classes at the college while running with the guys on the school's team. By spring my stress fractures had healed and I was able to run some respectable times on the track. Being healthy and fit rekindled my desire to run for a top program; I did extensive research and took a few recruiting trips that summer, and decided to pack my bags for Adams State College.

You had to be a running junkie to know Adams State. Mentions of it kept popping up in the lists of national champions I devoured in *Harrier* magazine, and through articles I found while looking at microfilm at my local Long Island library. Its campus was in Alamosa, Colorado, on a dusty plain in the remote foothills of the Rockies, at seventy-five hundred feet. In cross country, the winning team is the one that produces the lowest score. A cross country team has seven runners, with the top five finishers scoring points that correspond to their place, and the sixth and seventh runners not scored, but able to displace other teams. In 1992, under Coach Joe Vigil, Adams's five scoring runners finished 1-2-3-4-5 at the NCAA Division II national championships, the only team in NCAA history to achieve a mathematically perfect score of 15.

It was a monumental achievement, the kind that stuck in the memory of a young running junkie like me.

Vigil had retired and was succeeded by Damon Martin by the time I showed up on the mesa in Alamosa in 1997. Martin would become every bit as successful as Vigil, winning thirty-nine NCAA national championships in cross country and track and field, but even as a newer coach, he made us feel unbeatable.

Martin had a gift that was more than his grasp of the sport's technical side, a way of tapping into and heightening his team's emotions in a way that was uncanny. Before workouts, my teammates and I would gather in a classroom in the school's athletic building. Martin stood in front of us, his excitement rising, his delivery so powerful it was unlike that of anyone else I'd met.

"I want to rewrite the record books!" he said, and we left his meetings for hard 1,000-meter or one-mile repeats at Cole Park thinking, *Why not?*

The talks charged the atmosphere around practice and meets. We always showed up in the right mindset because of it. We wanted to break the world record for him, and we would leave no stone unturned in pursuit of that next personal best.

It was why on my cross country road trip I pulled off Interstate 40 to explore the runner's mecca of Flagstaff. I understood why it had that reputation after spending a few days running through stands of pine trees on soft dirt trails that my grandfather would have approved of. The scenery was amazing, but I couldn't stay long. I pushed on. Near Lawrence, Kansas, I checked into a motel because it had two amenities that appealed to me. The nightly rate was cheap, and behind the motel was a flat dirt road that stretched for miles. In other words, it was perfect.

In running circles, I had heard humidity called the poor man's altitude. Inspired by reading about the harsh conditions elite Kenyan runners trained in, and determined to build my toughness, I set out in the midday heat, running five miles out on that road and five miles back. I broke the mileage up into slow, easy paces, fartleks that alternated between intervals of fast and slow, and miles at my aerobic threshold. This was before GPS watches; I measured the route using my car's odometer, marking each mile with rocks, and when I ran past each marker, I'd click the Timex stopwatch that I had palmed. At the time, full of early-twenties hubris, bringing water on my runs was an afterthought. This was, in hindsight, dumb. It was kind of like another time when I convinced myself that I should run nothing but hills. I left Kansas after a miserable week, still headed east to North Carolina, showering at truck stops and public pools along the way.

The itinerary of that summer trip was a lot like mine in my twenties and thirties. I didn't stay in one place for long. But if it looked aimless to some, I didn't care, because I was doing it my way. Some stops were memorable, others were terrible. But in their own way, each pulled me closer to running, and toward an answer to the question that had brought me to Flagstaff in the first place. How do we run faster?

After my second year at Adams, I went home for summer break and found my BMX bike in the garage. Riding again felt good. I took the bike out to a trail on the eastern end of Long Island. Speeding up before a jump, my foot slipped off a pedal and my heel slammed into the ground. Before long, my knee had swelled up.

Another torn ACL.

Schoolwork alone wasn't enough of a reason to stick around campus, so I set off to work.

Without a plan for my future, I spent the rest of my twenties in the corporate world, not the running world. Running was still a passion of mine, though. I remained a student of the sport, reading books like *Daniels' Running Formula* by legendary Cortland State coach and exercise physiologist Jack Daniels; in later years, we corresponded by email, as I quizzed him on his coaching methods. I stayed fit, running in local track meets and road races throughout California, but I wasn't doing it with purpose. With my connections to biking, I'd gotten a job with Fox Racing, in Morgan Hill, California, just south of the Bay Area. Sales wasn't something I enjoyed, but I moved up quickly because finding success in that field was no different from how I approached improvement in running. *How am I going to sell more stuff?* I resolved to make more phone calls than anyone else, to visit everyone on my list five times more often than the regular sales guy.

My experience compensating for poor schoolwork had taught me how to work with different personalities and make people believe in what I was saying. But at my desk, managing my accounts, constantly overhearing coworkers gossiping, talking about random things—it was grinding me down. It felt like the biggest excitement was when the food truck pulled up outside the office at lunchtime. This was the opposite of the electric atmosphere I'd encountered while training at Adams, where the coaching had opened up my sense of what was possible, and where ambition was rewarded.

I hate my life. I don't want my life to be this.

Within a few months, I'd earned a promotion from inside sales to outside sales. But I didn't aspire to be a sales manager or a district manager. That wasn't going to make me happy. I wanted to be back outside; I needed to be back around running and coaching.

By 2007, eight years after my last official college race at Adams, I was running for a team again, at Concordia University in Irvine, California, which competed at college sports' NAIA level. Long before the COVID-era rules that extended eligibility to graduates who had missed out on a season of their sport, I was the original Super Senior.

I had some success, earning indoor all-American honors, but by the next year I had already moved on, an hour south along the Southern California coast.

At Cal State San Marcos, I used my last bit of college eligibility to run one season of cross country. But that wasn't what drew me there. It was that I could do it while training under the program's coach, Steve Scott. He was one of the milers whose name and times I'd memorized in high school reading *Track & Field News* and then his book, *The Miler*. He'd run under four minutes in the mile 136 times, more than anyone else in history. In his 1980s heyday, he seemed to do everything fast—even setting a record by playing eighteen holes of golf in 29 minutes. By the time I got to campus in late 2007, his US record in the mile of 3:47.69 had finally been taken down by Alan Webb—but only after standing for twenty-five years, an eternity in track and field. Steve had reached the pinnacle by being a training machine, yet he seemed wary of pushing his athletes as he'd pushed himself.

"I can't give you this workout because I did that," he told me once. "And there's no way."

To be fair, we were at the NAIA level, far from the top college ranks of NCAA Division I. And there truly was no way I could handle such a workout because I'd shown up to San Marcos coming off yet another injury, a stress reaction that kept me stuck on an elliptical, unable to run consistently for the previous seven months, since the indoor season the previous winter at Concordia. Yet by the end of the fall cross country season at San Marcos, I was an all-American.

That's when my apprenticeship under the great miler really began.

The mile is an unusually difficult event because it demands speed, strength, and endurance. To be world-class, you can't be good at only one of them, but need all three. Steve created mile-specific workouts to simulate its demands: 800 meters, followed by a one-minute rest, then a 400, another one-minute rest, capped with a final 400. After a full rest, up to about ten minutes, the circuit started over. In all, Steve liked to do the 800-400-400 three times and average our splits together to come up with what Steve believed was an indicator of a runner's true mile potential.

But to reach my potential meant finding my limits, and Steve knew how to push me past them. Boy, did he ever. I'll never forget one day at the track. We ran a four-mile tempo around a 5:05 pace, then a five-minute rest, followed by a mile in 4:20, and after five minutes' rest, another mile in 4:17. After another five-minute rest, I ran an 800 in 2:04, and after a final five-minute rest, a sub-60-second 400. The volume destroyed my legs; I wanted to toss my watch in frustration the next day when I was so sore that I could barely move on my usual eight-mile run. As exhausted as I was, workouts like that changed my perception of what I was capable of running. The next time I raced, when I hit that moment you always do when you question whether you can keep the pace, I believed.

My goal was to tap into Steve's knowledge and experience to translate something, *anything*, that had worked for him into my own running. After all, only Steve knew what "fast" like a 3:47 mile felt like. I would track down his old races on YouTube and ask him to narrate what was happening on the track and in his memory. He told me about winning the silver medal at the world championships in 1983 and even let me hold his medal. He told me about finishing 10th at the 1984 Olympics and fifth at the 1988 Olympics in the 1,500 meters, and the disappointment that lingered. He told me that the miler who leads the first lap never wins.

"The mile is won in the last 150 meters," he said. "I promise you."

His insights were unbelievable.

My own improvement, meanwhile, was not.

My times in the 1,500-meter had hit a plateau.

"I don't know what's going on," I told Steve one day. He didn't know what to tell me. That was a lesson, too. If an athlete has a bad or confusing performance, one of the best things you can tell them to sustain their belief and confidence is that it's not their fault, and that you, as the coach, are going to figure it out. Even if, in the moment, you don't know how.

I was trying to figure out how to stay in running as a postcollegiate athlete. At the 2007 US Cross Country Championships in San Diego, mutual friends introduced me to Scott Simmons, the coach at Queens University, a Division II school in Charlotte, North Carolina. He found my number a few days later and invited me to join his staff as a volunteer assistant. I packed my few belongings into my car and started another road trip East. Scott's offer intrigued me because he had created success at a school with little history of it while also coaching successful pros. I felt a kinship with this obsessiveness in the search for getting faster. I wanted to learn from his blueprint.

Quickly, it became obvious Scott wasn't afraid to do things differently. During muggy Charlotte days, he'd show up to practice and hand athletes gloves he'd outfitted with slots to hold packs of ice in the palm, because he'd read that cooling the periphery of the body could cool down the whole body. His athletes had their blood tested regularly, which was my introduction to learning the importance of levels of hemoglobin, iron, and ferritin. He rented motor homes and drove the team into the Appalachians to run at Beech Mountain—at about fifty-five hundred feet, one of the highest points along the Eastern Seaboard—because he wanted to learn about the short-term effect of training at elevation. He chafed at the widely accepted notion of what "base" offseason training looked like. Many coaches believed a runner's foundation is built on their loading up with heavy mileage before the season starts. Not Scott; he didn't believe in a high volume of mediocre work, focusing instead on speed, year-round. He noticed how some athletes ran their best in the middle of the season while still training their hardest, not at the end, as their workload decreased, and it made him rethink how to taper. I hadn't put the pieces together like that before, but when I saw his methods, they made sense.

We didn't always agree on workouts, which I sometimes thought could be too punishing or too predictable, but I always recognized the underlying logic. "Running is learning to run with pain," he'd say, and that meant designing frequent points in training to simulate a race effort. That's how I learned the concept of the "hammer" workout, such as ten 400-meter repeats at 59 seconds each with one minute of rest in between, but with a couple of "hammer" repetitions at faster speeds, around 53 or 54 seconds, in the middle.

After being around Simmons for a while, I was out for a run with some of the Queens athletes when I realized I'd been thinking only about the athletes I was with and their training. This had never before been the case, my thoughts always centering on how I felt, or how I was training. It was a bolt-of-lightning realization—that my own running had become secondary to that of the athletes I was working with; maybe, I thought, coaching would be my calling.

A great coach once told me that a lot of coaches in the NCAA are monkey see, monkey do. Scott's methods challenged that. I wanted to be different, too, and when I found athletes who bought into how I saw coaching, who were willing to go beyond their preconceived notion of their limits, it hooked me even more.

Once, during a goal-setting session at Queens, a male runner who ran about 15 minutes in the 5K said he wanted to run 14:10. We left the meeting for practice, and I overheard him bragging. I thought to myself that this guy was in love with the goal but didn't understand the commitment needed to achieve it. Meanwhile, we had another guy, Michael Crouch, who had about the same level of success and told us his goal was to run 14 flat. The difference was Crouch didn't just talk a big game, he had a vision and a plan to make it happen.

A few years later, in 2009, I was at Stanford University standing along a fence before a 5,000-meter race when Michael ran up to me with a wild look in his eyes. He told me he was prepared to hurt as much as he possibly could.

"I'm going to run harder than anyone else out there," he said. "I don't care."

This kid's going to do something crazy, I thought. And he did.

That night, Crouch ran 13:40.89. By the time he graduated from Queens, he'd won multiple national championships and broken school records. You can't run sub-14 if your body isn't physically able to handle that speed. But your body won't do that without the mind also believing that it can.

That race single-handedly changed the way I thought about coaching. Being willing to push beyond my competitors, beyond even what I thought was possible, had been second nature to me since I was a kid racing 5K's and getting up early to train gate starts on my bike. But that wasn't enough if I couldn't get athletes to be all in, too. Michael was the blueprint for what was possible with the right mindset, plan, and commitment. It was why when I left Queens in 2010, it wasn't important for me to hear about athletes' goals, but how much they would sacrifice to reach them.

Trying to extend my running career had taken me all over, but also not very far. After Charlotte, I moved to Eugene, Oregon, which called itself TrackTown, USA. In the 1960s, Eugene had been the center of the American jogging boom, thanks to the University of Oregon coach Bill Bowerman, whose search for running knowledge had taken him to New Zealand, among other places. A statue of Bowerman stood near the 100-meter starting line of Hayward Field, the university's iconic stadium, which by 2010 had again become the nexus of the sport. It felt as if everyone who wanted to be great in the United States was moving to Eugene, trying to run for the Oregon Track Club Elite. You could spot pros running at Hayward or on the city's bark trails, named after legendary distance runner Steve Prefontaine. There was an aura about the club, and I wanted to get close. I lived with only what I could pack into my car and found myself there around current and future Olympians.

I was trying to work up the ranks, and Andy Downin, a former pro runner who coached a small group in Eugene, allowed me to join them as I continued to chase a sub-four-minute mile. We quickly butted heads over training philosophies. I never felt as fit as I could be, and expressed that to him. He told me he couldn't coach me without my buy-in to what he was doing. He wasn't wrong.

Without a training group to focus my attention on, I started testing out my training theories on myself, which untethered me from Eugene. When an opportunity came to train with a small group of established pro middle-distance runners in Lafayette, California, just outside the Bay Area, I moved south. But I couldn't break through that line separating a fast amateur from a true professional.

I'd had success. I'd been an all-American in college at the NAIA level, and in the years since I'd left Cal State San Marcos, my fastest mile had dropped to 4:02. My sales background came in handy while building connections within the professional world, and relationships with agents and organizers helped me talk my way into races like the Fifth Avenue Mile in New York. But I didn't see it reflected in my race times—and it was because I was a bad athlete to coach. I was the example of how to screw it up. Every one of my coaches would probably tell you that I believed I needed a perfect day to perform my best. When inevitably the perfect situation didn't arrive, I'd get impatient. Instead of listening to my coaches, I questioned their philosophies and workouts. I didn't at the time realize that there is no such thing as the perfect day, that mental toughness means understanding you can—no, you *had* to—perform even when conditions weren't ideal.

It took me years to realize how much I'd learned from Downin without realizing it, and that his style would actually have made sense had I not been so hotheaded and in a hurry for results.

Instead of sitting back in a pack to conserve energy and trusting my training, I'd make rash race plans. At the 2010 Brussels Grand Prix, held in Belgium every summer, I went into the 1,500 meters so frustrated by my stalled progress that I had only one thought: *I'm gonna take the lead two laps in and not let anyone pass me the rest of the way.* Sure, it worked that day, when I ran 3:46.68 to win, but the strategy wasn't sustainable. Neither was my training. To figure out how much my body could handle, I'd do workouts that would make no sense, like running 200s at faster-than-race pace with 60 seconds of rest, as many as I could complete. It wasn't exactly a smart workout, but I wanted to understand how it felt to get a headache brought on by an extreme buildup of lactic acid.

By my early thirties, I was running 3:44 for 1,500 meters, which translated to close to a four-minute mile, a lifetime best. Yet I'd accepted that I was never going to make a living as a runner. The sting was softened by the epiphany I'd had a few years earlier in Charlotte while running at Queens, when I realized I wanted to coach. But how could I draw insights from top coaches without being a top athlete myself? What if I made a documentary? I envisioned calling it *Track Shack*. In my head, I would bring a camera and follow training groups in North Carolina, Colorado, Oregon, or California.

I didn't have the credentials for a top program to hire me as a coach. But my stops to this point had shown me there were other ways of creating an opportunity.

CHAPTER THREE

THE TRACK ON THE campus of Nike's headquarters in Beaverton, Oregon, is a red oval set inside what looks like the middle of a forest. In 2011, it was the home of two of the country's most successful distance-running groups: Oregon Project and the Bowerman Track Club.

I'd moved from the Bay Area to Portland because the clubs there were producing some of the world's fastest runners. The Oregon Project was coached by Alberto Salazar, who in the 1980s had broken US records on the roads and the track. When their Olympic-medal-caliber athletes, such as Galen Rupp, Mo Farah, and Kara Goucher, showed up to meets, they had a noticeable presence; runners would stop and stare at their sleek warm-ups and logo, which was a mixture of a skull and a laurel wreath.

Meeting Bob Williams, a former University of Oregon runner and Oregon Project assistant, was an early break. He agreed to coach me a little, showing me things that I immediately made part of my routine, like a warm-up that used ropes to stretch. Bob introduced me to Kenny Moore, an Olympic marathoner in 1968 and 1972 who'd become one of the best writers about the sport. Most important, Bob took me to train at Nike's track. And by email, Bob also introduced me to Salazar.

I'd always had this strong belief that I could manifest my crazy idea of learning from the sport's best coaches into reality; in a weird way, I always had confidence it would work out. And with my permission to use Nike's track, I began doing what I'd always done: hang around, work out, meet new people, and become a sponge. I wasn't there every day, and when I was, I tried to stay out of the way of the elite training groups. But I made a point of being around, nonetheless, sometimes to watch the workouts of my girlfriend, Tanya. We'd met at a cross country meet when I was at San Marcos and she was already an NCAA Division II all-American for Cal State San Bernardino. With her last bit of collegiate eligibility, she went to Queens when I joined the coaching staff and won a pair of 10,000-meter NCAA championships. Between her training and my own, it gave me opportunities to be at the Nike track.

My running credentials weren't impressive enough that Alberto was obligated to give me even a second glance. But one day, after I was done cooling down, Alberto showed up and was talking about *The Fighter*, a new Mark Wahlberg movie. I'd seen it, and we struck up a conversation. We just got along. When I'd see him on campus, he'd say, "Hey, Sean." It happened enough that I asked if we could meet. I had so many questions: Why did Oregon Project athletes do so many drills to work on form? Why did they use an oxygen tent to mimic altitude, as opposed to simply spending a few weeks at altitude? Alberto kept a measuring wheel in his car to make sure a workout course was always dead-on to the meter. He was obsessive about details. I took note.

Alberto had this noticeable presence when he walked on a track. Maybe it was because his athletes knew how hard he'd been willing to push himself, often racing himself to collapse in the 1980s. I'd been to some college workouts where it was immediately apparent that I couldn't run fast there, even if you paid me a million dollars right then. But in Oregon's rainy air, there was electricity. Athletes crushed workouts that seemed impossible at the start, only for the incredibly fast times to become their new, accepted reality as they happened over and over.

Alberto said to me once that for Farah to win a 10K, he had to run the final lap in 52 seconds, at least. Alberto was teaching me the idea of learning how to reverse engineer a race; all of Farah's training pointed toward allowing him to close with a devastating kick. Everyone who exercises creates lactate, and at an easy pace the body recycles that lactate into new energy. But at a certain point when the intensity increases, the body creates more lactate than it can reuse, and the lactic acid builds up in muscles. That certain point, in running, is known as the lactate threshold. The best runners train their bodies to get used to that threshold and increase how much energy and power they can create, even when their body is redlining.

Yet entering the final lap of a race, Farah's heart rate and lactate couldn't be allowed to limit his performance; the coach and the athlete had to figure out together how to run that 52, no matter how much it hurt. I heard the echo of my grandfather's advice: Everyone just limits themselves, setting barriers well before their true potential. I knew constant improvement, past a certain point, was impossible. But track and field and cross country are weird things, and you can always go a little harder, dig a little deeper.

In June of 2011, Nike wanted a pacer for Kara's 5,000 at the Prefontaine Classic, held every year at the University of Oregon in Eugene, and they asked Tanya. It meant I got to tag along and watch inside Hayward Field from a reserved space with Oregon Project members. Farah, the star of the Oregon Project who would go on to win gold medals in the 5,000 and 10,000 meters at both the 2012 and 2016 Olympics, was on his way to the first sub-27-minute 10,000 of his career when I made an observation about some of the racers. Alberto looked at me and said, "That's exactly right." It gave me confidence that we were seeing the same thing; it reassured me that I could coach.

Years later, in 2019, the US Anti-Doping Agency banned Alberto for four years for doping-related violations, after which Nike scrapped the Oregon Project (though none of Alberto's athletes were ever found guilty of any violations or rules being broken). Salazar's four-year ban was upheld in 2021, but he has always denied the claims. Let me be clear: I did not witness athletes doping during my time observing them and their coaches from 2010 to 2011, and I categorically condemn doping, as well as abuses of athletes in all forms.

Jerry Schumacher coached Nike's other pro squad, the Bowerman Track Club. Bowerman Track Club's roster of professional runners was headlined by Chris Solinsky and Matt Tegenkamp, who had starred as collegians under Schumacher at the University of Wisconsin. I really came to know Jerry after going to Seattle to race a mile. Some of the Oregon Project and Bowerman athletes were also running at the meet. Jerry needed someone to bring his runners through the first mile of a 3,000-meter race at a certain pace, and I volunteered to be the rabbit. When he approached me afterward, he first thanked me. Then he said he'd noticed that I, definitely not a Nike athlete, had been hanging around Nike's track training a lot recently: What was my deal?

At times, I'd wondered the same thing.

For the two years I'd lived in Oregon, I slept on an air mattress. In my spare Beaverton apartment, I kept only what would fit into my car in case I needed to hit the road again. But whenever people heard about the odyssey of my twenties and early thirties, moving from place to place, and suggested I settle down and get a career, it annoyed me. I rejected it. I *had* worked, saving up enough money that, along with a part-time job at a running store, I covered my costs. Once, a guy who worked for a different shoe company asked a friend what was wrong with me, and when I was going to get a real job. Hearing that made me want to go my own way even more. You might be working some job you hated, I thought, but the freedom of my vagabond lifestyle allowed me to do what I wanted, testing training ideas on myself to see what I might want to keep when I became a coach. People didn't see a career path, but I was convinced that I was building one. I'd met some of my best friends within the running community from traveling around. That I didn't have some monetary things didn't mean anything to me. I didn't want to climb the traditional ladder of going to graduate school, becoming a grad assistant, and then getting a job and moving up. I was never going to learn anything being around one coach for that long. I wanted to talk to everybody. I was in Oregon for that purpose. What I wanted was to build my running knowledge, not a life.

After our interaction, Jerry and I exchanged numbers. A few weeks later, he agreed to get lunch.

We must have spoken for three hours. Most runners train on a seven-day schedule, with a long run every weekend and speed work and easy runs sprinkled in between. Jerry told me about building a training schedule around a ten-day cycle instead. You can fit tempo and race-pace workouts, along with a long run and easy days, in a seven-day schedule, but you're rushing it. If you don't feel good on a workout day, or if life gets in the way, it's easier on a ten-day schedule to take an extra easy or recovery day. It was one piece of wisdom I held on to for later.

Hanging around the coaches was educational in other ways. I observed their contrasts. Where Alberto built his runners' foundations on speed, Jerry believed training could be oriented too much on race-specific work and believed drawing out a runner's maximum effort was a combination of building their aerobic strength, their speed work, and their race training, with an emphasis on strength and endurance. For that reason, Schumacher had his milers train with the club's 5,000- and 10,000-meter specialists, running three or even six times the distance they'd cover in their races.

"Listen," he told me once, "you have three different systems and you just got to figure out how to constantly use those systems. It's that simple, Sean."

I felt unbelievably lucky to have access to these different schools of thought playing out on the track, right in front of me. My idea for a documentary never happened, but this was like living out my own personal *Track Shack*. Anybody could read a book on training. I never did. I wanted to be side by side with coaches and athletes to observe that relationship directly. Numbers are everything in running—maximum aerobic capacity, heart rate, paces, hemoglobin levels. But I'd always felt that reaching winning times was more art than science: knowing when to push an athlete past what was comfortable, and when to pull back, just from analyzing someone's stride, or how they look as they warm up. It's not something you're born with, but something for which you develop an eye. One analogy for coaching is that it's a mixture of the improvisation of cooking and the precision of baking. Another is that it's like watching two comedians deliver the same joke, but one's funny and one isn't. There's an art to the delivery, and observing the best coaches instilled in me the subtleties I couldn't learn any other way.

I realized that the same things that had stalled or even hindered me as a student and an athlete might be assets. Unable to rely on getting good grades in school, I had learned how to deal with people by reading their demeanor. I liked to think it was hereditary, a trait passed down from my father, who spent his career as a detective figuring out who was telling the truth and who wasn't. Bouncing around between schools, training groups, coaches, and cities had left little consistency in my training, and yet without all that moving around, I wouldn't have been exposed to an array of different philosophies. Some runners are molded by just one or two influential coaching figures; my irregular path allowed me to learn what I liked, and just as important, what I didn't, from dozens. Questioning my coaches—constantly asking, "Why? Why? Why?"—had led to clashes. Yet later on, I'd learned that challenging accepted practices and established norms could spark innovation. Returning to running after years focused on BMX gave me a different perspective from someone who had exclusively run.

There are great running coaches who did it by being totally immersed in a particular system. But stepping away from it for a while gave me a wider lens to look through for inspiration. It's why I also turned to MMA for inspiration and education—the precision around diet and sleep in MMA amazed me, leading me to think about how to apply it to running. From basketball coaches, I learned of the need to not be stuck to a plan mapped out months in advance but to adjust workouts and schedules in the moment, based on instinct.

There is no one way to coach, just as there is no one way to learn. I learned by seeking information from the source and watching coaches work. And watching workouts at Nike solidified something I'd believed for a while, that speed wasn't just about an athlete's individual talent, but their training atmosphere. I stood on the track within the trees watching that combination of great coaching and great talent and thought to myself, *It's not happening yet, but this is what I'm going to do.*

Just not immediately. Tanya and I were on the move again. We relocated to the California beach town of San Clemente in Orange County so that Tanya could go to graduate school. I didn't want her to work during her studies, so I went back into sales, first for a high-end sports-sunglasses company, Rudy Project, then selling running shoes for Saucony, and work boots for Caterpillar. Selling running shoes kept me involved with the sport, and Caterpillar paid good money. Both left me unfulfilled.

Over the years, I'd stayed in touch with my old coach at San Marcos, Steve Scott, and after work I would drive forty miles south to campus, where I could still get on the university's track. Running hard, late on warm nights under the lights, having the track all to myself, brought me a sense of peace. This was the world I wanted to be back in.

I started a company I called Mile High Running Camp so I could coach youth runners at altitude in the summer. It was rewarding work, but it was only seasonal. When Tanya finished graduate school, she got a great job, but it required us to move three hours north to Thousand Oaks, on the edge of the Los Angeles suburbs. Knowing we would be there for at least two or three years for Tanya's job, I felt stuck. What was I going to do now? I knew I wanted to coach, and I knew I'd probably need a master's degree to do it, so I went to grad school and earned my master's in education and a teaching certificate.

But college coaching jobs close to our new home weren't plentiful, and high school jobs weren't what I wanted. High school meets were often so disorganized that I couldn't stand going to them. But my options were slim. Hadn't I really enjoyed the seven previous summers I'd spent working with teenagers at The Running School in upstate New York, one of the country's longest-running and most popular running camps? As maddening as the high school meet experience could be, the more I thought about coaching teenagers, the more I realized the impact I could have on them and how fulfilling it could be for me. California high schools had huge populations, and there had to be seven good athletes in a school of several thousand, I thought. Maybe I was being naive, but as I considered my options, I began to believe that if I could get some halfway decent athletes, I could get those kids to the top of the state ranks.

So in the winter of 2016, I emailed more than a dozen high schools in the area asking if I could help coach their runners. Only one person wrote back: Marty Maciel.

Maciel had coached boys cross country and track and field at Newbury Park High School for years. He invited me for lunch at a burger spot near the high school. He listened to my background, and after a bit of discussion, he agreed to bring me on as an assistant. I figured if I was going to coach high school, I was going to go all in, the only way I knew how.

Full throttle.

CHAPTER FOUR

SITTING IN A RARE patch of flat ground in the hills high on Newbury Park's western slope, the Dos Vientos Community Center was designed to be a meeting space. Outside, the building was surrounded by a playground, courts for sand volleyball, and fields for baseball and soccer. Inside, there was a preschool, an open gym, and multipurpose rooms for rent.

On a late-spring day, I walked through its tiled hallway and into a long, narrow room with a poured-concrete floor and a row of windows facing west. The 2016 cross country season at Newbury Park was about to officially begin.

In California each spring, schools are allowed to begin meeting with prospective athletes ahead of the fall sports season, and this was our introductory meeting to explain Newbury Park's offseason training and offer a program overview. It wasn't my first time around the Panthers. Months earlier, after Maciel responded to my email, he'd asked if I would start by joining Newbury Park's coaching staff during the 2016 track season. It was a good way to learn the runners' names and personalities, and for the runners to get to know me.

Runners I'd met that spring began trickling into the Dos Vientos meeting room. At the far end, in front of a floor-to-ceiling mirror, was a table with the sign-up sheet. Rows of seats were arranged in the middle. When I arrived at the community center that day, I knew what I was walking into. This wasn't the Oregon Project. This was a *project*.

Newbury Park is a town within a town, a string of housing developments that, for the past fifty years, have been built on the western edge of Thousand Oaks. Tucked inside a row of coastal mountains, it's an affluent but easily overlooked place of about forty-five thousand, one that drivers might pass on Highway 101 without even realizing they'd just flown by the last stop before leaving behind the Los Angeles suburbs. Going any farther west means driving down a steep grade that drops you down the back side of the hills and into a valley of wide, flat agricultural fields abutting first Camarillo and then its neighbors, Oxnard and Ventura. Going southeast over winding mountain roads leads you to Malibu.

The success of the Panthers distance-running program was also easy to overlook. There had been little since the school opened in 1967.

Despite an enrollment that hovered around two thousand, which put Newbury Park in the biggest of the five divisions governing high school sports in California, the school's boys cross country team hadn't qualified for California's state championships since 1991. Their girls had never qualified. Getting to the state meet is a bizarrely complicated process of league championships, sectionals, and prelims run by the state's high school governing body, CIF—the California Interscholastic Federation. Within that qualifying process, Newbury Park had rarely advanced past even the first step because California was always known for being one of the toughest states in the nation for cross country. Advancing out of the CIF's Southern Section, which covered most of Southern California, to reach the state meet usually meant running against four teams ranked in the entire country's top ten.

In the school's hallways, such mediocrity was met with a shrug.

The parents of a promising incoming freshman named Jace Aschbrenner told me that when they'd toured the school with other prospective eighth graders, they'd mentioned to the principal that their son was a runner. How good were the school's cross country and track teams? "Oh, we're okay" was the response. "But we have TO in our league," the principal added, meaning Thousand Oaks High School, a rival only a few miles away. TO *was* good, but I hated that mentality, that unspoken resignation to being on a different, lower level.

I thought through all of the training methods I'd gathered over the previous two decades. Those first few months at Newbury Park, and all of the program's history, or lack thereof, told me that training wasn't going to be enough here. There was going to have to be a 180-degree turn in team culture, attitude, and goals. You can't become fast without first believing that you can.

The meeting room at Dos Vientos filled up with about seventy people, including athletes and parents. I saw Tanya, who would be helping me with the summer program, in the back of the room. I've never been good at delivering prepared remarks, but I wanted to get across how passionate I was about coaching the students and that I wanted anyone who signed up to match my commitment.

In front of the room, I pulled out wooden blocks I'd painted yellow and black, the school colors. My block represented the 100 percent effort I would give. Next to it, I placed a second block of equal height, representing the athletes' commitment. Across the top, I placed a third block, creating a strong foundation.

"This is when it works," I said.

Then, I took away the athletes' block and replaced it with a shorter one. The once-balanced foundation fell apart. "This doesn't work if we don't match each other's effort."

The longer my remarks went on, the more excited I got about what we could achieve. Without having planned to do so, I made a bold promise: "If we do everything I say, and we get a total commitment, Newbury Park is going to win a state championship in four years."

I kept elaborating, talking about building one of the best teams in the country and breaking national records. I was starting to lose the room, like, Who is this new guy, and why is he dreaming so big? I reined in my speech. It was hard to read the reaction afterward, but I could tell I got the attention of at least a few. I'd surprised myself, too. I left the meeting psyched.

"How was that?" I asked Tanya after leaving.

"I think it was great," she said. "I think everyone is excited."

It had been a risky thing for me to promise. In fact, it was a crazy thing to promise. One of the most powerful lessons I'd learned from my years running and being around coaches was never to tell somebody they can do something if you don't believe they actually can. In coaching there's a fine line in this way. The job is to get athletes to believe they can do things they've never done, to redefine what is possible. But you have to understand each athlete and their potential to meet those goals. Trust collapses if you overpromise and can't deliver. Instinctively, I think most people want to believe in a new plan. However, if you make big promises, you had better produce results.

I actually believed what I'd said during the meeting, though. I'd looked ahead at the schedule and noticed that the Southern Section Finals, in November, which would determine the teams that made the California state meet, would be held at a course in Riverside, east of Los Angeles. Looking through a few years of past results had shown me that our top five runners would need to average about 15:26 for three miles there to qualify for the state meet. That was about 5:08 per mile, which didn't seem *that* hard. I set up our season's training around that goal of making the state meet, and also for breaking the school record for average time, another benchmark that I thought was attainable. I was confident, even bordering on cocky, that this was possible because I'd watched as pros and semipros I knew had gone on to coach high school teams. In case after case, the teams' improvement—just by being coached by people who knew what they were doing—was both astounding and predictable.

People get mad at me when I say this, but while I think it's extremely hard to be the best in high school, I also think it's really easy to be a state-championship-contending level of good. The limiting factor? Coaches are too scared to go hard with training. Football players work hard in practice every day, without a lot of time to recover. Running intervals hard, while also getting treatment and recovery time and supplemental training like weights and plyometrics, is not going to physiologically burn out a teenage runner.

Marty was good at keeping the team together, but he came from a wrestling background and wasn't a runner himself. From being around Newbury Park in the spring as a track and field assistant, I didn't think anyone had made the athletes truly think about what they could be. To that point, the program's idea of greatness was qualifying for a state meet. I wanted what used to pass for the program's biggest ambition to be our floor for expectations. Why can't we be the top team in California? Why can't we eventually be the best in the nation? I wanted the boys to know, as their coach, that I would believe in them, even if no one in our county, let alone state, did, and that I'd work like crazy to get us there.

Getting fast, though, meant starting slow.

Half a mile from Newbury Park High School, up Reino Road, sits a city park called Pepper Tree Playfield. It isn't much to look at—grass field, playground, and a parking lot. Its geographic convenience had led it to become Newbury Park's home cross country course. Measuring almost 1,300 meters around its perimeter, it did the job. In June 2016, it hosted my first day coaching cross country at Newbury Park.

A few days earlier, the coaches had been sent a list of runners who'd signed up for fall cross country. Among the incoming freshmen were Jace Aschbrenner, who'd run 5:18 for 1,600 meters in eighth grade, and Nico Young, who'd run 5:06. The times were promising for eighth graders, though not among the fastest in the area.

That day at Pepper Tree was my first time meeting Nico. He had braces and at five feet one and maybe 110 pounds stood a full head shorter than Jace, his classmate. Nico was the oldest of three brothers and lived about ten minutes north on Highway 101 in Camarillo, a bigger city that sat on the other side of a mountain range from Newbury Park. His family didn't like the academics at the high school he was slotted to attend in his district and got an interdistrict transfer to Newbury Park. I learned of this later, as I came to know the family. All I saw during our first practice was that these soon-to-be freshmen were already competitive and might be something.

NICO YOUNG

I started running youth track when I was five years old, as early as you could. It wasn't intentional. Neither of my parents had run, and they didn't know anything about the sport. I was just running around my backyard with one of my friends when I was five one day and my mom's friend was like, "He looks like he's fast. You should put him in track." She put me in track and I ran the 100 when I was, like, six. I never ran anything above the mile when I was in youth track and never ran cross country, but I liked the environment, I liked the people that it attracted, so I felt it was a given that I would run in high school. I really knew nothing more than that at that point.

I certainly didn't know how to comprehend racing hard for two miles. At Pepper Tree, we did a two-mile time trial and I sort of tried, but didn't really try that hard, because I was unsure how hard to run or how fast to go. I ran 13-something for two miles, about 6:30 pace, and it was definitely difficult. What was clear was that Sean was very motivated and knew what he was talking about, from the first meetings that we had with him.

Before the summer of 2016, the school had subcontracted its summer training to an outside academy in Thousand Oaks. Runners couldn't be required by the school to attend summer practices, but I could let those who did know my standards. For as much as I was trying to sell the runners on big ambitions at our first meeting, I was really trying to get them to trust my methods—and, by extension, me.

It started that summer with running six days per week. Before our runs, taking inspiration from Jim Wharton, an injury-prevention guru whom I'd met while coaching at the Running School, I had everyone stretch their legs with an eight-foot-long length of rope, a durable poly blend used to tie boats to a dock, found at a local hardware store. I cut the ropes individually for each team member and taught them the routines that had been passed down to me.

Boys had to run two miles in 14 minutes or less to make the team. The cutoff was a slight ruse. I never actually meant it as a way to cut anybody, aware some might never reach that time no matter how hard they tried. It was to set a clear goal: I wanted them to make the brave attempt to do something difficult with the confidence that they wouldn't go it alone. Running is often put down as a "niche" sport. (Essentially, all that means is it's something that has a hard time being televised.) In fact, it's anything but niche. No sport is more open. Are some runners going to have a bigger, more efficient aerobic capacity? Of course. But getting better, faster, and more resilient doesn't require being a genetic outlier; it just requires making the commitment to keep going when everyone else wants to stop. Anyone can do that. Anyone can decide, like Michael Crouch had shown me back at Queens, that they're willing to find their limits.

I couldn't promise the high schoolers now in my charge that all of our runs would feel good, or that all of them would be quality workouts. But what I knew from my own running and from watching some of the best coaches was that the difference between good and great was showing up the day after the bad run with the unshakable belief that the next would be better. If that sounds like an individual pursuit, something that can only be brought out from within yourself, well, I wanted to build the kind of team I'd wanted to run on in high school, one where we would all push one another.

The hardest challenge was figuring out how to adapt the workouts and workload I'd seen professionals handle to kids still growing into their bodies. I couldn't assign fifteen-mile runs on the weekend because you don't want to hurt someone that young by making them do too much. Our older athletes were capable of running fifty miles per week, but incoming freshmen like Nico and Jace stayed at forty miles, with their long runs eventually working up to a maximum of eight miles. I knew some coaches who sketched out months of practices ahead of time, but that never struck me as wise. How would you know, as a coach, what your athletes would be feeling like that far ahead? I started coming up with practice plans two or three days ahead, but often ditched those plans at the last minute after seeing how we warmed up and sensing that we weren't ready for that day's initial idea.

Every run has a purpose. Sometimes it might be running dog slow for three days because you need that for whatever reason, or you have an emotional time in your life and you're going through something. I always believed it was my role to pick up on the emotional wavelength of a team and adjust where needed and switch on the fly. Obviously, bodies this young would not respond like those of experienced pros. But I was convinced they could be trained a lot harder than they, and most high school coaches, believed.

Pushing the runners to adopt a no-limits mindset was even more important. Early on, I wanted to establish that I would treat them like professionals, showing them the respect of explaining in detail the workouts we were doing, and what had, in my experience, led me to design it that way. I was looking for the athletes who weren't scared to push it in training, because you learn and make more gains in training than you do in races. Training is where confidence is born. Racing is where you hope to execute a plan built on that foundation of confidence. In return, I made it clear I would demand the respect of their full commitment, no matter whether someone was the number one runner on varsity or struggling on junior varsity.

Like Scott Simmons at Queens, I'd come to reflexively hate the word *base* when it was used to describe summer training. Yes, you can get really good by loading up runners with mileage early in their training; some high school programs design their seasons to look like going downhill from a mountain peak—running the bulk of their mileage in the summer and a little less with every passing month to taper for championship meets.

But mileage alone wasn't how Newbury Park would train, under my philosophy. We would be working all systems, all year round, just as my mentors did. Your body takes three months to adapt to training, which was why we started our hard workouts in the summer. From there, our training progressively built to our highest mileage in September and October, in the middle of the season. Our runners had to learn what it took me years to realize: There is no such thing as the perfect day. If they could perform on race day during some of their hardest weeks of training, they might realize that what had seemed hard before wasn't quite that way after all.

By August, with our first meet only weeks away, the team had clearly gained fitness. Less clear was my own role.

I was frustrated. I thought I had the authority to coach the boys as I saw fit, but Marty wanted to implement some of his own training methods. To me, it sent mixed messages, enough that I considered walking away. I would feel bad about leaving while still laying the foundation of our program, especially after the big promises I'd made. But I had high expectations for our team, and I didn't see how I could pursue them if someone else was telling me what to do. And I didn't want to start the season if I didn't see a way to finish it.

I emailed Marty in early September, letting him know why I didn't think it would make sense for me to continue. I missed the boys' first meet, in Santa Barbara, as I decided what to do. Marty asked me to come by the school the following Monday to talk it over with him. We met at the track. While the team stretched underneath the bleachers, we talked for ten minutes, walking the infield grass, talking through my concerns.

"Let's do it," he told me. Marty wanted to handle the logistics, but going forward, I would be the head boys cross country coach and could run the program as I saw fit. He told me that he was planning to retire soon, anyway. He recognized my passion for running and training and trusted me to guide the kids the right way. He just wanted what was best for the kids.

It's hard to coach a team for years, then let some guy come in and take over with your blessing and tell him, "You can just do everything." It said a lot about Marty.

When I rejoined the team, there were less than two weeks to go before the Woodbridge High School Cross Country Classic on September 16. The 3-mile race, known simply as Woodbridge, was no ordinary season opener for a new coach. Held in Norco, about an hour east of Los Angeles, Woodbridge is not so much a race as it is a distance-running festival, where more than fifteen thousand runners compete in dozens of races over multiple days. Some cross country courses are set up to show who's the strongest. Woodbridge's course, wrapped around a huge complex of flat grass fields, revealed who had pure speed.

We showed up as a small fish in high school cross country's largest pond. And we looked terrible. Bringing pop-up tents to high school meets is the norm, and it's not hard to understand why. Teams are there for hours and need a central place to get ready, hang out, or just stay out of the sun or rain. Woodbridge was a sea of tents emblazoned in team colors, with schools' names and logos. It looked amazing. We showed up with . . . a blue tarp. Runners from other teams warmed up together in customized shirts and pants. Our warm-up gear was comprised of mismatched clothes, not matching black and yellow. No one even had a T-shirt that said NEWBURY PARK. It was embarrassing, but that wasn't the end of it. We also couldn't field our full team—Jace, one of our promising freshmen, couldn't run because of an obligation with the Boy Scouts.

It was an ominous start because that wasn't even the hardest part.

Our boys were entered in the so-called rated race, the most competitive of the entire weekend. We would be state-meet aspirants competing against established state-title powers.

It had all the makings of a humbling day. Instead, it became our first breakthrough.

A senior named Ethan Duffy finished eighth overall in 14:57, and the rest of our team flew in behind him. Ethan Ronk was next in 15:09, Nate Garner in 15:11, Nico Young in 15:59, and Clay Nishi, our fifth and final scoring runner, in 16:11. Our sixth and seventh runners finished less than ten seconds after Clay. Overall, our runners averaged a finishing time of 15:29, breaking our school record. We finished fourth overall, only one spot behind Temecula's Great Oak High, perhaps the state's most successful running powerhouse.

"This is good enough to get to the state meet," I told our boys afterward. "This is what we need."

Nico's time stood out to me. The tiny freshman in the too-big black-and-yellow jersey had been running youth track since he was five, but he didn't know how to *train*. At the start of summer workouts he'd run about 18 minutes for three miles. Less than three months later, he was breaking 16 minutes. I thought, *This kid's going to be really good.*

Woodbridge showed us where we were lacking. Only 38 seconds separated the top five finishers of El Toro High School, the boys champion in the rated race. Second-place Bloomington (a 47-second gap) and Great Oak (22 seconds) ran as packs, too. But worrying about tactics could wait until the following week because we left Woodbridge with the runners experiencing their first sense that perhaps my belief in them wasn't as crazy as it sounded during the season's first meeting. Their mindset seemed to change, a sense of *maybe* setting in.

And for me, too. Because throughout the season, I thought that *maybe* I wasn't cut out to coach at the high school level. I'd hated it the first couple of months. I wasn't seeing the level of commitment I'd expected. One issue was soccer. My rule was that if you wanted to be on varsity cross country, you couldn't miss any practices or competitions to play soccer. Parents sometimes thought their kids should be doing everything and that it was bad to specialize in one sport. I never understood why it felt as if cross country was constantly second tier. Once you get to high school, there is nothing wrong with focusing on a sport. If anything, I told the parents, specialization teaches you dedication. Not everyone agreed.

Though Newbury Park was surrounded by trails and parks a short drive away, training on soft surfaces to reduce injury risks was difficult because I couldn't get clearance from the school to take our practices off campus. Running in town had shortcomings for other reasons. Coaching running takes more faith than any other high school sport because it's the only one where your athletes leave your sight for long stretches of time. There was the girl who hid out during training runs at our local Trader Joe's, multiple times. There was a time when a few athletes ran off to a friend's pool. I was often pissed when I got home from practice. All of the time that I wasn't spending working on getting my teaching credentials was spent thinking about training, only to find athletes who were supposed to be on runs messing around at Pepper Tree on the playground's swings. I reminded the runners who joined just to earn a PE credit or be social with friends that water polo—where you could float in the water and not get cut—was an option. Our school's water polo team didn't like hearing that.

I had to remind myself that these were teenagers wanting to have fun. And that I, too, had complained when I was a teenager about training methods I didn't agree on with my high school coaches. I saw a bit of my younger self in the runners I was struggling to reach. I was trying to produce the things I hadn't had, the things that I felt had kept me from running my fastest—answers to tough questions about training, a team culture in which it was aspirational to give a damn.

I'd need help to pull it off.

Ethan Duffy didn't start running until his sophomore year of high school, but when I arrived at the start of his senior season, right away it was clear he was our number one runner. It wasn't because of raw talent. It was because the more we spoke, the more it became obvious how badly he wanted to be really good. Ethan was smart, too. Knowing that his times weren't necessarily fast enough to get him to his first state meet as an individual and that his aspirations hinged instead on qualifying as a team, Ethan realized we had a chance, but only if his teammates bought in.

"I'm not letting you guys take my senior year away," I heard him tell his teammates once.

Nico and Jace, our freshmen, had also shown that they were willing to work as hard as I could push them. When Ethan didn't like his performance after one race, instead of cooling down at the prescribed 6:50 pace, he took off on a training run at 6-flat, and Nico and Jace went after him to keep up. That was telling. Their commitment, Jace's Boy Scouts weekend notwithstanding, was evident.

Still, as freshmen, what they said held little weight with the rest of the team. We needed an upperclassman to lead, and Ethan was an alpha personality whose teammates didn't mess with him. I believed in him: He became my liaison, reinforcing my messages to the team. And he believed in me: Under our new training regimen, his time at Woodbridge as a senior was forty-nine seconds faster than the year before. The team would never have been as good without Ethan, just as Ethan's senior-season ambitions depended on the team around him being good.

On October 8, we drove north to Fresno for the Clovis Invitational. Like Woodbridge, this was another measuring-stick race. The course was at Fresno's Woodward Park, which had hosted every CIF state cross country championship since the first, in 1987. If we wanted to advance to state, here was our preview of what it would look like. At 5,000 meters, it was a little more than 100 meters longer than the 3-mile races that were on the rest of our schedule.

The meet was an eye-opener, for reasons we didn't want: We weren't very good. Our performance at Woodbridge helped us make the cut for the most competitive race at Clovis, but little else about our

Woodbridge performance carried over. We finished eleventh overall, and ninth among Southern Section teams. That forecast a potential problem. Five weeks later the Southern Section Finals would be held in Riverside, and the top seven teams would advance to the state meet back at Woodward Park. We had a gap to make up.

We needed more speed and more information. One year, in college, I'd largely trained in dry conditions throughout the season. On the day of the cross country national championship meet, however, a storm moved in and left the course soaking wet. We struggled to manage the change. I never wanted any athletes I coached to go to a big meet so unprepared.

I had an idea. We rented buses and drove 100 miles east to the Riverside Cross Country Course for a scouting session. It was an old golf course that had been turned into a three-mile loop of essentially all-dirt paths, cutting through little ravines. I had our runners do a nine-mile run that covered the course three times. Once we were done, we discussed how the race would go at each portion of the course.

In early November, Newbury Park's boys finished second at the league finals, 4 points behind Thousand Oaks, but we won the overall boys league championship because of our results in previous league meets, combined with the final. It was the school's first Marmonte League title in twenty-one years. The runners' hard work had paid off.

I remember some parents being almost overjoyed afterward, and I couldn't understand why. Winning our league was a baseline expectation, not a cause for celebration. I wasn't ready to celebrate yet.

On November 19, 2016, from where I stood along the fence at the Riverside City Cross Country Course, I could see Newbury Park's boys line up at the starting line of the Southern Section Finals. In about sixteen minutes, we would find out if we'd finish in the top seven and extend our season one week to the state meet, or if our season was over. The runners looked young, nervous, and inexperienced, but I was confident that they could qualify. Next to me, I overheard two people talking.

"Nobody will ever beat Great Oak," one said.

Great Oak. Everyone in California was chasing the school from Temecula. It was a huge school with cross country rosters that sometimes had 100 or more kids. The program wasn't known for producing the fastest individual runners but for the way its coach, Doug Soles, trained his team to be effective at running in tight packs that condensed the time between their first runner and their fifth to mere seconds. Their mascot was the Wolfpack, after all. They carried themselves like champions because they were. Their boys had won the state's Division 1 title in 2014 and 2015. They had also won the 2015 Nike Cross Nationals, high school cross country's version of a team national championship. Their girls had won state titles in 2010, 2012, 2013, 2014, and 2015 and looked as if they weren't going to release their grip on the state anytime soon, either. When Great Oak showed up to races, everybody stared at them and their head-to-toe Nike warm-up outfits. Their shoes matched. The initials on their red singlets read like a mission statement: GO.

I interrupted the conversation of the two people next to me: "We'll beat them. Mark my words, in three years, we'll beat them."

I don't know why I said three years. I don't know why I spoke up, period. They looked at me as if I were a moron. I must have looked like one: An overconfident new coach at a high school with zero tradition. They just kind of smirked, turned away, and watched the race.

I was dead serious.

The gun went off. It was hard to tell where my guys were, but I knew our number one runner, Ethan, had gone out way too fast. Now I was worried about the rest of the team. This wasn't unheard of; I get nervous watching my athletes run, especially at the start of a race when hundreds of legs are tangled together in an all-out sprint, and superstition makes me worry that my watching will cause a nasty fall. As a runner, my nerves would dissipate as soon as the gun went off; as a coach, with no control of the action, the nerves only escalated. It never gets easier.

We had watched video of this course countless times so that the team would know every mile marker, every quarter-mile marker, as if it were as familiar as Pepper Tree. One mile in we weren't in qualifying position. The course took runners out into a field where I couldn't see their position or read their body language. I ran to a spot about 800 meters from the finish line and started looking at the live results on my cell phone as runners passed the two-mile marker. We were around eighth place, right on the cutoff line.

JACE ASCHBRENNER
We were on the course's backstretch, by a fence, when you're just in no-man's-land, and you turn with half a mile to go. You're just exhausted. Something clicked: I felt, *This is bigger than myself*. Making state was possible, and we could rewrite history books by getting there. It was everything Sean had talked about with our team, and it was what replayed in my head in the moment. I was this little fourteen-year-old kid, thinking, *I've got to go!*

Eight hundred meters to go. Ethan passed by on his way to a nineteenth-place finish in 15:05.

"We're gonna do it!" I yelled.

I was trying to yell positive things, even though the standings were shifting so quickly I had no idea what place we were in. I looked at another of our older athletes, Ethan Ronk, our number two runner.

"You're doing it! Let's go!" I yelled. "We're gonna make it! We're gonna make it!" His eyes lit up and I could see him get a burst of energy. He finished in 15:17.

Jace, our number three runner, finished in 15:26. Yes! In four months, he'd taken three minutes off the time he'd run for his summer tryout over two miles. Results indicated we were in seventh.

Nico, our number four, passed on his way to 15:43. We were

eighth—then the stats page corrected us to seventh. Our fifth runner, Nate Garner, finished one second behind Nico. Our places added up to 252 points. Would that be enough?

I was gripping my phone. I hadn't moved. Sometimes there are errors in the results, but 99 percent of the time, these are the final results. Or so I hoped.

Down the dirt course, I sprinted toward the finish, leaping over rocks. I was screaming as I reached the runners, who looked lifeless, not knowing where they stood in that limbo zone between what they hoped for and what was real. I spotted Marty.

"We made it, we qualified!" I said.

"Do you know?" he said.

Frozen by the possibility I was wrong, I stopped. When I looked at the phone again, the results page said *FINAL*. We were in seventh place by a mere 13 points, the difference between only a few runners placing a few spots higher or lower.

"We made it!"

The same athletes who had been silent were now screaming. I was so proud of the guys, and I told them so as I sent them out on a two-mile cooldown. Seventh place was not going to make headlines, but for us it felt like our Olympic moment, one I will never, ever forget. I'm never big on celebrating just qualifying for something. But that was a milestone because no one thought we could qualify for the state meet. I don't even know if the parents thought we could qualify. We didn't even have hotel rooms booked in Fresno. That would be a problem for our booster club to solve. All that mattered was that when the gun went off at Woodward Park the next week, Newbury Park belonged on the starting line.

We showed up to Fresno the following week looking like a different team. We now had Newbury Park warm-up T-shirts. More concerning, from my perspective: We also didn't resemble the hungry team that had battled so hard the previous weekend.

Getting to state had taken so much out of everyone's emotions that by the morning of the state race, what was left was a team that acted as if the pressure was off. They weren't nervous because getting here felt, to some, like enough. We'd surpassed most expectations— even our girls team had laughed when, the previous spring during track season, I suggested that I thought the boys could make state. I don't think the boys believed they could finish on the podium as a top-three team. To be truthful, I didn't either, as I made my team-score projections.

Yet I wanted us to have the mentality that we belonged in that conversation. After all, teams struggle, seemingly out of nowhere, at big meets every year. It's just a fact. When someone blows up, it creates opportunities for those who are prepared. But that day, I couldn't shut out the thought *We're so not focused. This is not good.* I had a pit in my stomach, and watching Marty try to switch up our season-long warm-up added to my frustration. We didn't know how to act on the biggest stage.

Ethan Duffy ended his final cross country season with a 24th place finish at state, in 15:47 over 5,000 meters. Ethan Ronk, a sophomore, was our second runner, in 39th (16:02); Jace was our third, in 94th (16:31); and Nico was 103rd (16:36). Only five freshmen in all of Division 1 were faster than our two. Everyone ran what they probably could have and should have, and I was okay with the effort.

We finished ninth. I was proud of our progress in one season together, when getting buy-in from the runners and parents had been a constant battle. When I saw how happy the runners were afterward, I struggled with it, because a top-ten finish in California's Division 1, the classification with the largest schools, was a very good feat. And yet . . . they had to want more than this. I debated whether I should say that to them right then, or if I should just let them enjoy the moment. I don't know if it was the right thing to do, but after they cooled down and we were cleaning up our belongings, I called them over.

I was proud of them, and I wanted them to know it.

"But," I said, "I want you to want more than ninth place."

There was silence. I almost thought one of the younger guys was going to tear up. The message I wanted to get across was that I was only saying this because I deeply cared, and I believed that if we could do this in only our first season, then our future had huge potential. I reiterated that I was proud, and that we could do a lot better. And we were going to do better.

As we drove home, I noticed that Nike Cross Nationals were the next weekend in Portland. I didn't know what it would take to qualify. But I wanted to find out.

CHAPTER FIVE

WE WERE AT THE same Riverside course, running the same Southern Section Finals, living through the same anxiety. All that stood between Newbury Park making or missing the 2017 California state cross country meet was a familiar razor-thin margin in the standings.

But the result?

Crushingly different.

One year after our breakthrough moment in Riverside, we hit our lowest point on November 18, 2017, finishing eighth at the Southern Section finals, one spot and 21 points short of qualifying for the state meet. There would be no return trip to Woodward Park that fall. There was only the blank expression on Jace's face as he walked back to our bus and the question of how this had happened. I was the coach who always wanted to have the answers, and in the immediate aftermath, they weren't coming easily.

Our prerace projections that pegged Jace, now a sophomore, as a clear top-ten finisher—high enough to qualify individually for state—weren't based on wishful thinking. Only two weeks earlier at the 3-mile Marmonte League Finals, Jace had won in 15:11. The following week at Southern Section Prelims in Riverside, Jace had won again, in 14:57. Our hopes for finishing in the top seven of the team standings and snagging a spot at state were dependent on Jace scoring a low number because Nico wasn't going to be anywhere near the front of the pack. The previous spring, before his freshman track season, he'd badly injured his hamstring and had to resort to cross-training, spending weeks in a pool. His diligence could only accomplish so much. By the time cross country season started, he still wasn't healthy because he was going through a growth spurt. His fall season turned into a sporadic mix of resting, running, and riding an elliptical. The most memorable thing for me about his sophomore season wasn't his running but meeting his twin brothers, Lex and Leo, who were three years younger.

It's hard to forget the first time I noticed the twins. I looked up during a league meet we were hosting early in the season at Pepper Tree; the twins had climbed a tree and were watching from a branch. They looked like these crazy kids, always smiling, always fiddling with cameras. Someone mentioned they were really good youth runners. At first glance they didn't look like they would necessarily be elite. I kept seeing them through the season, though, such as when the team would occasionally head over to the Young house for breakfast after long runs on the weekends. Lex and Leo would jump their mountain bikes off homemade ramps in their backyard, a pair of adventurous kids with seemingly endless energy who loved doing their own thing. Would they be any good at running? I had no idea.

Was our team, for that matter, good enough to fulfill the ambitions I'd set for us?

In early November, the Southern Section Finals went out unexpectedly, and almost comically, slow. Halfway through, at a mile and a half, so many runners were still within ten seconds of the lead that it looked like a neighborhood run club out for an easy Saturday jog. With half a mile to go, a group of thirteen, including Jace, opened a gap of a couple seconds on the rest of the pack, but dozens and dozens were right behind. Such a plodding start meant the race would be decided by who had the fastest kick. During his sophomore year, Jace had proven he was our workhorse. He'd replaced Ethan Duffy, who had graduated, and passed Ethan Ronk, now a junior, as our most reliable top runner. His commitment was total—he wasn't going to Boy Scouts anymore. He wanted to be the best, and it showed in his training. Jace could wear down other runners. But he didn't have the speed to outkick them in the final meters, and we hadn't trained him to be a kicker, either. As the race reached its final 400 meters, the lead group splintered again as seven runners took off—and Jace was no longer among them.

Jace finished in 15:07, an improvement of 19 seconds and thirty-one places from his 2016 finish at the same meet. But the day had been anything but a success for him, or anybody else. Over the final half mile he had faded to twenty-fifth, with Ronk barely beating him to the line for twenty-fourth.

It's why I couldn't shake Jace's look afterward. He had put so much trust in me to turn him into one of the best Division 1 runners in the state, and I'd let him down. My race plan should have been for Jace to go to the front and push the pace if no one else would, not allowing a pack to form. It would have been hard for him to hang on like that. But he would have been far better off doing that than trying to keep up his position in a kicker's race. Instead of telling him to push the pace in the middle of the race, I didn't adjust.

The first two sentences you say to an athlete after a bad race are extremely important. You have to pick your words wisely, and you might need to give them space and not talk with them for a while. But when you do talk with them, the first things you say will affect how they move past that bad race, for better or worse. My own experience led me to believe that.

All I could think to do after this race was to start off by apologizing.

I had taken qualifying for granted and trained with our focus on performing at state, and not enough on finding the best race plan to get there. We trained for many scenarios, but not one with a pace so slow that it would create a bottleneck at the front. I met the team afterward and told them it was my fault.

Upset at myself for being overconfident, upset at how the race had played out, I didn't sleep much that night. The thought I kept coming back to: *What do I do?* I'd never set out to coach high school athletes. I'd basically fallen into it. I wondered if they were too young to develop as I'd imagined, or if I was the right person to help them.

I called my mom, who had become a running fan while following my decades in the sport. I needed a sounding board.

"Maybe I can't do this," I said. "Maybe coaching high school isn't for me."

I didn't for one second regret my unorthodox path to coaching in high school, one that had allowed me to learn from collegians and pros, but it certainly left me feeling like an outsider in the high school ranks. That feeling was exacerbated by our 2017 failures. Did I need this? I wasn't any less conflicted as Tanya and I drove an hour east to Crescenta Valley Park. I'd helped coach Tanya as she continued running after college, and this was the day of the Southern California Cross Country Championships. Her down-to-the-wire win by two seconds in the 6-kilometer open division, beating women years younger than her, changed my mood. So did a conversation I had at the meet.

I'd met Christian Cushing-Murray during my travels through the running world. Once a pro runner who'd run a 3:55 mile, he'd never stopped trying to stay fast, even as he'd become a high school teacher and coach in Southern California. All of that experience knowing how to ride the ups and downs of high school coaching made him a wise figure, and one I needed that day.

"Sean, listen," Christian said. "You are helping them. You can't let your happiness be decided by the success of a bunch of teenagers. You just can't do that. You cannot let that define who you are."

It was important to hear that. The sun had still come up that Sunday. I'd made strategic mistakes at the section finals that I regretted, but we still had promising runners with promising futures. Frustrated by not qualifying for state as an individual, Jace wanted to race in the Foot Locker West Regional on December 2 at Mt. San Antonio College, in Walnut, east of Los Angeles. Mt. SAC, as it's known, is famous because its course has a series of, in my opinion, overly brutal hills. I never understood why it was so revered. Making it to Foot Locker nationals was a big deal; for years, its champions were a who's who of future distance stars at the collegiate and pro levels. I thought it was great that Jace wanted to go for it because it was only a couple more weeks of training and it might wash away the bitter taste of our high school season. He had another really good training session, and he and Nate Garner, a Newbury Park senior, prepared for the race.

The leaders went out that morning and Jace was with them, until all of a sudden I couldn't find him. Where the hell was he? Turns out he'd stepped off the course, a DNF—did not finish. He wasn't hurt, and I couldn't tell exactly what had happened, but it seemed as if he'd put a lot of pressure on himself and, after starting really fast, was dead by the time he hit the course's hills. Another unhappy ending to close out 2017.

Ever since the section finals in Riverside, I'd been rethinking every bit of the race in detail. Cushing-Murray had been advising me to take a step back. From that vantage point, our failure to qualify couldn't be seen as a shock. It had been building for months, the end result of a difficult year, for both me and the runners.

Nine months earlier, in February, my grandfather died. I flew to New York and, the day before the funeral, went to Bethpage, the state park he used to take me to for three-mile repeats. I'd barely run for weeks because of a broken foot and had only recently gotten out of a walking boot. But I needed to clear my head, and Bethpage felt like the right place. Tanya came with me for her own run; I did eight miles. My foot felt fine afterward, and within hours I had a crazy idea.

The next morning, before the funeral, I went to a track and ran eighty-six laps, one for every year of his life—just shy of twenty-two miles. I probably hadn't run that many miles combined over the previous two months, but when I have an idea in my head, I'm stubborn. A few family members came to the track, jogging a few laps at a time beside me.

"One down," I said after the first lap.

"Two down," after the second. I didn't want to forget where I was.

My hamstrings seized in pain. I hadn't run in so long, and it wasn't as if I trained for marathons to begin with. All of a sudden, I had decided *now* was the time for the longest run of my life? With about a mile to go, my grandmother showed up, and the last four laps became as hard physically as they were emotionally. It was difficult losing my grandfather. His coaching had made me want to start running as a kid, then return to it as a teen. After my time at Adams State, when I hurt my knee and stopped running for a while and began working in sales, he was always urging me to get back into running, always encouraging, without judgment. He didn't care that I'd bounced around between schools, only that I graduated.

He was thrilled when I used my eligibility until the last drop at Concordia and Cal State San Marcos. I majored in business because of his advice. I was lucky to count so many elite coaches as mentors, but my grandfather left the first imprint.

Why did I think it was normal to go to great lengths? Probably because of my grandfather's willingness to drive me out of a Northeastern snowstorm to Virginia for a workout, and because of how consistently he traveled across the country to watch me run in college nationals. He also had a commonsense approach. Coaching was learning the attributes of everybody on the roster, he would say, and then figuring out how to make the bad stuff good and the good stuff even better. It sounds simple, but it's not.

Peaks and valleys.

The year ahead would prove his advice right, again.

Marty Maciel had come from a wrestling background, but he knew the value of training at altitude. Most summers, he took Newbury

Park's teams north to Mammoth Lakes, about seventy-eight hundred feet up in the Sierra Nevada just outside Yosemite, for a week. It was the right idea, but to me, the wrong location. There, the team stayed in dorms at a community college and there were few ideal places to run. Logistics were hard for the athletes and their parents. Runners were forced to train on pavement or hard gravel. We wouldn't be going back in the summer of 2017. I had another spot in mind: Big Bear Lake.

At about 140 miles east of Newbury Park, Big Bear was half as far as Mammoth. Rental housing there was cheaper and nicer than dorm life. Our team drove east, skirting downtown Los Angeles, then through Arcadia, home to one of the country's top track meets every spring, and kept going as our vans followed winding roads high up into the San Bernardino National Forest. It wasn't as though we'd stumbled upon an undiscovered gem in the world of distance running. The former American record holder in the half-marathon, Ryan Hall, had grown up there. Brenda Martinez, a world-class 800-meter runner I knew who'd grown up close by, started a professional training club based in Big Bear, a club that included Boris Berian, a former Adams State runner who later won a world indoor title at 800 meters.

Yet if elite runners knew all about Big Bear, our runners did not. I wanted to make the experience memorable. Professionals are obviously single-minded about running as a job. College athletes show up to campus taking their sport seriously, too. But high school kids are different because the range of experience is so different. On the same team in which you might have a state-title contender, you might have others trying running for the first time, and many who may never run competitively again after graduation. So we didn't set out for Big Bear expecting to reap long-term benefits from elevation after one week—it's just not enough time for the physiological effects to take hold. It *was* enough time, though, to create an environment where a team could mesh while spending all day, every day, together. This wasn't a professional training camp. Taking our training seriously was important, but so was enjoying ourselves afterward.

To rent big, amazing houses, Tanya and I put down some of our own money, along with money I'd pulled in from my Mile High Running camps at Big Bear, which I'd still been holding over the summers, for high school runners from all over. We could lower the costs for the athletes and their families that way.

While the elevation around the lake was about sixty-eight hundred feet, the dirt fire roads ringing the hills around it climbed much higher. Most of our running was done in Holcomb Valley, which sat a few miles north of the lake at seventy-four hundred feet. One day was reserved to go up the hill to Skyline Drive on the lake's south side. Skyline stretched up to about seventy-eight hundred feet, and the out-and-back run we did there that followed the road's uphill grade was probably one of the hardest runs our athletes would ever do. Skyline traced a ridge, and if we drove it farther west, it would dump us out at Bluff Lake, a little patch of water at seventy-six hundred feet surrounded by pines and wildflowers. We could loop the lake trail a few times to get in a slow three miles.

We worked hard. We also found time to play. Just off the western shore of Big Bear Lake, where the water hits the Bear Valley Dam, sits a rocky island where small houses were built between boulders a hundred years ago. Some call it Treasure Island, some China Island, but we knew it as a perfect place to jump from the rocks into green water below, just across from some docks. It was probably a cheesy team-building idea, but I would stand at the edge and tell the guys that this was a metaphor for running. Some would jump off a rock about thirty feet off the water. We moved to lower rocks.

"Now, you've got to do a flip," I said.

The runners' reaction was a hard no.

"I'm telling you," I said. "It's a metaphor. Everyone will help you do it."

Nobody flipped. Admittedly, it was pretty high, about twenty feet.

So, thinking it might be inspirational, I pointed to an even higher point. "I'll flip off *that*."

We spent hours at the rocks. But as we were leaving to pack up and go, someone noted that I hadn't flipped either, and that it looked as if I were all talk. The runners stared at me as I stood there on the rocky outcropping I'd pointed to earlier. I hadn't done a flip in probably fifteen years. *Oh, shit.* I had no idea if I could pull one off. But if I was going to sit here and ask these teenagers to work up the courage to push their limits in the coming months, here was a chance for my actions to back up my words.

"Start a countdown!"

"Ten, nine, eight, seven, six, five, four, three"—*If I don't do this,* I thought, *I'm going to look like an idiot in front of the team*—"two, one."

I jumped. I over-rotated a little bit but I was surprised it was a decent flip at all, because my fear barely got me off the rocks. I was, to put it mildly, terrified. I had to act as if it were no big deal. Moments like these at camp were fulfilling.

They were also fleeting. As the 2017 cross country season neared, our chemistry still wasn't right. A few upperclassmen didn't have the mentality that to become exceptional at something, it has to become a life-changing habit. That's what it comes down to. You have to identify as a runner. Not *Oh, I run* but *I am a runner.* You have to want to make it part of your life, even if that means sacrificing elsewhere.

It frustrated me because I didn't see this as punitive. If runners put in that effort, they could have gotten fast enough that recruiters would have called offering scholarship money. Jace and Nico saw that commitment as worth making, but not everyone did. The two finally confided in me with the problems on the team—who was causing them, the upperclassmen who were telling the rest of the roster that I didn't know what I was talking about and shouldn't be trusted. In later years as Newbury Park found success, people assumed that my teams must have been perfect, or that I was lucky all the time. But in our second season there were still kids cutting practice, going to hang out with their girlfriends, and avoiding the work, such as when one athlete said that he was skipping practice to go to a physical-therapy appointment. That was news to the physical-therapy office when I called to check. When I would tell their parents about it, they would put the blame on me. This wasn't the kind of team environment I envisioned creating.

It raised one of the reservations I'd had after joining Newbury Park's coaching staff, when some parents voiced concerns about the students needing to run year-round. I was worried Newbury Park was too white-collar, meaning too many vacations, too many ski trips. Those are great opportunities, and if a family wanted that time, I was not going to tell an athlete not to go. But I did tell parents that long breaks without running would not get their kid to their potential. While they were not training, everyone else was getting a leg up on them.

It left me restless. In the spring of 2018, after our dismal 2017 cross country season, I was approached by Trabuco Hills High School, about two hours south in Orange County, about an open job coaching their girls distance runners. Tanya and I had enjoyed our years living in Orange County when we'd moved to San Clemente. The school offered to bring me in as a coach and would try to get me a teaching job as quickly as possible, because I had by then finished my master's degree and earned my teaching credentials.

It appealed because it offered a fresh start and a better livelihood, too. I told the Trabuco Hills athletic director on a Friday that I would take the job. The plan was to inform Newbury Park the following Monday.

I thought it would be easy to turn the page once I'd verbally accepted. But that weekend, I didn't sleep. It just didn't feel right. I'd let very few people know what I was planning, but Jace's parents were among them. They were upset—not at me, exactly, but that I was leaving. As the weekend went on, my gut kept pointing me back in the direction I came from: *There's no way I can leave. I'm not doing this.*

On Sunday night, I called Jace's parents: "I'm not taking the other job."

The change of heart wasn't even because I sensed our team at Newbury Park could be great. It was just that something didn't feel right about leaving. Christian Cushing-Murray's message after section finals had reminded me of the perspective that coaching high school involved peaks and valleys. And yet, while coaching at that level was never my intention, my belief hadn't changed that if I was going to do something and ask for my runners' all-in commitment, then I had to be absolutely all-in myself.

Trabuco would have gotten me whatever job I needed, teaching-wise; but I figured I could hold on for one more year for a position to open at Newbury Park. And as chance would have it, a few days later Newbury's girls track and cross country coach stepped down. I realized I wanted to coach our girls, too.

I couldn't leave. There was unfinished business. We were too close to being too good. And I believed that because of something I had seen earlier that spring.

CHAPTER SIX

THE THING ABOUT RUNNING is that some races take only a few minutes but have a way of sticking in your memory forever.

A race on May 12, 2018, was one of them.

In California's convoluted qualifying system for the state track and field meet, which was separate from the fall cross country season, the Southern Section Preliminaries represented only the first of three meets that eventually decided who would compete in Clovis, just outside Fresno, at the state's track and field championships. But for Nico Young, his performance in the 3,200 meters that day represented the moment that I realized this sophomore, still shorter and skinnier than just about anyone else in the field, would push himself to his limits like no one else. As it unfolded in front of me on a cloudy day at Trabuco Hills High, of all places, I was standing against the fence at the track, screaming my lungs out.

Earlier in the spring of 2018, Nico had run a personal best of 9:19 in the two-mile, a time that made him a candidate, but not a favorite, for state. Before the Trabuco race, I'd advised him to run conservatively—hang back, stay in the mix, but reserve enough energy to make a move with two laps to go. Then the race started, and that plan went out the window. The race went out extremely fast, the leaders coming through the first mile in about 4:24, far faster than we'd anticipated. It was also only one second slower than Nico's 1,600-meter PR at the time. And yet Nico was right there with the leaders.

Oh, God, I thought to myself. *That's way too fast.*

But I could tell Nico was locked in. His head was cocked a bit sideways, and I could see the determination on his face. Others who saw him at that moment probably thought his pained expression meant that he was about to blow up. My gut told me otherwise.

I turned to Tanya and said, "He's committed now. There's no turning back."

Pushing into the final lap, Nico was not only still hanging with the five runners who had broken away from the pack but was somehow looking stronger with every stride.

He was sixth with 400 meters to go.

Then fifth with 300 left.

Fourth at 200.

This kid is insane!

Coming off the final turn of the final lap, Nico ripped past a Great Oak runner into third. Nico wasn't going to catch the leader, but even though he was caught at the finish for fourth place, he smashed his personal best by 14 seconds, running 9:05.17. His place qualified him for the next stage. Nico's time also established a school record and, when the season ended weeks later, ranked as the fourth best among all high school sophomores that year. Since we'd met at Pepper Tree in the summer of 2016, Nico had shown promise and toughness.

But in this race, he'd held that red line as I'd never seen from a high schooler, proof of a special aerobic capacity and uncommon guts. Riding the red line is one thing, but showing guts in competition is another. Putting it all together, against these odds, with these stakes—that's moxie. To be successful, you have to have a certain amount of talent and you have to put in hard work. But at the end of the day, it also matters who is going to be tough. Nico Young was tough.

His parents weren't at Trabuco Hills that day, so I called his mom, Lynne, after the race.

"He's gonna do great, huge things like this," I said. "He's arrived."

In California, you don't make a state meet off one race. Nico was going to have to keep this up to make state. It was hard, but I had evidence that he had it in him.

I'd seen him do hard things for the entire previous year.

Fourteen months before Nico's breakthrough at Trabuco Hills, on March 16, 2017, I wrote an email to Lynne. A few weeks earlier, I'd taken some Newbury Park runners to an indoor meet in Seattle, partly to keep the kids racing during the lull before the outdoor track season began and partly as a way to make it fun for the kids and their parents by traveling and competing outside Southern California. Nico couldn't make the trip, however, after slightly tearing his hamstring running 200-meter repeats at Pepper Tree. When track season arrived, he tried to tough it out and felt pressure to keep scoring points for the team. But he was in pain and didn't know what to do, not wanting to let teammates down. I was only the head distance coach, not the head track coach, but to me, competing with an injury was the absolute wrong thing to do, and I wrote Lynne to say so.

> *In my opinion, I think he should just do pool workouts for 8–10 weeks to let his hamstring fully heal. I know he won't want to hear this diagnosis, but I truly believe Nico is going to be one of the best HS runners in the State his Junior and Senior year and just want him to be healthy and injury-free.*
>
> *My senior year of HS, I tore my ACL playing football in P.E. and had to get surgery. I had to get surgery at the end of November and miss my XC state championship. Everyone told me my year was done, even spring track, because of the healing time and time off of running that would be required. However, I would not accept that answer. I missed 4 months of running, but I was able to cross-train and stay super fit and I ended up*

running huge PR's that spring in track and placed top 5 at the state championships. If Nico can be patient and is willing to cross-train, I'll help him with a program to stay fit.

Nico's family had access to a pool in their subdivision in Camarillo. The pool, not the track, became his new training ground. The weather wasn't warm when he began in the early spring, and the pool wasn't yet heated, so Nico wore a wet suit while he aqua-jogged by himself, his mom or his dad keeping him company from the pool deck.

"You don't have to do this every day," his mom would tell Nico, to which his reply was always the same.

"No, no, I want to."

Hearing that told me a lot about the kid. Assigned solo cross-training like this, most teenagers would have half-assed their accountability and effort. But nobody, and I mean nobody, worked out harder than Nico. Anyone who met him thought he was the calmest kid in the school, and he is unfailingly polite. But he is also one of the most competitive people I've ever met. He has a real problem with losing. When Jace, not Nico, had been named the Ventura County freshman of the year after the 2016 cross country season, I could tell Nico was upset that it hadn't been him.

"Well, how do I get it in track?" he asked. I had to break it to him that there wasn't a top freshman award for the track season. But I loved his attitude.

An athlete's motivation is like a fingerprint, unique to them. Some want recognition on social media. Some want their parents to be proud. Some don't want any attention. A fundamental part of a coach's job is to understand each athlete's motivation. How else do I convince any of these kids that what they're doing is correct, that they should believe in our training, that they're going to get great results? That's the trick, and the relationship between the athlete and the coach is the most important part of cracking it. I don't mean that in the sense that we need to sit together over coffee. What I mean is that there is a connection in which I understand what they need to perform, and they understand me, my boundaries, and how they expect me to coach them. You have to know when to step back, when to push forward, when to say something, and when to say nothing. The best coaches aren't those who are rigid; they're the ones who see coaching as three-dimensional and who can change on the fly, adapt to the athlete. Articles and message boards obsess over tactics, race strategy, and training. Those make up just the tip of the iceberg.

There is also a common misconception that running is an individual pursuit. That is only partly true. It is a relationship—between you and your coach, yes, but also between the runner you are now and the runner you want to be.

The most overlooked and hardest problem to solve is how you first figure out your athletes, and what mentally drives them forward, or what keeps them from taking that step. I always felt my nontraditional background, racing BMX, and incorporating the way basketball coaches and MMA trainers did their jobs made me open to different ideas. Working in sales provides a quick lesson in understanding how people respond to incentives. I never wanted to approach an athlete from the narrow perspective of a running coach evaluating a runner. It took a while for me to understand Nico because he was so outwardly humble and soft-spoken. But I'd realized that while Nico wanted fast times and coveted winning, he hated losing even more. It's a subtle distinction, but an important one. I think wanting to win manifests itself in races. But hating to lose? That's the fuel that gets you in a Southern California pool in a wetsuit in the dark of winter.

A "rule" I've always gone by is that when you're cross-training, you have to work about 40 percent harder to maintain your fitness. I sort of made up that figure, but I'd heard other coaches I trusted suggest something similar. For someone like Nico, ten or eleven minutes cycling on an elliptical counted as running a mile, but my real target wasn't time. It was heart rate. I explained to Nico that while pool workouts would be monotonous, the best part was that the no-impact training on his legs meant he could do "hard" workouts on consecutive days. Some days spent running in place in the pool looked like this: a very easy 25-minute warm-up, before a transition into running intervals of two minutes hard, followed by two minutes easy, for about ten reps. Follow that with an easy 20-minute cooldown, and pretty soon you're around an hour and a half of good work. Or, he would jog in the water easily for a 30-minute warm-up, followed by 30 minutes of solid work that would keep his heart rate at around 170 beats per minute. That's a pretty high heart rate, by design, to simulate in the water what his body would be going through on the ground during a tempo workout.

Cross-training isn't perfect; it's not the same because you don't work the same muscles you'd use on land. Yet aerobically, you can be a beast. Keeping up Nico's fitness wasn't the only goal. We also needed to keep him focused. I shouldn't have worried about his focus, though. He would text me every day, his messages detailing exactly how the workout went and what his heart rate was. He would have done it for a year straight if he had to.

That doesn't mean it was easy for him. As he was cross-training in the spring of 2017, I would see him at Newbury Park's track meets, cheering on his teammates. But he would be sitting there with schoolbooks, unable to run, and I could tell he was sad. Halfway through the meet he would leave to do his pool workouts. That diligence made me want to increase my own as his coach. Here was this fourteen-year-old kid giving me all this information that I often couldn't get from a professional. I owed it to him to help him. And that's why I thought that maybe it was for the best that he got hurt. Seeing his intensity and resilience during his recovery made me realize how much he wanted to be great.

The work produced an impressive foundation of fitness, but it couldn't protect him against more setbacks. The hamstring took away his spring, then growing pains limited his second-year cross country season. The strong and lanky sophomore was a different animal compared to the scrawny freshman I'd met a year earlier, but the tendons and connective tissue had yet to catch up to the changes in the musculature; his knee started barking at the newfound stress his muscles were capable of absorbing. When Nico's parents saw doctors about it, one blamed it on the backpack he was wearing at school. No one could figure it out, and his season became a series of health-related stops and starts. He ran the big meets we circled every season. At Woodbridge in mid-September, Nico was our fourth finisher, 44 seconds behind our first, Jace. Nico was our fourth runner again at Clovis in early October, 51 seconds off our number one, Ronk. But by the Marmonte League Finals and the Southern Section Prelims in November, Nico couldn't run. He gave it a try during the Southern Section Finals but was seventh on our team, and 149th overall.

His season came to embody the whole team's. We just couldn't put it together.

But as the spring of 2018 arrived, things started coming together for Nico. He understood training better. He understood the sport better, too, becoming a fan of top professionals like Galen Rupp, curious to learn how they'd gotten so good. Able to train from the start of the outdoor track season, his running was more consistent than it had been in more than a year, and all of his work, dating back to the wet suit in the pool, began to pay off. Seven weeks after opening his sophomore season of track by running 9:52 over 3,200 meters at a March dual meet, a low-key meet between us and just one other team, Nico didn't just win the league championship in 9:19, he won by nine seconds, while Jace picked up third in 9:32.

Yet as much as he'd improved, I was convinced there was much more in the tank. Nico had accumulated consistent work, punctuated with eye-opening track workouts, such as seven 800s with two minutes of rest between intervals, averaging 2:14 per repetition. It was all coming together. Nico was ready to run under 9:10.

Whenever we talked about his potential, I was careful to keep what I said measured. Because he didn't have a deep, technical background in training, he was a little naive, and he believed what I told him. If I'd suggested he could run a time I didn't really believe he could, only for him to fall short, he would have been crushed. But I was confident he could go under 9:10. Then, on that amazing, cloudy afternoon at Trabuco Hills High that left me screaming from the side of the track, he did it for the first time. It was a breakthrough in more ways than one. Running faster doesn't start with leg turnover and aerobic capacity. It starts with belief that it can be done and the courage to go for it. Once Nico neared the sub-nine barrier, he did it over and over.

I heard Jace put it best later: "He broke through that glass ceiling of elite running for us."

NICO YOUNG

I don't know why I was so committed to running because I had yet to run anything really that fast and had very little evidence that I would be able to be good at all of this. I debated quitting running and going to play tennis because, to me, tennis seemed like a fun sport. It was a random thought, and I don't know if I ever would have done that—but if Sean hadn't been the coach, there is a good chance that I would not have kept running. When he said that Newbury Park's runners, under his coaching, would have to run almost every day, my mom and so many parents said, "We're not having our kid do that, that's crazy." But then we did it and eventually everybody accepted it as the new normal. There was an immediate trust because of his experience around big-time runners. It just gave us a clear goal and purpose of what we were going to do that season.

I would do two workouts in a row, or a workout every other day. It helped me create the aerobic strength that I didn't have before then, because I really had barely run. My sophomore year of cross country, I ran very badly at the CIF Southern Section Final because I had been injured so many times that fall, and I just couldn't train.

I know now it was because I was going from five-one my freshman year to five-eight my junior year and five-eleven when I graduated. But at the time I was running slower than I did as a freshman and was like, "What the heck is happening? How do I manage this?" It was difficult. I think that's one thing that scares people about going all in is you can go all-in and give it everything and still not get what you want. And you have to be proud that you still did that. It makes it even more meaningful to enjoy every moment, focus on the process of trying to reach the goals that you want, but that's scary for a lot of people. Improvement is never linear. It wasn't linear for me; it's just like a big squiggly line where, hopefully, the trend is up. When my growth spurt stopped, that's when I stopped getting injured, and every week after I was able to consistently train, and that's what allowed me to have a good end to my sophomore track season.

I was already somebody who really wanted to be the best at one thing. Once running started to become something that I thought I'd be really good at, I had no problem at all going all in on this, and having a coach who had the same perspective as that was tremendous for sure because it validated that what I was doing was right and that it was good for me.

Nico ran 9:07.65 one week later at another state-meet qualifier; a week after that, he went 9:07.01 to advance to the state meet. At the state meet in Clovis he finished fifteenth, in 9:09.56. Finally, this was the Nico that I saw as a freshman who I felt could be a star. From that point on, he never turned back.

But he didn't know that in the moment. Taking in his fifteenth-place finish, he was disappointed, mostly because the race was won by another sophomore, Matt Strangio from the Sacramento area.

I tried to make Nico feel better: "So what? He's not going to be better than you next year, I promise."

These weren't empty words, and I meant no disrespect toward

Strangio's talent. The sum of my experience and my time with Nico left no doubt: Nico was a monster.

Two weeks later, we took a group to the New Balance High School Outdoor Nationals, a quasi-national championship held annually in mid-June in Greensboro, North Carolina. Because it wasn't a meet that fell within the season on California's calendar, we entered the four-by-mile relay, running as Newbury Park Elite Track Club. For the four members of our relay, I cut them new ropes, with threads of alternating purple and white, to use for the stretching that had been part of our warm-up since my first day at Newbury Park.

We had to fight our way into a faster heat. I called the race director when I found out our team had been put into a slow section and told them we weren't coming if we weren't switched, because faster heats and better competition generally lead to faster times. Our runners deserved it after producing one of the country's top times at an earlier relay. Other teams had combined individual miles to make a composite time, in effect creating a hypothetical four-by-mile time. You can't do that. The race director understood.

Nate Garner opened up for us a 4:25.3 mile, and Nico followed in 4:20.6, even though he was still a little tired after the state track meet. Jace was our third leg, in 4:28.5, and Ethan Ronk anchored us in 4:25.3. We left with a sixth-place finish in 17:39, about three seconds per mile off the leaders, but more important, with experience at a national meet.

It was the whole reason we brought the team. I never wanted our runners to be overwhelmed by the spectacle of a "big" meet, so I purposefully reiterated that while national meets were often our big-picture focus during a season, they also shouldn't be treated as anything other than a regular race. There's a misconception that you have to run *great* at nationals if you want to win. No, you have to run *well*. Because many other teams are inevitably going to disappoint—choking when the gun goes off or otherwise failing to execute what they'd practiced. I tried to adjust my coaching to anticipate something going wrong for us on race day; our runners must have heard me say countless times that you have to be able to win without your top runner. On a big race day, there are already enough details to think about—I didn't want the spotlight of a big stage to overwhelm our athletes.

As I had told their parents before, I wasn't a fan of athletes taking long vacations with their families and not running. But as Nico and his family left for Hawaii that summer, I told him not to jog a step. Qualifying for the California state cross country meet in the upcoming fall would be a grueling process. It took a physical toll on a runner who still wasn't physically developed. When he returned, I figured we could slowly build him and the rest of the team up for summer training. He returned a new Nico.

In early August, a full month before races began for his junior year, Nico was ready. At a community 5K in Baldwin Park, a suburb about sixty miles east of Newbury Park near Pasadena, he finished second overall in 14:55—the fastest high schooler in the race—smoking a good field, beating racers from schools such as Great Oak. It was more evidence in support of my belief that Nico was the real deal, a gamer who could show up in big moments, and that he had top-end speed, because he'd come through three miles in about 14:20. I knew at that point entering his junior year that he had a shot to win an individual title at Nike Cross Nationals.

My confidence entering the 2018 cross country season went way beyond the team's having Nico, however.

You don't need to be that talented to have a successful team in high school. But to be the best, you need absolutely everything working in your favor. And in our team that summer, I saw the pieces. Jace was an extremely hard worker, too—and now that he and Nico, as juniors, had the standing to take over as leaders, they set the standard for everyone else. Our team was young but committed. The training that we were doing made me believe this was the year we would win the state meet.

The big takeaway from our disappointing 2017 was that our runners' potential could only be realized if they were healthy. We entered 2018 healthy, with our top priority being to stay that way. It was even more important because as our key runners began getting older, they took on heavier workloads. Long runs now stretched up to twelve miles for Nico and Jace, something they never did as sophomores or freshmen.

Also new was the addition of morning practices. CIF rules didn't allow multiple practices to be held on consecutive days, so we started introducing morning workouts two days per week. On days with windy afternoons in the forecast—which, because of where Newbury Park sat in the Conejo Valley, was often—we would move our hard workout to the morning hours. But usually, we'd gather the varsity team and anyone else who wanted extra work at 6:15 a.m. at the high school's track to focus on the types of things every runner *says* they do but actually do sparingly—weights, plyometrics, drills, and resistance-band exercises to strengthen their glutes and ankles. The junior- and senior-year athletes who were able to handle higher weekly mileage would add a three-mile easy run in addition to the supplemental training. Soon, we added a third morning session, with Monday, Wednesday, and Friday workouts. Attendance wasn't mandatory, but we could count on most of our top twelve boys—and top eight girls, now that I was their coach, too—to show up for nearly every session.

Finding soft surfaces for our athletes to run on as often as possible was a key part of keeping them healthy. It wasn't as if locations were scarce; we had parks and networks of trails only a couple of miles from the school's front door. But if we were doing a six- or eight-mile run, more than half of the workout would be spent running city streets just to get there. It didn't make sense to do it that way, and I hated that during our first seasons we'd been limited, because of the school's aversion to change, to training at Pepper Tree, with its hemmed-in confines, or on the concrete sidewalks around the high school. My reasons against it were many. Basketball and football coaches are only a few feet away from their team at all times during practices, but our runners would have to stretch under the bleachers, then I'd get in my car and follow along their route as best I could. Running on the streets and crossing intersections wasn't safe and added more pounding on their legs. The runners had to pause at stoplights, and it could never become an actual training run. In a larger sense, it also sapped all excitement from practice. I'd thrived on Adams State's electric atmosphere before hard workouts, and I'd seen the way Alberto could make the practice track in Portland feel like a championship final.

I took the issue to the school and made my case again. I wasn't going to be complacent. I didn't want our team to be thought of as receiving special treatment, but if I believe in something, I'm going to fight for it and ask, "Why not? Why can't we?" At last, it worked. Logistics had to be arranged, but parents who could spare the time bought in as well, and soon we had parents carpooling runners to new locations every day.

Finally, we could leave behind the streets for the ideal routes that were in our backyard the whole time. Three miles south of campus was Rancho Sierra Vista/Satwiwa, a park whose trails fed into the Santa Monica Mountains. The dirt trails were wide and fairly flat and went straight to Sycamore Cove Beach, almost eight miles away, a perfect setting for long runs. Dos Vientos Community Park was almost three miles west of the school and up a big hill, and its fields were perfect for 1,000-meter repeats through a loop that went around a beach-volleyball court and through the outfield of its baseball diamonds. Coaches would later tell me that they just didn't have the luxury of training off campus like we did. We didn't either, I told them. Only after I had tried three times did the school decision-makers finally listen. Any high school coach knows you have to get the parents to agree, too. The persuasion strategies I'd learned from my sales background didn't hurt in this area.

Our locations expanded over time. Driving west on the 101, we'd dip down into Camarillo, where I'd found Pleasant Valley Fields, a sports complex with one well-maintained soccer field after another bleeding into baseball diamonds. We'd stretch in a little patch of grass near the park's clubhouse, then use the fields for 100- and 200-meter speed drills. A slight uphill separated one set of soccer fields from another, and it became a place to practice accelerating going up or down a course. A dirt loop ran about a mile and a half around the perimeter, which allowed our runners to do several loops and get four to six miles in easily. There was even a trail that split off from the fields if we needed longer workouts.

Don't get me wrong: It wasn't as if we'd re-created running an ideal high-altitude Big Bear fire road. But I loved the place. We actually got a complaint from Camarillo High School for using this field, saying we had our own parks in Newbury Park. But the loops were open to the public and we never interfered with anyone who'd reserved a field. The complaint implied that we were trying to gain an edge over a county opponent, but we were just trying to do what was best for the kids.

It annoyed me enough that I scheduled a workout at Pleasant Valley once a week after that.

It wasn't a surprise to me that our runners had gained speed, because during the previous spring and summer they had also gained leadership.

It wasn't an accident that one followed the other.

The custom of naming a team captain never sat right with me. It felt as if it often went to an older athlete by default, when merit should count for something. But even I knew that respect was earned by more than running fast. When it comes to teenage dynamics, age matters. Now that they were juniors, Nico and Jace's teammates deferred to them with a level of respect that hadn't been there before.

The two were alike in many ways. Both would graduate as valedictorians two years later. Both had been some of our hardest-working and most committed runners since they showed up as freshmen. I knew our state championship ambitions wouldn't be possible if I alone wanted it badly; we needed locker room buy-in. Nico and Jace were all the way in, and because they were upperclassmen, it was easy for the others to see their level of hard work as our standard. It was cool to make running your way of life. It became cool to take our rope stretching and recovery seriously; to drink half your body weight in ounces of water throughout the day to stay hydrated; to show up for morning drills; to wear split shorts; to complete the toughest workouts. One of my most deeply held beliefs is that there are talented kids across the country, but their potential is never nurtured, let alone realized, because they're not in a program that amplifies their desire to be great. People would ask how to be the best, and I would tell them they needed to do these things.

During my first two seasons, cheating a workout was a way for some to project themselves as above it all. That didn't fly with Nico and Jace. Jace was a talker, comfortable with stepping into a room and telling teammates, "This is what we're doing." Nico didn't say much, if anything, and I didn't mind, because when someone tries to be vocal and it's not authentic, athletes can smell it. That wasn't who Nico was. His authority always hinged on his example. It rubbed off on our newest runners.

We'd added a group of talented freshmen, including Daniel Appleford and Colin Sahlman. Colin and Nico had known each other since elementary school, when they were teammates on the Camarillo Cosmos youth track club. I'd first learned of Colin when I saw him run a mile in less than five minutes as an eighth grader. He was quiet, with a huge head of hair dropping to nearly his shoulders atop a rail-thin body. With his frame, and seeing how smoothly he ran, I thought he had a chance to be a star right away. I had heard he might be coming to Newbury Park, but I had no idea he was enrolled until he began showing up to summer practices.

Colin's first race for Newbury Park came in early September and confirmed my initial feeling. It was a junior-varsity race, and he almost won it—except, near the end, he went the wrong way. Instead of going toward the finish, he went straight. It made me chuckle when he had to turn back, but it suggested that once we got him running, he could possibly score for the varsity as a top-five finisher.

Because of its sheer size and where it fell in the season schedule, Woodbridge always marked an opportunity to serve early notice about who was ready to contend. Nico did just that in early September. In the 3-mile race, his season opener, he ran 14:01 to win the sweepstakes division, the fastest time among the thousands who competed that weekend. Jace wasn't fully healthy, and we held him out as a precaution, wanting to ensure we could keep him healthy for the state meet, but our top five runners averaged 14:41, anyway. Our fifth finisher? Colin, the freshman. Woodbridge can be chaotic. More than two hundred runners were in our race. But Colin held his own in 15:06, finishing eighty-fifth overall, 25 seconds clear of the next-fastest freshman. The only team faster than Newbury Park was Great Oak. If we could make state, they wouldn't be standing in our way anymore. A drop in enrollment at Newbury Park had moved us down from Division 1 to Division 2. But Great Oak was still a model of success that we were chasing in many ways.

NICO YOUNG

I hadn't really done anything that was prominent on the national stage yet, and I remember all the talk going into the race was about one runner who everyone believed would win, and even I was like, "Oh, yeah, he's gonna win." Sean told me, "You definitely can win." I went into the race with that mentality: No one's gonna beat me. He told me I can win, so I'm gonna win. And I won. I remember watching the replay after the race, and the announcers didn't even know who I was. They were like, "What is happening? Who is this random athlete who is winning this race?" After that, I feel like everything changed. Because then, I was put on the national stage—it was clear that my goals should have been bigger for that season.

That race was when I realized people were paying attention to what I was doing. I barely use social media, but the next day I remember going to my Instagram and my username was something crazy like NinjaManNico or something—and I had, like, hundreds of follow requests because I had a private account. I was like, "What the heck just happened?"

Three weeks later we went to Clovis, which along with Woodbridge and the state-meet qualifiers, was one of the handful of meets we circled on the calendar every year. Fresno is nearly a four-hour drive from Newbury Park, and we stayed in a hotel the night before. Passing through the lobby the next morning, I overheard a group of parents wearing Great Oak gear.

"How much are we going to win by today?" I overheard one parent say. "One hundred points? Two hundred points?"

It didn't bother me that they were cocky. People could have accused me of being the same. I didn't care about that. It frustrated me—no, motivated me—that it was simply assumed on their part that they would automatically win, and that many programs in California gave them permission to assume that. Our enrollment was smaller, but I wasn't going to accept that Great Oak was unbeatable.

That day, Nico finished third, running the 5,000-meter state-meet course in 15:09, behind only Great Oak senior Tyler Tickner and the winner, Liam Anderson, a senior from the San Francisco area. Nico didn't have a good race and hated coming in third. We were second again in the team standings to . . . Great Oak. Their top five runners all finished in the top fifteen and were separated by only 23 seconds, less than half of our one-through-five split. My disappointment ran deep. I knew they were better but had still thought we had a shot to beat them. Yet the gap between us was 101 points.

It was an eye-opening reminder of how much work still was ahead of us.

Undeterred, Nico kept rolling. He won a 3-mile league meet in

14:46, and another 3-mile league final in 14:26 in early November and was completing workouts that wouldn't have been out of place on a college team, including mile repeats in the 4:30s. Jace was right with him. They were the politest kids I knew and both wanted the same thing—the team title I'd so boldly promised two years earlier. But they made each other better because on race day, or in a workout repetition, each burned to be the fastest. Every once in a while Jace would run a workout faster, and Nico would be crushed. I had to remind Nico that his average was still faster, that he shouldn't be worried about losing a few intervals out of, say, a dozen. He'd nod, as if he hadn't viewed it that way before. Just because he was uniquely self-motivated and emerging as a real candidate to win an individual state title didn't mean his confidence couldn't get bruised. The first words I told him after a race or workout that fell below his standard were extremely important to his confidence. He needed to be lifted up. "Peaks and valleys," I assured him.

The dynamic had changed. This wasn't 2016 or 2017 anymore, when Jace was reliably the faster of the two. As a junior, Jace would still have been the number one runner for virtually any other team in the state. On ours, he happened to be second to Nico. It seemed to me that Jace was struggling watching Nico progress so rapidly while Jace was hurt early in 2018.

When we held him out at Woodbridge, I pulled him aside. "You know you'd be up there fighting with Nico right now, right?"

"I know."

I'd wanted Jace to come to the meet despite being unable to run because I felt the environment we'd built as a team, around the example of both Nico *and* Jace, was positive. We wanted him at the race. I knew it was hard for him to watch, and that he wanted to be out there. But everything I'd learned about being around Jace suggested he understood that our goal was bigger than one individual, and that he was already improving our chances of making my state-title promise a reality that much more likely.

JACE ASCHBRENNER

I ended up being the top guy on the team as a sophomore, which is every kid's dream to be the number one guy on varsity and you still have two years to go. It actually ended up being, I think, somewhat harmful for my mentality as a runner, because it really developed an ego in me, the idea that "The team is counting on me, and I need to do this or else everyone fails because I'm the best one here." The sophomore version of me was inflated, and I really had to get knocked down a peg, and that actually happened at Foot Locker regionals where I dropped out of the race after going out in third place. There were guys in that mix that were future NCAA all-Americans. Meanwhile, the crazy little sophomore in me thought, "Oh, I got this, we can do it." And that kind of thing really broke down my ego, which was one of the big steps to understanding what it meant to be a leader on the team.

My junior year, Sean did talk with us a good bit about how this team was on our shoulders and how Nico and I had to lead our teammates and help them understand what he'd been helping us understand for the last two years. I remember watching Nico run 14:01 at Woodbridge, and that was incredible. But, I think, even more incredible than that was watching the team come together without me there on the field, running. That was the end of my ego era of sophomore year, the realization that this team can do well without you running, and yet you get to contribute to this awesome thing that's happening.

We weren't taking any chances. I didn't want to be overconfident about making state, as I'd been in 2017, but with the school's drop to Division 2, I believed we would not only make state but, with the shape that Nico and our top runners were in, could win it. I also knew that qualifying for Nike Cross Nationals for the first time depended on how fast we ran at state. At the end of every state meet, all of the times from all the divisions are combined to show how everyone stacked up as if there had been a single, huge meet. Taking it one step further, the top twenty or so teams from that ranking were then separated and merged yet again, as if only those teams had raced—theoretically, to show who was the best of the best. Whichever teams finished first and second earned automatic bids to go to NXN; everyone else would have to run fast enough to earn an at-large bid.

Trying to mimic the up-and-down hills of Clovis, held in Fresno's Woodward Park, led us to run 800s at Lang Ranch in Thousand Oaks, and 600-meter loops at Conejo Creek South Park. But those locations didn't reproduce how the Woodward course also switched surfaces from grass to hard-packed dirt, to pavement. The only option, in my mind, was complete preparation. And that meant training at Woodward Park itself.

Just as we'd driven the team to practice on the course in Riverside that was used for section prelims and finals, I came up with plans for a day trip nearly four hours north into the state's Central Valley, driving right back home after our workout. Following the course, our athletes ran four one-mile repeats—including doing the final mile twice.

The same-day up-and-back had been hard on the athletes. So a few weeks later, we went to Woodward Park again. I raised money to pay for a hotel and rental vans, and we put everything under the name of my running camp so that the school district couldn't object. After school on a Friday, we picked up the boys and girls who would probably make our state team, along with a few parents, and then we drove to Fresno for the night. The next morning, we woke up, worked out on the state course, and drove home. Coaches from other schools who heard about what we'd done thought I was crazy. *Yeah,* I thought, *our team is crazy—look how fast our times are. Why not maximize that talent?* The trips weren't mandatory for the runners, but they got to hang out with their friends on them. It was fun, and we were getting crucial preparation because there was more riding on how we performed at state than just the meet itself.

I hated that our school's enrollment numbers had dropped us down to Division 2. Qualifying for Nike Cross Nationals hinged on running a fast time. Division 2 wasn't as competitive as Division 1, and that meant we would have no other teams pushing us, while schools such as Great Oak and West Ranch would be in the state's bigger, faster race. To run a time comparable to those of Great Oak and West Ranch, we probably wouldn't be able to rely on other teams helping us set a fast pace. It would fall to our runners alone, and our runners would need to know Woodward Park as well as they did Pepper Tree. Even before our team trip to Fresno, Tanya and I had driven up to Woodward earlier in the season to familiarize ourselves with its 5,000-meter course. By the time the team drove home, we'd run it three times. We knew every nook and cranny, taking note that the hardest mile was the second, when the course crashed down a short, steep hill, around a rock, changed surfaces onto a road, then went back up two crazy hills. While watching videos of past state meets, we noticed how nearly every runner went wide around the rock. If we could hold a straight line in that section and not travel any more distance than was necessary, a title and NXN berth could come down to those few seconds gained. I even checked with the meet director to see if our strategy was allowed; it was.

Our weekends scouting Woodward made me think of Alberto's mentality. If we could beat our opponents on all these little things, it would equal a big difference.

CHAPTER SEVEN

ON NOVEMBER 8, I woke up to the start of cross country's championship season. Winning a state title had consumed my thoughts since practice began in June. It was everything we'd worked toward. Two rounds of qualifiers to advance out of the Southern Section, plus running well at the state meet itself, stood between us and a trophy.

Suddenly, that focus felt inconsequential. Instead of getting ready to drive the team from Newbury Park on Friday afternoon to Riverside, where the first section qualifier would be held the next day, I was reading headlines about a mass shooting that had taken place hours earlier, only five miles away from our high school.

Late on the night of November 7, a twenty-eight-year-old man showed up at Borderline, a bar and grill off the 101 Freeway in Thousand Oaks, and opened fire, killing eleven. A police officer who'd responded to the shooting was killed by friendly fire as well, before the shooter turned the gun on himself. No one expects to wake up to news of a mass shooting in their neighborhood. That morning, I tried to address what had happened with the team. The shooter had gone to Newbury Park High a decade earlier, and I wasn't sure if it would be on the kids' minds. We barely had any time to process what had happened before we had to think about another unfolding disaster.

I'd heard reports about a fire starting near Newbury Park as we drove away from campus. By that evening, after our team had finished its premeet warm-up and meetings, I learned two wildfires were now hemming in the town. The Hill Fire had started in the Santa Rosa Valley to the north but then moved far enough south that evacuations had begun, and the 101 had been closed. A few miles east, meanwhile, a new fire had started in the hilly, open space between Simi Valley, Chatsworth, and Agoura Hills, burning through industrial buildings on Friday before becoming much larger and much more dangerous. Santa Ana winds that arrive every fall in Southern California had pushed the blaze south toward the 101, and eventually over it, into the Santa Monica Mountains. From what we could gather from our athletes, it seemed to have missed their homes. As I watched the news at midnight Friday as they rested up for Southern Section Prelims, some new footage startled me.

"Tanya, we—we gotta go," I said.

"What are you talking about?"

"That's our house!"

Behind the reporter on our TV, we could see our block, with the townhomes where we lived. The background showed what looked like caution tape. At the time, we had five cats. It was about to be a long night. Tanya drove the two hours from Riverside to our home. DO NOT ENTER signs were already posted at the entrance to our neighborhood. No one stopped her as she went through, went inside to round up our cats, then drove two hours back. Once back to Riverside, she crashed in the hotel, and I went out to the van to stay with the cats, who were by this point going crazy. I can't say I really slept that night.

Saturday was a blur. Even though Newbury Park was now favored to advance after dropping down to Division 2, there were still real stakes riding on the Southern Section Prelims. In this race we focused not on fast times but simply on doing enough to advance to the following week's Southern Section Finals. We got the job done, winning with 120 points, 24 points better than the second-place team, as our top five runners finished within one second of one another, the definition of pack running. Much more stressful was the uncertainty awaiting us back home.

Twenty minutes from our school campus, our vans headed south on State Route 23 into Thousand Oaks, then merged west onto Highway 101, while surrounded by pockets of fire all over many of the same hills where we'd spent miles and miles training. Smoke filled the sky. The Woolsey Fire was now threatening Malibu, all the way on the coast. We could forget about running in Newbury Park—we wouldn't be able to run even close to home. Nearly every one of our athletes could return safely to their homes, but evacuation orders were in place all over the county. In Thousand Oaks alone, more than three-quarters of the residents had to leave. That included Tanya and me. After dropping off the vans, we drove east into the San Fernando Valley and stayed at a hotel. The following night, we slept in our cars because we wanted to be close to our neighborhood and check on our home. After the second day, when many of our neighbors had returned, we did, too. I still wasn't sleeping much. The Southern Section Finals were just one week away. The state meet, where we had a realistic shot at the championship, was two weeks away.

Where were we going to train?

When the encroaching fires shut down schools across the area, it provided us an unexpected advantage. With runners just sitting at home, we had the time to drive our team to areas unaffected by the smoke and train there. I went around Los Angeles looking for good air and soft surfaces. The best option, to me, was an area by the Rose Bowl, in Pasadena. I didn't even ask for the school's permission because I knew they would say no. I just called the parents and we organized car pools. We didn't need much, just enough room for about eight boys and eight girls, because the junior-varsity season had ended. In our team group chat, I texted the runners our workout's location.

Ping.

A notification popped up that I wasn't expecting. From Nico.

By text message, he was pushing back, questioning why we were driving an hour away just because it was windy near home.

What?

I sent Nico a direct message away from the chat: "Nico, if you don't want to go, you don't have to be on this team. I'm the coach, I say what we do, and if you don't want to go that's OK, but you're not running on this team."

I felt bad coming at him so hard. But I'd spent ten hours driving around looking for locations, trying to do something good for the kids, whose alternative was sitting around watching fire coverage. I was surprised, too, since Nico had always been more game than anyone else when it came to pushing ourselves—until he sent me a long apology, which included the backstory. The pushback came from Nico, but it hadn't started with him. A senior on the team had evidently asked Nico to contact me to say that the team didn't want to go.

But the opportunity was too good not to seize, and the team got on board with my plan. We were going. I had a special workout planned.

In 2018, at forty-one, I was years removed from competition. But I was still fit enough to run a 4:30 mile. In Pasadena, we went through our normal rope-assisted stretching and warm-ups and then discussed our workout of mile repeats. I had two specific instructions: Take off your GPS watches and just follow my lead. I would pace the boys for the first half mile.

Sometimes, I think, you have to do something crazy and stupid to try to blow an athlete's mind about what they're truly capable of handling. I needed our boys, who were fast, to know they could run even faster than they thought.

With me leading at the front, we hit 800 meters in 2:01. I thought nobody had a watch on, until I heard a senior, Ethan Ronk, excitedly speak up behind me in the pack: "We just went through—"

Before he could finish, I shushed him, while still running, before he could blurt out the time. I stepped off to let the boys finish the mile. They ended up running about a 4:25 mile. Our workout continued, but a point had been made. Cross country meets usually begin in fields, with each team allotted six feet of space on the starting line. You could do the math: With dozens of teams running at state and Nike Cross Nationals, hundreds of runners burst off a starting line wider than a football field until they funneled into a two-wide column of racers. We always wanted ours to be at the front, pushing the pace and dropping their competition. To do that, we had to train their bodies to run the first 400 meters at a dead sprint, and to keep pushing through 800 before settling in. If you don't train like that, you die a mile or two into a 3.1-mile race. I was very aware of my own running mistakes, like when I would go out hard and fade in college, and I wanted the Panthers to learn from them. It was crucial they did. Hopped up on adrenaline and nerves, runners at the state meet take the first mile at Woodward Park faster than almost any other race. In 2016, my first season, Newbury Park's runners couldn't have gone out in a workout like that in 2:01. They had to be built up, and with Nico and Jace more mature, it was time.

I gathered the runners after the first mile of our Pasadena workout.

"I want you guys to understand what you just did," I said. "You all went through 2:01. And then you just came back and completed a regular workout afterward. And you're fine."

They would have been tentative about going out at such a fast pace for the first half mile and finishing in 4:25 had I suggested it to them ahead of time. It's incredibly hard to go past your preconceived notion of what counted as fast, even for professionals. Alberto Salazar once told me a story about a time when Mo Farah and Galen Rupp had finished what they thought was a workout. Alberto told them to jog at an easy pace for ten minutes, then come back to him. When they came back, he told two of the fastest distance runners in the world that he wanted one more interval: 49 seconds for a 400. They were incredulous—that was a blistering pace even for elite distance runners, after they'd completed an already-intense workout. Alberto held firm. They ended up running 49.1 and 49.2. In his retelling, it had opened their eyes to the reality that they had a finishing kick that could close with anybody in the world. As a coach, you can't do that every week. But every once in a while, you have to do something that shocks the athletes to change their belief.

After taking the team to train in Pasadena a second time, I got in trouble with some of the leadership at Newbury Park High, who said we couldn't go. But I didn't understand their reasoning. In my capacity as head coach, I wasn't driving the kids to Pasadena; their parents were. Yet I was told that rules were rules, and that I couldn't do that anymore. So . . . we went back again. Our cover was almost blown when former head coach Marty Maciel, who still helped out, almost gave our athletic director a heads-up about our plans.

Not a word, I told him.

For the first time in three years, advancing to the state meet didn't come down to a nail-biting few seconds or points. In 2016 and 2017 we'd gradually tapered our weekly mileage in the final weeks of the season to ensure we were fresh at Southern Section Finals. In 2018, projecting an easy finish among the top seven state-meet qualifiers, we timed our taper for one week later, at state.

Back in Riverside, Nico won the section finals in 14:24, 11 seconds faster than the second-place finisher, with Jace coming in fourth, in 14:42, and Ethan Ronk eighth in 14:57. Our top five runners finished in the top twenty-four, rounded out by Kyndall Long, a senior, and Nick Goldstein, a sophomore, with Colin Sahlman running sixth.

Newbury Park won Division 2 with 51 points, 53 fewer than second place. It was a strong showing—two points better than even Great Oak's first-place finish in Division 1.

Afterward, I met Great Oak's coach, Doug Soles, for the first time. "Hey, congratulations," Soles said. "I'll see you at NXN."

This guy knew what he was talking about, I thought, and if he was saying we're gonna go to nationals in Portland, we're gonna go.

One week later, we pulled into Woodward Park. Our girls team hadn't qualified as a team, nor had any individuals, but I'd been waiting for the boys' return to the state meet since 2016. In a parking lot, I noticed a group from a high school near Newbury Park appearing at state for the first time in a long time. What caught my attention was that they had made shirts commemorating their trip to the meet. I pointed it out to our runners. They were going to do poorly the next day because they were just happy to be there, just like we had been in 2016. We wouldn't be happy until we'd won a title.

Scouting the course earlier in the season had helped me identify where I wanted to stand on race day.

After the gun fired and 204 runners sped off the line, I ran to a dirt parking lot next to the course, about 2,000 meters into the race. No other coaches were around, which was surprising because it's the most important part of the race. From studying the mile splits of past races, it was clear that the pace sagged in the middle mile, as runners went up and down hills—specifically, from the start of the second mile to about the 2½-mile mark. If we could run that section hard, but not so hard that our team would fall apart by the third and final mile, it would exhaust our opponents, mentally and physically. This is why we'd trained to know the course, and to understand exactly when we had the opportunity to separate from the pack.

I waited for our runners to pass.

"You guys are too fast!" I yelled. "Easy! Easy!"

In a code we'd worked up, "Easy!" really meant "Go!" Eventually, people around me picked up on it. But you should have seen the looks on the other athletes' faces as Nico, Jace, and Ethan put the hammer down. We had one last marker where our runners had trained to surge, with 1,000 meters to go. Nico cruised by with a gap behind him on the way to winning the Division 2 state title in 14:59.2. He was Newbury Park's first individual state cross country champion in twenty-seven years. The time would have beaten the Division 1 winning time run by Matt Strangio, the runner who had won the 3,200-meter state title in track the previous spring. Across all divisions that day, only Liam Anderson of Division 3 Redwood High School, just north of San Francisco, ran faster, by four seconds.

Such a result wasn't predestined. This was earned. As a freshman, Nico's fastest cross country 5K was 16:28. As a sophomore, hobbled by injuries, he'd gotten only eight seconds faster. I thought about the runner who'd spent a whole track season in a wet suit, ripping through interval workouts in a pool, and the one who'd shown guts on the track the previous spring. Nico had incredible aerobic capacity, but also an incredible capacity for grueling work, and only now was everyone else seeing what we knew around Newbury Park. His 14:01 from Woodbridge three months earlier was the fastest 3-mile time run by any boy in the state that season. In the entire United States, only two runners, both seniors from Texas, had run faster.

But our mission didn't end with Nico's title. The top three runners from La Costa Canyon, a high school north of San Diego, had finished before our second. The team title would be close. We all waited on the placement of our fifth and final scoring runners, along with the sixth and seventh, who could also disrupt the standings and set back the competition, if they ran fast enough.

Our number two was Ethan Ronk, who finished twelfth in 15:30. He was a strong runner, but also inconsistent. It was hard to know what to expect from him. At state, he came through though, followed five seconds later by Jace. La Costa Canyon's fourth runner finished in thirty-fourth place. Two seconds behind were our fourth, fifth, and sixth—Kyndall Long, Colin Sahlman, and Nick Goldstein. For good measure, another freshman, Daniel Appleford, finished as our number seven, two places before La Costa Canyon's number six. Both Newbury Park and La Costa Canyon had averaged 15:34 for the course, but we'd been faster with our top runner, and faster with our fifth. We'd won our first state championship, by a score of 77–90.

When I spoke to the team for the first time in 2016, I'd promised a state title in four years. We'd done it in three. If you had asked me then how I'd feel after winning our first state title, I would have thought that the moment would be rife with emotion. Yet, I didn't feel a tremendous sense of anything because my mind was already on to the next challenge. Our finish had put us in contention to make the national championships. Over the next four hours, the NXN committee would be deciding which teams would receive the at-large bids to the race. If I felt anything, it was nerves. Would we make it?

Our combined overall time of 77:51 was the second-fastest all-time in California's Division 2, but it didn't necessarily guarantee us a Nike Cross Nationals berth. For that, we had to wait and see how our time compared across California's divisions. Automatic berths went to Great Oak, which won the Division 1 title with a time that was a minute faster than ours, and the runner-up, whose time was 46 seconds faster than ours. Nike only had five at-large bids.

But we got one. Doug Soles had been right. It was time to see where we stood among the nation's best.

When I was in high school, Nike Cross Nationals didn't exist. The Foot Locker Cross Country Championships had been the sport's biggest stage for high schoolers since it started in 1979. Its list of past participants and top finishers was like a cheat sheet for spotting future Olympians: Meb Keflezighi, Adam Goucher, Molly Seidel, Ryan Hall, Jenny Simpson, Grant Fisher.

By the time I arrived at Newbury Park, Foot Locker still had prestige. But more and more, judging who was the best team often happened at Nike Cross Nationals. High school sports rarely have a true national championship because of the mess of different states, calendars, and competing national events, just as in track and field, where a number of shoe companies host their own "championship" meets in June, forcing athletes to pick which one to attend. With

Foot Locker more of a spotlight on the best individual runners, cross country became the only sport with a true national championship, as Nike Cross Nationals evolved from its start in 2004. It was always held in December in Portland, Oregon—meaning it was usually held in wet, rainy conditions. During its early years, the course was run on a track used for horse racing. Eventually it moved to Glendoveer Golf Course, in north Portland.

In 2018, twenty-two teams qualified from eight regions, some automatically, some with at-large berths based on time. The meet wasn't sanctioned by the National Federation of State High School Associations, which meant schools couldn't compete under their high school's name, or in their regular uniforms. The yellow Under Armour singlets I'd inherited when I became coach were ditched for sleek black kits provided by Nike with NEWBURY PARK (but not NEWBURY PARK HIGH SCHOOL) across the chest. GREAT OAK became TEMECULA XC, its fire-red jerseys replaced by maroon.

NXN isn't the type of meet where you show up the day before, prepare alone with your team, and run. Nike flies teams out, puts them up in hotels, and outfits them from head to warm gloves to toe in the Swoosh. Teams receive their gear during a literal unveiling, on a stage. The company hosts meetings with motivational speakers, and activities where the teenagers mingle with big-name Nike-sponsored runners. There were photo booths. I heard some of our runners describe being there as surreal. A coach can only downplay an experience like that so much, but I tried to show that we were there to race. Our plane arrived late to Portland. By the time we got to Nike's campus, someone with NXN told me our team had a meeting to attend in 40 minutes. I told him we couldn't go. We had seven miles to get in that day.

"You're really running seven miles two days before a race?"

"Yes."

"Well, you still have to go to the meeting."

"Okay. We'll be there."

We didn't go. It made the kids worried.

"Guys," I said, "they're not gonna kick us out."

It rained early on the morning of the race but then stopped, with only gloomy clouds by the start. The course wouldn't be a muddy mess—at least at the front. Before the race, a coaching buddy of mine from New York asked how we were going to do. On our best day, I thought we could finish as high as fourth. I wanted to finish on the podium as a top-three team, but we weren't at full strength, with Ethan Ronk running on a strained hamstring.

As for the individual title, I reserved higher hopes: "I have a guy that could win it."

"What do you mean?"

"I have a guy that could win individually."

Because this was our first time at NXN, my buddy preached caution with expectations: "Listen, just get him a top-twenty-one finish to be all-American. Don't send him out there to the front."

I understood where he was coming from, but I knew Nico would be going out there to win this thing.

One mile in, the leaders came through in 4:43, running five wide at the front with a giant mass of pink, orange, black, yellow, and blue singlets right behind. Nico was among them, just a stride off the lead. The pace was conservative. No one was ready to spread out the field with a move. As a team we stood seventh. At the halfway point, the course dropped down into a fairway and into rolling hills that made the course's back half a test of strength. Two miles in, Nico was in first place in 9:44, but seven others were within a second of him, and I yelled at him to attack. He surged—that was running with guts. Great Oak's team was second, and we were sixth. Nico, and Cole Sprout and Easton Allred, both from Colorado, were running stride for stride at the front of the pack. Liam Anderson, from the Bay Area, who had won at Clovis in October, lurked right behind.

Allred made his move and Anderson and Sprout followed. Fourteen minutes in, Nico was a clear fourth. As the leaders climbed the last short, steep hill and entered the final straightaway, with fans ten deep yelling on either side, the title race was down to just Anderson and Sprout. Anderson had something left, finishing in 14:57.6. Sprout was passed by Cole Hocker in the last stretch and finished third. Nico caught Allred at the line for fourth in 15:04.7.

Fourth place was the real deal. Once you get top five at a national meet, every school is going to be interested in you. I was even more optimistic because Nico was still underdeveloped, with room to grow, both physically and as a racer.

A sign above the end line that read FINISH ON EMPTY was appropriate. As the pack piled in, so many runners dropped to the grass that incoming finishers could barely walk. I was trying to pick out our runners in the crush. Jace finished in 15:53. Kyndall Long was our third, Nick Goldstein our fourth, and Colin fifth, in 16:22.

Purcellville, from Virginia, won the boys title, 37 points ahead of Great Oak. Newbury Park was sixth. For the first time, I wasn't disappointed. Afterward Doug Soles and I talked about our teams' finishes.

"That's a great showing for the first time," he said.

Our guys had earned the right to feel proud. Winning state had felt like redemption, and finishing sixth at nationals was confirmation that we were onto something. But I didn't want the team to be content. We had only one year left with Nico and Jace in the program to attempt something so crazy even I didn't want to promise it back in 2016. I didn't want to just win the state meet, but nationals. Winning nationals would require us to go even more all in. To change the belief of an athlete or a team, every once in a while you have to do something that shocks them.

And I had an idea.

CHAPTER EIGHT

WHEN I SHOWED UP for college at Adams State, high up on a plain in the Rocky Mountains, our coach, Damon Martin, made us feel as if we had an advantage simply by stepping foot on campus.

He had a saying that he'd tell the distance runners at Adams: Find an Olympic distance-running medalist and, in almost all cases, they had most likely spent at least some of their training at altitude, just as we were. As someone who had grown up at sea level, the notion that spending time at elevation could give a team a competitive advantage was powerful. From then on, spending time at altitude was nonnegotiable to me as a coach. If improving at distance running was marked by peaks and valleys, as my grandfather had said, then it couldn't hurt to find a literal peak and train there.

By February 2019, I wanted Newbury Park High School to aim high—national championship high. That month, I made my case to the parents for my plan. Things had changed since NXN. After our state championship and sixth-place showing at nationals, Newbury Park High hired me for a full-time job teaching business. And I felt we had unfinished business with our runners, too: That summer, I wanted our top boys to train at Big Bear Lake not for one week, as had been our custom, but for one month.

I asked team parents, and parents only, to meet at the high school, because I had a case I wanted to make directly to them. In front of the room, I clicked on a presentation. Great Oak spent one week of their summer training at Mammoth's high elevation. It was a proven piece of their winning foundation, just as our week at Big Bear had given us momentum heading into the 2018 cross country season. I felt we had the rare opportunity now to do something outside the box. Why not do something so crazy for high school if we're allowed to do it?

Professionals based in low-lying coastal running towns often spent several months of their winter and spring training high in the mountains of Park City, Utah; Boulder, Colorado; and Flagstaff, Arizona, because of the undeniable physiological benefits. The more time spent at altitude, the longer your body holds on to those benefits. Research had shown that training at altitude for about four weeks produced a red-blood-cell enhancement that could be maintained for another four to eight weeks after we returned to Newbury Park. It wouldn't make or break our preparation for, say, Nike Cross Nationals, in December, but it could give us a boost early in the season.

Philosophically, I remained opposed to the traditional summer "base" training, which for many programs simply meant running a ton of miles. I didn't want the team running 100 miles a week; I didn't even want them coming close to 80. As our varsity runners got older, we gradually added to their workloads, but rarely ran beyond 60 miles per week. Why? We prioritized quality work. If we spent one tough month acclimating to elevation, our runners could maintain their usual, relatively modest mileage while still getting stronger because their bodies would adapt to more efficiently deliver oxygen. Running a 3-mile cross country race at the paces we were projecting would never be considered "easy" by any means—but knowing you've crushed demanding workouts at seven-thousand-plus feet for a month also delivers a different kind of confidence when you step to the line.

The opportunity for building bonds also couldn't be replicated if we stayed in Newbury Park all summer. Who could turn in reliably strong efforts under tough physical circumstances? Whom could we expect to speak up when it was time to dial in their teammates' focus? Who could break the ice when the pressure built? Spend a month around your teammates, and you'll find out all of that and more.

And did I mention the cost would be minimal? I projected we could do it for about $650 per person for the whole month. That cost would cover breakfast, lunch, and dinner every day. If the athletes wanted souvenirs or to go into Big Bear's little downtown for smoothies, that was on them. But it was a steal of a deal. Top running camps ranged between $1,000 and $1,500 for one week; meanwhile, I wouldn't be making a cent off this. Actually, I would be pouring in money from the Mile High Running Camp I was still doing every August, to keep costs down. The camps brought in about $15,000 every summer, money that went right back into covering costs for our high school program.

I told the parents we would take our top twelve boy runners—twelve because that's how many I could fit in a single van that would include me and another parent chaperone—to Big Bear for the first three weeks, before the rest of the roster would join them for the fourth and final week, no different from the team's traditional one-week summer stays in the past. At least one other parent would be present for the entire stay, and there would be an extra room for other parents who wanted to come up and spend a few days, too. Incoming freshmen wouldn't be allowed because I wasn't about to take fourteen-year-olds for a full month. That meant no Lex and Leo Young, even though they were varsity candidates. As eighth graders essentially only running for fun without any real training, Lex had run 4:46 in the

1,600 and Leo had run 4:55. That told me they would be good, but I didn't know if they could run faster than Nico because while their times were solid, they were, by themselves, hardly a guaranteed predictor of success. A lot of kids run those times and never go on to do anything notable in high school.

I'd envisioned the meeting as a presentation. Basically, I ended up pleading with the parents.

"Listen, every one of you as parents have said you want to be national champs next year. And at the team banquet at the end of cross country, we all came to this conclusion that everyone wants to be better. So, how do we become better? This is my solution."

The reception, when I finished, wasn't exactly silence. Neither was it close to an ovation.

The consensus was that a month was far longer than they were comfortable with. It felt as if no one wanted to be the first to commit.

Then one did. The father of Zaki Blunt, who would be going into his sophomore year in 2019, raised his hand.

"You can take my kid the whole summer!"

Everybody laughed, which broke up the awkwardness. No, seriously, though, he followed up, the idea sounded great, and he thought Zaki, who wasn't one of our top seven runners but was among the twelve I'd had in mind, would love it.

We had one on board. Progress.

Others started to change their feelings. *Two weeks, maybe. But not a month.*

The concern was all that extra time spent in one house. What would the kids do when they weren't running? Would they get bored? Start infighting? Get in trouble? Was there enough supervision? They're going to want to come home, right?

I was biased but also not worried about twelve kids being bored. If the kids truly wanted to do this, they would be signaling a commitment to leaving their family for a month, and the family's commitment to them. It was a commitment to try to be the best we could be.

When other running coaches in the area heard we were attempting to spend a month at Big Bear, 99 percent must have told me that it was crazy. There was no way, they would tell me, that they could do something like leave town for a month. It was the same excuse I'd heard when I'd pushed to leave campus for practice the year before: "I couldn't do that."

Well, we couldn't either—until we did. It was why, when I would hear other coaches, or people from our own high school, criticize our plans, say that we were crazy, my reaction was that I wasn't so sure about that. Crazy is only crazy until it's the norm. I looked at it this way: How important is it to you?

I knew some people viewed this part of me, the one that felt compelled to take whatever I was doing to the fullest extent, as a negative. But it was central to who I was. I'd run 5K's before kindergarten. I'd fallen so in love with BMX that I practiced my starts before breakfast. I wanted to coach and was willing to crisscross the country to learn from the best. The challenge of creating the best team in the country from scratch was appealing, not daunting. Some may have thought that was over-the-top. From my perspective, I thought it was ridiculous to do otherwise. Why sign up to coach a high school team if you were just going to give your athletes half effort?

In running, the idea of pushing the envelope can be taken the wrong way. Performance-enhancing drugs were a line that I or our athletes would never cross. But within the rules, we should absolutely push what is possible. That there was never a simple answer with me was almost a running joke between Newbury Park's athletic director and principal.

When coaches said they couldn't possibly be away from their families for one month, that their spouses would be upset, I understood. Sure, I was lucky Tanya came from a high-level running background and understood sacrifice. When we lived in Beaverton in an apartment without a real mattress, she hadn't cared. But even so, I still would only see her for a few days during the team's month at Big Bear, as she worked and helped out with our junior-varsity runners back at Newbury Park. That was going to be hard. Doing this would mean giving up almost all of our vacation time during the summer *and* it would cost us financially.

But as a team, our runners had an opportunity to do something special. I had competed on a run-of-the-mill team in high school. I wanted to create for Newbury Park what I would have wished for— an environment in which the athletes chose to be around one another, creating memories they'd never forget.

Right after the meeting I talked to the Youngs. They were all for Nico going. Now we had two. With Nico on board, I knew others would follow because everybody saw Nico's rise from a young runner with raw promise to elite caliber, and everybody who wanted to be good followed his example. When Nico showed up for morning sessions and did plyometrics and weight bands, others did; when Nico monitored his iron levels, others did.

The parents of Ryan Collier, a junior who ran on junior varsity, said that when they went home from the meeting and shared the plans with Ryan, he was ecstatic to be invited. They were thrilled, too. Now we had three.

Weeks passed. Spring was approaching. Only three months remained to figure out logistics if we were going, and I needed answers. I kept talking with the parents. It felt a little insulting that everyone said they wanted to do what it took to be the best, yet this plan was almost entirely shot down so quickly. At another team meeting before track season, I pulled aside Jace's parents.

"This is going to make them better physiologically, mentally, and it's a huge opportunity without training them too hard," I said. "If people don't want to go, that's okay. But that means you really don't want to win, because I'm telling you what we need to do in order to win, so it just comes down to that. And if it's not in the cards, it's not in the cards, but this is my plan. You want to know what we're going to do? This is what we're going to do."

A few days later, the Aschbrenners were on board. Now we had four.

Once the major players agreed, everyone else joined in: yes, yes, yes. That commitment to a plan that had never before been done, to go far beyond the usual expectations for summer training and to change our mindset about what was possible, hit me as incredibly meaningful. It wasn't just me anymore standing in front of a room detailing my seemingly crazy ambitions.

I was convinced that I could have gone to another high school and developed fast times. But I'm not sure I could have gone somewhere else and won big because the parents and the kids wouldn't want it as much as Newbury Park's. These kids, and their desire, were different. And that got me excited.

For three years, our team had been the Nico-and-Jace show. But very early, it seemed to me that our opponents would soon have to watch out for yet another fast, tough Newbury Park runner: Colin Sahlman.

Colin had impressed me during his freshman cross country season. Inside the skinniest kid on the team, there was toughness. He hadn't been able to run much in 2018 because of growing pains, yet he had still made the top five of a team that won a state championship and placed top ten at nationals.

The following spring, during his freshman track and field season, I noticed something else about Colin: Good luck to anyone trying to outkick him. On our team, even someone as fast as Nico—whose top-end speed was vastly and continually underrated—had to work on their kick, when a runner unleashes their final burst of speed at the race's end, either to pass competitors or hold them off. Not Colin, though. He had the kind of kick that you can't teach.

He'd shown flashes of it in cross country, but I became a full believer on March 28, 2019, at an otherwise forgettable little dual meet at Westlake High School. Colin ran 4:23 for 1,600 meters, which was pretty good for a guy who'd run about 4:48 the year before, as an eighth grader. But the time wasn't what made the memory stick. It was how he ran it. Before the race I specifically told him not to take the lead early but instead wait until there were 200 meters to go.

"Then, light 'em up," I said.

I'd said it in sort of a joking manner. Well, Colin lit them up. He closed the final 200 in about 26 seconds. Second place was 5 seconds behind. It was starting to click for him that what he once considered his best was just the start.

A few days later, in early April, we took a select number of athletes to the Arcadia Invitational, northeast of Los Angeles. Tucked between the San Gabriel Mountains to the north and Pasadena to the west, Arcadia High School had hosted a premier meet under the lights at night since 1968. Every year, Arcadia's 3,200-meter race became a de facto all-star race, the closest thing to one race hosting almost all of the country's elite. Because of its scale and the way we circled it on our schedule every year, Arcadia could be seen as a track and field cousin to the cross country meet at Woodbridge. Entered in the Rising Stars Mile, which featured some of the fastest underclassmen in the country, Colin won in 4:16.4 to break the race record by a second. A mile is 1,609 meters—meaning that only days after going as fast as he'd ever run in a piddly little local meet, he'd gone even farther and faster against even tougher competition.

Naturally, he did it with another monster kick. With 200 meters to go, Colin entered the race's final curve in fourth, a massive three seconds behind the leader. With 80 to go, he was still fourth, but had swung out into lane three to pass from the outside and began hauling. His kick was so fast and so unexpected that it left the race announcer laughing in disbelief.

COLIN SAHLMAN

Sean would always tell us not to put limits on ourselves. For me, especially my freshman year when he said he thought I could run sub-4:20, I was like—that's really fast—"I don't know about that." He told me, "I know you can do it; you can be one of the best freshmen in the country." And then when I did it, I was like, "Oh, he was right." After that, I fully trusted him.

As a coach, you have to develop a gut feeling for how much more your athletes can honestly improve, not only to give them the confidence, but also to not overpromise. Ever since I had begun competing, I felt I could watch a runner for a few minutes and intuitively begin to sense their potential based on their build, gait, and mechanics.

When I was in elementary and high school, I was much more a visual learner than one who learned through reading. I liked watching my history teacher act out a historic moment rather than reading about it. It's why it was so important to me to observe coaches as they did their job and watch the nuances of communicating and coaching. To me, that was an art. I'd been with Newbury Park's runners long enough by now to predict how they would race just by watching their strides during warm-ups. From that, I knew what Colin was capable of, even if that potential was hard for him to see at such a young age.

I've heard it said many times that I just think everyone can be fast.

No. But I do think everyone can be fast*er*.

I'm not someone whose head is always in the clouds; I realize that there has to be an eventual top end to how fast humans can run around a track or a cross country course. But once an athlete or a coach acknowledges they are limited, then they are.

Like Colin and the team parents who had to be persuaded about the Big Bear proposal, Nico had unnecessarily set barriers for himself, ones he got over with some convincing.

As soon as Nico finished fourth as a junior at NXN, top college distance-running programs such as Stanford, Northern Arizona, and Oregon recruited him harder. So much of the initial contact in recruiting happens through collegiate assistant coaches. Now, the head coaches were calling. Stanford's Chris Miltenberg was one. I've always thought highly of Miltenberg as a coach, and we chatted that spring, soon after he'd talked with Nico as part of a recruiting conversation. Miltenberg told me something that made me wince. He and Nico had been chatting about Nico's goals for his junior season of track. Nico had told the Stanford coach he thought he could run 8:54 for 3,200 meters. I firmly believe it should be up to athletes to come up with their own goals, but Nico had just sold himself far too short—and to a top NCAA coach, no less. Nico was too good to tell someone he wanted to run 8:54.

I sent Nico a message: We had to talk.

You are capable of running 8:40 or faster, I told him. I could see in his head that he was thinking, *8:40— and that's fast.* And it is. But he had to understand that it was both a huge goal, but also within reach. Our workouts during the spring had begun to convince him that it was. Arcadia was the place to test whether our belief was justified. Arcadia was the most important track and field meet for Newbury Park every spring. Unlike California's state meet, it didn't require weeks of arduous qualifying. And unlike the state meet, it drew elite competitors from out of state, especially in the distance races.

On a cool night, Nico lined up near the inside rail, part of a field that was so loaded it would reveal where Nico stood nationally. Liam Anderson, who'd won Nike Cross Nationals four months earlier, was running, as were Cole Sprout and Matt Strangio, both juniors, who'd finished third and eighth, respectively, at NXN. There were more familiar challengers Nico had seen at NXN, including Drew Bosley; Luke Grundvig; Carter Cheeseman; Charles Hicks, a future NCAA cross country national champion; and Joe Waskom, a future NCAA champion and world-championships qualifier at 1,500 meters. All had finished in the top forty in Portland. There was also Leo Daschbach, an up-and-coming talent from suburban Phoenix.

That kind of field had attracted a lot of media hype. I couldn't help but notice that seemingly 80 percent of people weren't picking Nico to win, and I couldn't help but get frustrated by that. Some media members tried to interview the top athletes from across the country before the race. As soon as they approached Nico, his expression tightened. No one would be interviewing him before the race, I announced. I probably sounded like a jerk, but I wanted it clear that these poor kids didn't need to be interviewed minutes before running. They needed to warm up and get ready.

Nico asked if I could go to the warm-up area with him. Normally, he warmed up alone. He seemed nervous. Really nervous. I was nervous. It was our third year together. But as I watched him run his strides, the short sprints distance runners practice to mimic a start, my stress level dropped. By his stride, I could tell he was ready to win. Tanya was standing next to me, and I told her so.

"How do you know?" she said.

Nico has a demeanor where you can just tell. It's the same to this day. *Oh, he was ready.*

Nico's start left him boxed inside a pack of more than two dozen runners, but as Sprout began stringing out the field from the front, Nico worked his way up and got on Sprout's heels after a 4:22 first mile. After ripping off consecutive 65-second laps, the two separated themselves from the pack with three laps to go.

Nico tried to overtake Sprout a few times on the last lap without success. I was by the fence as Nico came off the final turn into the last 100. He saw me.

"You can do this!" I yelled.

Arms pumping, pulling across his body, he passed Sprout with 50 meters left. Nico crossed in 8:40.0—exactly what we predicted, the third-fastest 3,200 ever by a high schooler, and 0.7 seconds ahead of Sprout.

For anyone who doubted Nico's speed, here was evidence they were wrong. And for Nico, here was evidence he should dream even bigger: He'd just run the fastest time of the season in the entire United States. If he had been satisfied with 8:54, that's probably what he would have run.

NICO YOUNG

I don't know why I was abnormally nervous for that race. We got there really early, I think that was part of it, and I put a lot of expectations on myself that *If I win this race, this is going to be huge for me.* Sean told me I could break 8:40, and when I ran 8:40, it instilled more confidence in me. During that race, he was climbing on the fence at 150 to go, screaming. I remember coming around the turn seeing him yelling at me to go around. Setting 8:40 as the standard made all the difference. Winning that race and beating the NXN champion of that year was when I went, "Okay, I know what I'm going to do next year." We're going to change the plans and try to do everything we can and run as fast as possible in every race.

We would always do, like, a workout about ten days out from a race that was a clear indicator of the shape that we were in. If I wasn't in shape to run something, Sean would tell me that, so there was definitely a big dynamic of trust there. Half of it was definitely believing that I could, and then because of that there was no sense of panic if it started to feel harder earlier on than I anticipated in the race; I still knew that I would be fine because he told me that I would be fine, because I'd trained for this specifically.

It dawned on me that Nico and Newbury Park were no longer just a fun story about a team on the rise noticed only by college recruiters and local fans. Within the running community, something was happening. Word was spreading about these fast times, especially from a school with practically zero history of them.

The fame the kids were getting was deserved. But it brought out nuttiness in a small number of others. For the first time, I began noticing anonymous, faceless accounts spreading lies about our program, suggesting Newbury Park's success must be attributed to drugs. Such a suggestion was completely detached from reality. Just as strange was the encounter I had with someone willing to show their face.

One night that spring, I came home from track practice to one of the strangest interactions of my time in coaching. Waiting on the porch of my home was a man in his fifties or sixties. He said he wanted to talk to me about Nico's training. He didn't want to talk so much as rant. The man was pissed off, saying our runners had blocked him on the social media app Strava, which allows runners to post their times and routes. He was convinced I was overtraining Newbury Park's runners, yelling at me about how I should be doing this, and how Nico shouldn't be training like that, and how I was going to burn him out.

"Who are you?" I finally said.

"I coach athletes in Connecticut. . . ."

"You live in Connecticut? Why are you here?"

It was one of many unanswered questions I had, even after we talked for close to a half hour. I was trying to be nice, but finally, I told him he had to leave and threatened to call the cops. He at last took off. I already had concerns about the way Strava allowed strangers access to our athletes' training, and my reasons had purely related to coaching. I didn't like how followers might be able to see an athlete's run or mile splits, but would never know the instructions behind that workout, a disconnect that inevitably led to speculation I'd see on message boards or social media.

Uninformed speculation was one thing. But the interaction on my porch made me even more nervous about strangers tracking our runners' whereabouts, especially the girls. I told the team that while I couldn't force them to get off Strava, I didn't want them public anymore.

Even after Arcadia, Nico wasn't satisfied. As he did during his sophomore year, Nico spent the next month passing through California's qualifying gauntlet to make the state track and field meet in the 3,200. Under the lights in Clovis, he dominated with his 66-second laps, winning in 8:47.27. He'd essentially run the last three laps by himself. Liam Anderson had run a tough race to surge late and win at NXN the previous fall, but now Nico was the one pulling away as the race progressed. Anderson was six seconds behind. One year after Strangio had won the state title in 8:56, he was ten seconds behind Nico's winning time. Jace finished eleventh. Our top two were as strong as any other duo in the country.

What I love about track and field is how it reveals what is special about an individual racer, and how the times stack up across decades; unlike cross country, where courses are hard to compare, there are no complaints about whether a track is a few meters short. But track season was over. I wanted the runners to get a short break, because by late June, we would be in Big Bear. Cross country is a complete team sport. Winning a national championship hinged on more than just our top two: How fast would our third, fourth, and fifth runners be?

At the state track meet, a coach I knew congratulated me on Nico's victory in the 3,200. Such moments happen only so often, he said. "Take it in while you can because it doesn't last."

It was friendly advice. It also wouldn't apply to Newbury Park.

CHAPTER NINE

WHEN I LEFT FOR my usual five-mile run, a lot was on my mind.

It was June 2019, and it was about to be our most important month since I began coaching at Newbury Park. In just days, we would be embarking on our four-week trip to Big Bear; I believed in my core that this season could be historic. I. Could. Not. Wait. A work project had taken Tanya to Arizona, so I went through our last-minute planning and found so much work still to do. I needed to cut a rope into sections for our rope-assisted stretching. I needed to finish packing and finalize the logistics of getting to our rental houses.

I headed out now on trails I'd run many times before, but this run was different. Overcome by dizziness, I had to stop and walk what felt like a dozen times before I cut it short by two miles and went home. Something had felt off for weeks, and I knew it because running had become so much harder in recent weeks. I saw an endocrinologist. We thought I might have asthma. We thought I had hypoglycemia. This, though, was something new.

A shower didn't ease the discomfort. I grabbed chicken and vegetables from the hot bar at Whole Foods for dinner and came home to watch a Diamond League track meet from Morocco that I'd recorded.

I couldn't shake it. As I ate, I forgot where I was one moment, then felt as if I was going to pass out the next. My left arm and neck went numb. *Oh shit.*

My breath labored as my heart rate skyrocketed, as if I were going after a four-minute mile. I'd never thought what was wrong could be my heart. Sweating and panicking, I called Tanya.

I told her that I thought I was having a stroke and that she needed to call an ambulance. She called back and told me she was having trouble because she was in Arizona trying to reach the right people in California, and at that point I didn't feel that I could wait. I looked at my cats and thought that I might not be back for a while, then stepped outside with the keys to my Jeep, which I'd bought only a week earlier. The hospital was in Thousand Oaks. As if on autopilot, I got in and raced to the hospital. I don't remember driving there. I probably shouldn't have driven.

As soon as I mentioned my heart, I was in an emergency room bed.

As I lay there, I started to feel somewhat better—until I saw the mother of one of the runners I was supposed to be taking to Big Bear in just a few days. She worked at the hospital, and I didn't want her to see her son's coach like this, only days before a monthlong trip that I had convinced everyone to agree to. I rolled over onto my stomach to avoid being seen. Escaping the doctor's attention wasn't as easy. When I told him that in less than five days I was going to Big Bear for a monthlong trip, he told me I wasn't going anywhere.

The hell I wasn't.

Night came. I quickly learned that the hospital was no place to rest. Sleep came in spurts. Doctors checked in incessantly, interrupting my sleep. Then, as I would relax enough to doze off, a bedside alarm would jar me awake, triggered by a resting heart rate that ran in the forties due to years of running.

Things seemed to have stabilized, but I couldn't leave for several days as I went through test after test. That meant missing the first two days of practices we'd scheduled before leaving for Big Bear. I told the team that a family emergency had come up, and Tanya and my assistant coach, Steve Hawkins, who knew what was really happening, stepped in to run practice in my absence. But the runners started to wonder what was going on. They didn't know I was literally lying in a hospital bed. As a coach, I always wanted to explain the what and the why behind our team's workouts and plans. In this case, however, I was not going to send the group chat a message of "Barely walking right now, this is bad!" There was no way.

A few days into my hospital stay, Jace's dad called. "Sean, what's going on? Is everything okay? Jace said you haven't been at practice."

There was no use in hiding the truth anymore. "I'm gonna be honest with you." I told him what my previous few days had been like. He was stunned and asked if I was all right before asking the same question that had been on my mind.

"What are we going to do about camp?"

"I'm going."

"You can't go."

"I'm going, it's fine."

But I wasn't fine. I'd suffered a heart attack, and leaving the hospital, I felt far from my usual self.

The episode had left me, someone who thought of himself as a fitness-oriented person, shaky. Then, tests at the hospital had left me momentarily unstable.

Trying to figure out what had caused the heart attack led doctors to perform a coronary angiogram. A catheter was put into a blood vessel and they searched for potential blockages around my heart. When they didn't find any, it was a relief. But when I was released, it was with the understanding that I would have to work to get back to baseline. Walking was difficult. At first I needed crutches, then I graduated to walking with a limp. There would need to be a change of plans. I called Todd McDonnell, the father of Tommy McDonnell, a junior, and Sam McDonnell, a promising sophomore on the girls team. Because Todd and I knew each other well, we had planned for him to spend a chunk of time helping out at Big Bear. After my heart attack, I asked if he could spend the entire month. I was under doctor's orders not to lift more than fifty pounds and would need help.

"No big deal," he said.

On June 24, a Ford Transit van packed with twelve boys, Todd, and me drove into the mountains. We crammed in as much luggage as we could and were followed by parents who had filled another SUV with more luggage our van couldn't hold. The house we'd rented for the first three weeks looked like a log cabin from the outside, but inside had an awesome modern setup: An air-hockey table, Pop-A-Shot basketball hoop, and pool table were in a room right off the front door, along with a pair of bunk beds. A spare room was reserved for parents who wanted to drop in and spend a few days. Where I slept wasn't a big concern. The runners needed their own beds, not me. In later years, I spent some nights on a little mattress under a pool table. Another time, I rolled out my sleeping bag in a closet that wasn't tall enough to stand in but was long enough for me to lie down. With its rooms and beds everywhere, the house was a little kooky and a little run-down. It was, quite honestly, perfect.

Our weeklong trips to Big Bear the previous two summers became the blueprint for our longer stay, except now those plans could be expanded. This was not your garden-variety LSD—long, slow distance—summer buildup. From the jump, we got to work. Once a week, we ran the punishing ascent up Skyline Drive at 6:30 mile pace, which is extremely difficult. We would do a long run at Holcomb Valley, north of the lake, which is also pretty hilly, and depending on the week, it might be an easy, medium, or hard long run. Tempo work was always on the menu. Knowing the runners were coming to camp after some type of break from running following track season, I didn't want to overload them early in our Big Bear stay, but it was common to run one mile, followed by a minute rest, three times at tempo pace. This work, for these boys, with years of conditioning under their belt, was easy. The goal was to ramp them up so that by the end of camp, they could run a workout of four miles straight at the same pace they'd been doing the tempo workout. For our faster runners, at altitude, that meant running about 5:20 per mile.

Nico was a physical freak, though. By the end of camp, he was running his four miles close to a 5:05 pace and making it look easy at seven thousand feet. I sent Mike Smith, coach at Northern Arizona University, one of the many recruiting Nico, a message to ask whether it was normal to see someone this young doing this kind of work at this kind of elevation. The answer: No, it's not normal.

Nor was this training conventional. What was shocking to everyone I explained our training to was that working on speed year-round *was* our normal, even if it wasn't the philosophy by which most coaches operated. Speed means different things to different people. It doesn't mean we're doing 400-meter repeats. It means we were sprinting year-round—40 meters, 50 meters, 60 meters. I had read research showing that if you stop doing speed, you lose your speed in three to five days. That's why people do strides—short, usually 100-meter bursts—after runs a few times a week. The problem, in my view, is that most people don't do them extremely fast. If you run a stride at mile pace, it won't help. We not only ran fast strides year-round, we also did workouts. At Newbury Park, we started 1,000-meter repeats, and mile repeats, as early as July.

Building that level of fitness was at the core of why we were at Big Bear. And yet, by now, the runners understood that under our progressive training philosophy, their highest mileage would come in September and October, during the heart of the season. We wanted to run well at Woodbridge in September and Clovis in October, but I'd subscribed to the observation Scott Simmons had made while we were together at Queens University in Charlotte, that sometimes runners run their best when they're training hardest, well before their season-ending tapers take effect.

Our days were split up into the serious and the laid-back. Everything related to running we approached with the purpose of commitment. When we stepped to the line for our hardest workouts, our runners had already stretched with ropes, run a few warm-up miles, and done dynamic stretches.

A lot of athletes can run fast immediately after picking up the sport. Running record-breaking times, however, isn't an accident; it's a result of intent. We had made sacrifices to come to the mountains for four weeks. Why not use it wisely? That message wasn't one I conveyed alone, but with Ethan Duffy during my first season, and Jace and Nico since. The runner-led shift that had started in 2018, when the team's leaders made clear through their actions that it was cool to think big and compete hard, was continuing into a new summer. I wanted these kids to be so damn good, but by agreeing to go to Big Bear for a month, the athletes and their parents had signaled they wanted it just as badly.

Training at altitude gets you fit quickly because it raises your fitness without having to increase your mileage. The natural effect altitude has on red blood cells is not insignificant. It's why schools including Northern Arizona, Colorado, BYU, Adams State, and Colorado School of Mines routinely produce top distance runners and title-winning teams, and why the majority of top American professionals either live full-time or train part-time in high-altitude places like Flagstaff, Arizona, or Boulder, Colorado.

Inside our Big Bear home, a small spare room lined with bookshelves became our place to understand how our runners adapted to elevation. As an inside joke to jab at some of the deranged online comments about our team, we stuck a sign reading NEWBURY PARK LAB outside the entrance. Before any workout or long run I would test the hemoglobin of runners who wanted to take part, using a device that slipped over a finger and used lasers without drawing any blood. It would register heart rate, as well, information that was sometimes relevant. Once, the CIF and the school received complaints that I was testing our athletes' blood, and I had to show them that it was noninvasive, that taking it wasn't obligatory, and that there was a reason for the tests.

Hemoglobin is a protein inside a red blood cell that helps deliver oxygen to muscles, which makes it one of the most studied areas of endurance sports, as scientists try to understand the relationship between hemoglobin and VO_2 max, which essentially means the maximum amount of oxygen we can use while exercising the hardest. We would chart the hemoglobin levels before and after workouts and then compare them. What I noticed was Nico recovered extremely quickly. Jace and Nico would run together, but their blood suggested that Jace needed more recovery the following day. And that was the reason why we tested, so we could avoid overdoing our training.

But the physical benefits of going to Big Bear for one month were clearly outweighed by its unquantifiable team-building value. We could probably have trained in the Catskills in upstate New York, at a fraction of the altitude, and gotten the same results. The secret was building an environment that could elevate our roster to something better than the sum of its already-talented parts. By the time the starting gun went off at Nike Cross Nationals in December, our red blood cell advantage would be gone, but not the intangible bonds we forged through being around one another at camp.

I'd blast music early some mornings in the living room. Maybe it was cheesy, but the kids would wake up, laugh, and our day would begin. It was usually almost lunchtime when we drove our vans down the mountain after our runs, back to the house. This was where parents had wondered how we would spend all of our free time. When you're asking runners to work as hard as I was, they deserve time to relax. We had days when we didn't run at all. Some days involved plans we'd made ahead of time, like for go-karting or renting ocean kayaks and taking them out on the lake. But mostly, it unfolded as I'd envisioned—like a normal summer for the kids, heightened by the opportunity to hang out with friends for weeks on end. They ate, went to the lake, or lay low at the house. Some played video games. Swimming at the lake was free. Doing flips off the rocks was free. Some guys would have a second run; others wouldn't. We had a pet raccoon. Fargo, as he was quickly nicknamed, wasn't supposed to be a pet, but I kept leaving him a plate of scraps from dinner, so he kept returning to our back deck. Inspired by a full moon, we went on a midnight hike into the woods, then I let the kids sleep in the next day, waiting until the afternoon to run. On July 4, we watched fireworks burst over the lake. And, as had now become tradition, we went to the Rocks.

One day, instead of swimming over to the Rocks from shore, we rented a big pontoon boat and motored over. It was Daniel Appleford's day to captain the boat, and without a place to anchor it near the island, I told him I was going to jump off the Rocks, then come straight back. I thought he might drive around the rock island while he waited. There was some miscommunication. As I was climbing up to the ledge where I was going to jump, I heard it.

"Nobody's by the boat!"

Slowly moving with the chop of the water, the boat inched closer to ramming the island. I jumped in and pushed it away, just before our little boat trip was about to get a lot more expensive. We could laugh about it later, once we got our security deposit back.

The days also had structure. We broke the team into smaller groups and assigned them rotating duties. Those on cooking duty would go to the grocery store with me, buy the food, and come home and work on dinner. If the kids wanted to keep their rooms a mess, well, that was up to them, but we would keep the rest of the house clean, and that meant garbage duty. Others handled other jobs. Tuesday was taco night at Dank Donuts, a little building on Moonridge Road with live music and long outdoor tables. The first four tacos for every runner were on the tab their parents had paid in the spring.

Fresh out of the hospital, I was shaken up the first couple of nights in the mountains. I found myself thinking, *God, this is nuts.*

If shopping for food with twelve teenage boys isn't chaotic enough, try it while moving at only half speed. As they loaded shopping carts with boxes of pasta during our first team grocery run, I, the coach obsessed with speed, drove the aisles in one of the motorized carts kept at the front of the store. Walking was still too painful, too slow.

I know now that I have an irregular heartbeat, called atrial fibrillation, and that it can be triggered by exercise. I still run most days, but usually for five miles or less. Maintaining a 6:20 mile pace feels easy some days, and on others I might feel my chest pitter-patter and have to stop three times in four miles.

When running is your life, having it taken away can feel disorienting. But knowing my limits is something I have to be conscious about now because it scares me, causing stress, which leads to migraines. At one point, I started losing hair. At camp, my attention was split between trying to hold myself together and keeping our team going full speed. The kids knew the outlines of what had happened, and I didn't want to lie to them or their parents. When their parents were nervous, I'd respond, "I'm fine." But during those first few weeks at altitude, I was scared I might drop dead.

When the kids took off down the trail toward the lake to go rock jumping, I struggled down the path behind them. When the rest of the team got into the lake to cool off, the stitches in my leg, where the catheter had been inserted, kept me from getting in. Before I left the hospital, the doctor told me that I had to promise to wait fourteen days before getting in the water. The potential for my stitches to interact with lake-water algae gave him even more reservations about my upcoming trip. I held to that promise. But fourteen days in, on the dot, I covered my stitches with a waterproof patch and added tape around its edges. I did not want it to become infected, and yet, after two weeks of watching everyone else have fun, I was going in the damn lake.

The two-week mark was a milestone in other ways. Walking became easier. I could climb rocks, and I went for my first run, joining Nico and Jace on a flat dirt road during their cooldown after a tempo workout. Going for a two-mile run had never felt so bad, and yet, after what I'd been through, I had a whole new appreciation for being able to stand there, exhausted and covered in dust, with this team. It was . . . perfect.

For our final week at Big Bear, we checked out of the house we'd stayed in the previous three weeks and into another home, where we were joined by the rest of the team, including the incoming freshmen, such as Lex and Leo Young. We held a mini talent show. In one act, the boys dressed in leis and sunglasses, playing ukuleles.

On one of the trip's final nights, the teams gathered in our house's huge living room and I asked their leaders what they wanted to accomplish that season. On a whiteboard, the teams started writing. It wasn't too surprising that a list of goals from a group led by a couple of future valedictorians in Jace and Nico was long and detailed. But at the top was that the boys wanted to win NXN. Their ambition was welcomed; I certainly fed it. But goals had always been secondary to what happened *after* a goal-setting session—how hard were you willing to work to accomplish them?

COLIN SAHLMAN

Sean said, "I don't want to have any influence over what you guys are saying or what your goals are. I want you guys to figure that out for yourself." Nico and Jace would ask us what we want to do as a team together and then they threw in ideas, too: Get eight hours of sleep; hold each other accountable in workouts; fuel your body right; little things like that, because we all knew we wanted to do everything we could to get to NXN. A big bunch of little things combined is not a little thing.

One year earlier, when we'd left our high-altitude summer training, we weren't considered a California title contender, let alone appearing on the radar nationally. Our seemingly overnight success during the 2018 cross country season, and the spring track season that followed, had brought a new level of scrutiny. Everyone we came across seemed to have an opinion about us and the program we were building. We were open with reporters: I gave interviews all the time about training methods, yet so much of what I heard about Newbury Park was completely uninformed; there seemed to be a school of thought that we must be doing something improper to run as we had, at a school with no tradition. As a way to mess with that crowd, I bought a notebook while we were in the mountains. Its cover was Newbury Park High yellow, and on it I wrote in black Sharpie NPXC SECRETS and posted the photo to Instagram.

The joke was that there was nothing written inside the notebook. The secret was there was no secret. Just consistency, belief, and speed.

CHAPTER TEN

IN LATE AUGUST, I took out the measuring wheel I stored in my Jeep's trunk. Our team was starting to gather at Pepper Tree. We'd run the park hundreds of times, but no matter the course, on days when we held our hardest interval workouts, I always measured the loops we would run down to the exact meter.

Except this one.

Ever since our sudden emergence as a state champion, media outlets had begun to take interest in Newbury Park. By August, weeks before the 2019 cross country season and our state-title defense officially began, a website that covered the news of high school track and field, MileSplit, asked to film one of our workouts. I agreed. It was a chance to send a statement and have a little fun.

At altitude, I had stayed away from hard intervals, what some call VO_2 max workouts because they test how much oxygen your body can use during exercise. Under our progressive training philosophy that increased our runners' workload over the course of the season, timed to sharpen us right before the state meet in November and Nike Cross Nationals in December, you have to pick your battles over when to go really hard. One was in July, in one of our first workouts after coming home from Big Bear. That day, Nico ran seven repetitions of one kilometer, with three minutes rest in between, and averaged 2:55 per kilometer.

By late August, the time had come for another 1,000-meter-repeat workout. MileSplit interviewed Nico and me beforehand, and then, away from the camera, I pulled the team aside to let them in on my plan: I'd purposefully marked the course short by a few meters for the camera. Was I confident our runners would still run ridiculously fast? Yes. Did I also want it to shock people a little? Also yes. MileSplit wasn't aware of any of this. Only the runners would know, so when they crossed the finish line, they would hear me bark out one time for the cameras, but added two more seconds for their real split.

Nico covered his first kilometer in 2:48, or the equivalent of a 4:30 mile. After our second rep, the boys got a three-minute rest. Nico cranked the third in 2:47. The team didn't let up the rest of the way; Nico averaged 2:48 for his seven repetitions, and Jace 2:51. The gap between what they'd appeared to run and what their actual split was was so tiny as to not be a misrepresentation of their general fitness. I also knew the times would raise eyebrows and put everyone on notice: Newbury Park was coming. Message boards and comment sections devoted to distance running lit up, some questioning how we could pull it off, others stunned that teenagers were doing this.

NICO YOUNG

Sean loves messing with people but in a good way like that. He enjoyed the attention of folks freaking out over something that we did, because it just elevated the group so much more and brought more attention to the team—and scared the competition more.

If the point of the ruse was to mess with people, the intent behind the workout was extremely serious. Our challenge with Nico was getting him to feel comfortable, even relaxed, covering the first mile in cross country in 4:25. Every mile in a 3-mile or 5K cross country race is a different challenge. The third mile is for holding on, the second for pushing yourself through pain. But the first is about finding a rhythm. The tendency is to run the first 400 meters too fast to get off the line in a field of several hundred runners and not get stuck in the middle of the pack, where it's harder to maneuver and easier to get tangled. We trained to start hard, but the necessity of doing so means you can't just run an evenly paced first mile. Years spent observing coaches, and becoming one myself, had made me very aware of running mistakes that I had made. But some mistakes I'd recognized as they were happening, like during college when I noticed that I would go out so freaking hard in the first mile, only to think, *Man, I'm just not used to doing this. We've never simulated this in workouts. And now I'm trying it in a meet?*

I couldn't expect Newbury Park's athletes to excel pushing their red line during my first years coaching cross country. I needed them to physically mature to handle such difficult workouts, and I needed time to build their trust in me. By 2018, we'd reached that point. By 2019, we could push it even harder.

"If you can go out at that pace, the best guy is going to follow you and you're going to destroy him," I said. "You're going to make him go out sub-4:30. He's never done that before, and you're going to destroy him. You'll have done it a million times at practice."

One of my cardinal rules was to never tell an athlete they could do something if I didn't believe they could. Inflating their self-belief beyond their abilities, only to see their confidence crater should they fall short, was a risk I wasn't going to take. But opening in 4:25 was realistic for Nico because he was coming into his own as one of the nation's best young distance runners, even if, at times, he still needed coaxing to trust his ability. He was so humble that sometimes he had to be reassured that he was truly that good.

A few weeks before our Pepper Tree workout, Nico had been one of a select few invited to attend Nike's Elite Camp on the sportswear giant's corporate campus west of Portland. I was mentoring Nico and wanted him to meet a mentor of mine, Alberto Salazar. Not possible, a camp official told me. So, I called Alberto. He'd heard of Nico, knew Nico looked up to Galen Rupp, and made the meeting happen. I was convinced that many more around the country would know Nico's name by December. In the race for the national championship at Nike Cross Nationals, Nico was what was known in the world of cross country as a *low stick*. The term goes back to small meets where score is kept by handing runners as soon as they finish a Popsicle stick with their finishing place written on it. Nike Cross Nationals used slightly more advanced technology for its results, but the point remained. From our 2019 forecasts, Nico's stick could very well have the lowest number: 1. If our top scorer could score just one or two points, it would create a much bigger margin of error for our other scorers.

It was a credible plan—but not a foolproof one.

The only problem is that runners who qualify for NXN as individuals and not part of a team don't count toward team scores. If Nico finished first, and individuals took the next eight places, then a runner representing a team who finished in tenth would technically count as scoring only two points. We pushed the pace to create fast races because we didn't believe anyone else could stay with Newbury Park and thus ensured that our runners were running freely near the front as we hit midrace. But if a bunch of nonscoring individual qualifiers finished early at NXN, then other teams with finishers deeper in the field could score lower points than normal. That would negate any advantage from our front-running strategy and shift it toward teams that didn't have a single outlier individual, but were capable of running in tight packs.

Teams such as Great Oak.

The proven power versus the upstart. We'd circled each other in

2018 when the Temecula school was still stronger. In 2019 we were again separated in California by our classifications—they remained Division 1; we stayed in Division 2—but the progress our runners had made since the last cross country season suggested that a head-on collision for the national title in Portland was possible.

JACE ASCHBRENNER

After we were sixth at our first NXN meet in 2018, it was fun and all, but the mindset instilled in us by Sean was that we could be better. One of the best things about California is that it was so competitive that we always had teams like Great Oak, La Costa Canyon, and schools like that who would always be competitive with us and show us what the national level looked like and what the top is. Going into senior year, the primary goals were to be state champions, to beat Great Oak, and to win nationals. It was fun to be on the team with goals like that. Whenever we won or lost, we won or lost together, and we were always able to just keep the goal in mind.

Turning Great Oak into the enemy wasn't a point I wanted to hammer into our runners. Although I made clear to our guys that we wanted to destroy other teams out on the course, we were just as strict about ensuring we gave our opponents respect. Great Oak was a power because it had earned it. Their coach, Doug Soles, had been nothing but cordial to me, even encouraging. Our athletes were friendly at times. But the competition was fierce. Great Oak's reputation consistently drew talent, and that talent rose to the occasion in cross country. In the fall of 2019, four scorers from their 2018 team that had won state and finished second at Nike Cross Nationals returned, and that didn't include Gabriel Abbes, who had been Great Oak's top runner early in 2018 before being sidelined by a foot injury. Abbes had returned, as had Chris Verdugo, their other top threat. And yet I believed they didn't have any individual outliers who could run at the front with just about anyone in the country, whereas we had two, in Nico and Jace. It was why I felt Great Oak probably worried about us more than I did about them. But in many ways, for all the contenders emerging from Utah, Virginia, Illinois, New York, and Rhode Island, the race for the national title might very well come down to two California high schools separated by about 140 miles.

We wouldn't need to wait until December to see how we matched up.

Someone asked me once how many cross country races are enough. For elite high-school-aged runners, my ideal was racing three times: once during the regular season, then the state meet and nationals. You don't need to run a 5K on a cross country course eight to ten times per season—that's counterproductive. You develop in training. I understand that athletes want to see the fruits of their hard work in races—and it's true, you can race more in track, at least I think, because you're generally racing shorter distances. But cross country? You have to look for windows to build a solid training block during the season if you want to perform at the end.

I would have skipped all of the CIF meets if we hadn't needed them to go to the state championships. The Ventura County Championships and dual meets were long-standing traditions that I didn't care for at all. It applied to the track season, too. For runners at the junior-varsity level, or maybe a 4:25 miler, a meet like the county championships is a good race for you because it was appropriate competition. But if you're a 4:07 kid, or four-flat—these aren't hard-and-fast ranges, just indicative of an elite runner—then you don't need to participate in all of those meets if you want to run well at the state meet and the national meets to follow. Our schedule was determined by our goals, which meant chasing records. Sometimes we even had to evaluate whether it was worth it to compete at the various national championships in track and field that are sponsored by the big shoe companies. If we felt we had an opportunity to do something special in cross country, and we would begin focusing on cross country in late June, as was our standard, was it worth it to compete at a track meet in mid-June? Not really.

My aversion to the traditional schedule upset some people. But if it wasn't going to help our athletes maximize their talents with an aim toward showcasing how good they could be on a national scale, it wasn't something I wanted to do, customs be damned. My coaching was never motivated by filling up our trophy case with prizes from the Marmonte League championships or from the county championships. I like elite times, breaking barriers, and winning national titles.

It rubbed off on the kids. They didn't care about the little stuff, instead focusing on the bigger picture of not only how far they could go among high schoolers, but how it was setting them up to run fast in college and beyond. By shifting our thinking toward that approach, it set the bar higher for our expectations. I know this will sound harsh, but I think a lot of high school coaches are too cautious to do that.

Forget my ideal of running three times in an entire season; California's onerous system of qualifying rounds for state forced us to run more than I wanted in November alone. We had to run one dual meet—though I would treat it as essentially a workout—our league finals, Southern Section Prelims, Southern Section Finals, the state meet, and Nike Cross Nationals. All of that racing meant we had to be selective about which meets we entered the rest of the season. We cared about only two: Woodbridge in September, and Clovis in October. Clovis was important because it was an opportunity early in the season to race on and familiarize ourselves with the state-meet course.

Why Woodbridge? Except for the state meet, no other meet in California rivals the electric atmosphere at Woodbridge, where thousands of athletes from the best teams in the state show up and race under the lights at night, everyone believing they are about to run a personal best. They think that because of the course, which has changed location four times in the meet's four-decade history, but since 2016 has been held in Norco, deep in California's Inland Empire, on pancake-flat terrain that loops around soccer fields for three miles.

For those reasons, when people asked me my favorite race, I always said Woodbridge. It was the perfect site to showcase our fitness and show everybody who we were.

And it was the perfect place for Nico to try to break the national 3-mile record.

By the time Newbury Park's vans arrived in Norco on September 20, race day, there were stories indicating that Nico was going to attempt to join the elite club of fifteen boys in US high school cross country history to run 3 miles in less than 14 minutes. That only fifteen boys had done it was partly because there weren't many good opportunities to do it, because for several years the sport had slowly moved toward accepting 5,000 meters, or 3.1 miles, as the standard for high school cross country. The other reason so few had done it since Craig Virgin set the national 3-mile record of 13:50.6 at the 1972 Illinois state cross country championships was self-evident: Running that fast as a teenager is absurdly hard to do. Debates rage about the sanctity of records in cross country. Course-specific variables such as hills make comparisons across the years less clean than in track and field, with its standard, flat 400-meter oval. Still, even though spikes, gear, and training methods had improved over the decades, Virgin's record never fell. Chris Derrick, who went on to a successful college and pro career, came within two seconds of breaking the record in 2007, on the same Illinois course. Three years later, Lukas Verzbicas, one of the most decorated high school runners ever, and also from Illinois, missed by less than four seconds.

Averaging 4:40 miles, Nico had run 14:01 to win Woodbridge as a junior. His training indicated that he'd go faster as a senior. Much faster. Before the meet, I saw Rich Gonzalez, the meet director at the Arcadia Invitational, who ran an outlet that covered high school running in California. He was involved with the sport at all levels, including Nike Cross Nationals, and he wanted to know my expectations for Nico.

"He could break 13:40," I said.

Newbury Park stepped to the starting line for the Boys Sweepstakes race shortly before 10:00 p.m., alongside thirty-one other teams and 241 runners from seven states in the final race of the night. Great Oak's boys had won the Sweepstakes team title in 2018, 2017, 2015, and 2014, but on this night their coach, Doug Soles, wasn't there to watch his team's title defense in person because he was in his Oregon hometown being inducted into his high school's hall of fame.

As in any big race, the pack funneled within a quarter mile from a starting line dozens of runners wide down to only a few at the front, led by Nico. He passed the first mile in 4:28, with two others trying to stay with him. It was a hopeless strategy. There was no one in the race I thought could be close to Nico. Everybody gets to the first mile fast, but at about 2,000 meters, or a quarter of the way through the second mile, it dawns on them that the pace is unsustainable. Usually, that's when the wheels come off.

But that's the part we trained for. That's when we trained to surge.

Not even six minutes in, the wheels were off for everyone not wearing a yellow-and-black Newbury Park kit. Nico was in his own world at the front, and Jace had moved into second, and with Nick Goldstein and Colin Sahlman not far behind, we had four runners in front of Great Oak's number one.

As Jace ran by one of the fences holding back the crowd, he aggressively clapped his hands and bobbed his head, all while holding his pace. I later found out that Great Oak's assistant coach, running the team in place of Doug Soles that night, was bothered by Jace's clapping, thinking it was cocky or aimed at Great Oak in particular. I just thought Jace was caught up in the moment, pumped up by the atmosphere and all of the fans screaming as the leaders ran past. He didn't mean any disrespect.

What was indisputable, however, was that Jace was having one of the best races of his life. The course record was 13:58. Not only was Nico in position to smash it, but Jace was, too. No team in US history had ever produced two sub-14 performances in the same 3-mile race. With every stride, watching Jace's upright style and Nico's stride, his twisting shoulders and arms seeming to pull him forward, we had a chance.

Nico passed two miles in 9:05, with Jace 18 seconds behind in second. Nick Goldstein and Colin Sahlman hadn't let off. Newbury Park had three in the top five, and four in the top nine.

Standing in the middle of the course's soccer fields, I watched it unfold until it was time to get to the finish line. Nico turned the corner into the final 400 meters, a dead straightaway directly to the finish. I was near some Great Oak parents when Nico came into view. After a long wait, Jace appeared around a corner in second. Another wait. Along the fence, heads turned back and forth, looking for the chase pack. It was 10 seconds behind Jace. If I could sum up the parents' reaction, it was "Where the hell are our guys?"

The crowd was so tightly bunched around the finish line that I couldn't see Nico finish, but I could spot the top of his head as he crossed: 13:39.7. It was a course record by 19 seconds and a national 3-mile record by a stunning 11 seconds. Around me, I began hearing a rumor that the chip on Nico's race bib that tracked his time had malfunctioned. People were claiming that he'd been disqualified. Parents from other schools tried to say he wasn't in the official results. It was all wrong. Nico's time was going to stand.

And so would the times of the rest of our team—because no high school team in history had ever produced a faster team average over a 3-mile course. All together, they had averaged a record 14:14 per runner.

Jace was second, all by himself, in 14:04.8. We believed he could be right around 14-flat, and we weren't surprised that he'd come close. Goldstein was next in seventh, in 14:25, and Sahlman tenth in 14:26. Our fifth scorer was Daniel Appleford, twenty-fourth in 14:36. We'd put four runners in the top ten and all five within the first twenty-four. Great Oak's top finisher, meanwhile, was Christian Simone in fifth, with Aric Reza in eleventh. All of their top five finished within the top thirty.

The results distilled our schools' differing racing philosophies. Breaking barriers required taking it out fast. Fifty-seven seconds separated our first and fifth scorers at Woodbridge. Great Oak, of course, held firm in a pack near the front, its top five spread out by only 20 seconds.

To say I was excited was an understatement. But I was not surprised. I'd seen our summer training. I'd seen our runners' ridiculous times at altitude. We'd not only dethroned Great Oak on a course it had ruled, but dominated in a way that, even when taking out the individual, nonscoring qualifiers, hadn't made the score much closer. Newbury Park's 36 points was nearly half that of Great Oak's 69. We were each other's only competition. Third place scored 234.

Doug Soles had been getting updates in Oregon. His text message to me arrived at 11:11 p.m.

"Congrats, Sean. Damn impressive race by your kids tonight."

"Thank you, lot of hard work, you guys continue to set the bar," I wrote back. "We'll see you at Clovis."

"Sounds good. We look forward to the rematch."

For the majority of the season, until it was time to prepare for the most important meets, Newbury Park's training was built on the ten-day schedule that Bowerman Track Club's Jerry Schumacher had introduced me to. That schedule was broken down into certain runs done at certain paces, and understanding each athlete to know which paces would help them improve most was vital.

My college and postcollegiate career was my own evidence.

Running a lot of tempos—hard, long runs—absolutely fried me. You had to know which athletes responded to which methods. Sending your runners out on a run without any instruction on how fast they should run? A football coach wouldn't run a play without any instruction first. But the belief that pure mileage is the most important metric for success is still prevalent, and I think that's misguided, to put it nicely, and a disservice to athletes.

Our fastest athletes ran their recovery days at 7 minute pace, their easy days at about 6:20 pace, and their training runs at about 5:45 to six-flat pace. Paces for a tempo run varied depending on the athlete, the surface they were running on, and the temperature, but our top guys were roughly at 5:05 pace—the rule was about one minute slower than your fastest mile. On a recovery day, I wanted our runners to go slowly. Easy isn't slow, it's just an easier run, and for an elite high school boy 6:20 pace fits the bill. Where high schools mess up is programming a workout, followed by an easy day, followed by another workout and easy day. There is tremendous value in those other days.

It's not just the workouts. It's not just the long runs, which we did only when I felt it was appropriate, instead of weekly. It's not solely the tempo work, or the speed development. You have to know how to implement all of those because we build the aerobic system throughout the week, not just in workouts. The ten-day schedule creates the time to use more recovery days as needed, and the time to use all the systems, just like Schumacher said—race pace, tempo, long run, and speed. Try to do all that in a seven-day schedule, especially in California, where state rules prohibit athletes from taking part in any organized activity with their high school teams on Sundays, and runners have to do workouts back-to-back and never recover. Only when we reached the prime racing portion of the schedule would we switch to a seven-day schedule.

By October 12, race day at the Clovis Invitational, we had ramped up our training and were doing some of our heaviest work. I wanted to go to Clovis anyway to race the state-meet course and reintroduce our runners to its peculiarities. The 5K course begins on grass, and within 400 meters it transitions to a ridiculous stretch of pavement that starts with going over a sidewalk curb. But what makes it great is that once runners get to mile two, it gets really hilly, with a lot of changing surfaces. It makes for a first mile that is usually blazing fast and a second that is much slower.

Anytime we lined up, we wanted to race well. That included at Clovis. The challenge was that with the heavy block of training, guys were tired. We couldn't afford to show it, though. Great Oak was going to be there, and Doug Soles had told MileSplit ahead of the race that his runners were ready to "give everyone the show with Newbury Park they are hoping for, win or lose." And in the race for the individual title, Nico would face some of his toughest competition.

There was Matt Strangio from Jesuit High, east of Sacramento, who'd won the state track title at 3,200 meters as a sophomore in 2018, then returned the next year to win the 1,600. He was a known quantity, easy to spot in Jesuit's red singlet and yellow shorts, because of how often he and Nico had raced.

There was also a new threat from Arizona named Leo Daschbach. Only two weeks earlier, in late September, Daschbach had averaged 4:35 miles to hold off Cole Sprout and win the Nike Desert Twilight in 14:14.26. It was called the second-fastest high school 5K in history, behind only Dathan Ritzenhein's record of 14:10.40 from 2000? In any national-caliber meet, Sprout was always likely to be near the front. That Daschbach had waited Sprout out and passed him with a kick right before the tape showed that he wasn't just the best guy in Arizona—he'd won state titles at 800, 1,600, and 3,200 meters the previous spring—but was now part of that nationally elite club, too.

We entered every meet with a plan for Nico. At Clovis, I wanted Nico to go out really hard to put fatigue in his competitors' legs and doubt in their minds. I always want my runners to be able to cover competitors' surges, or short bursts of speed. One thing I'd noticed about Nico was how unbelievable he was at doing that midrace—redlining a ridiculous pace in some moments, while still capable of easing off just slightly and being comfortable. It's kind of like the old Kenyan way, where they would constantly shift paces in races to try to mentally and physically break their competition. You have to be able to match moves and change pace at any point, and we trained to help our athletes add that capability from a physiological level.

One of my favorite of those workouts is the 30/40 workout, made famous by Steve Prefontaine when he was an NCAA champion at the University of Oregon in the 1970s. In this workout you run continuously 200 meters in 30 seconds, followed by 200 in 40 seconds, for six to twelve laps. Typically, a runner who is in four-minute-mile shape can do this for twelve laps. I adjust this workout for my athletes depending on their current mile fitness. So, for instance, if one of the boys was in shape to do a 4:40 mile, which is a pace of 35 seconds per 200 meters, I would do this workout at 35/45 pace. The first time we do that, we might aim for six laps. Eventually, we get up to twelve laps at that pace. And we always do it on the track, even during cross country.

Nico was ready to employ this skill at Clovis, and there was no one Nico wanted to drop more than Daschbach. Between the Nike Desert Twilight and Clovis, Nico said that he had heard an interview in which Daschbach indicated that he could win at Clovis. Nico was the politest kid ever, and it wasn't an act. This was a guy who had to be convinced at times that he was as good as we believed. But the interview had upset him.

"You're gonna destroy this kid," I told Nico. "Game on. You're going to win this race the hardest way possible. You're going to take the lead at the mile and then you're going to keep surging. Let them catch you and keep surging. Just keep messing with them. Nobody can match you on this."

I was nervous. I wasn't kidding when I'd told him it was a hard way to win. If he could do it running that way, against that field, it was the clearest sign he could win nationals.

Spurred by the extra motivation, Nico came through the first mile in 4:30, completely locked in. Nico, Strangio, and Daschbach formed a pack all by themselves at the front until after the two-mile mark. Strangio had fallen back. It was now only Daschbach and Nico. I'd told Nico ahead of the race that with 1,000 meters to go, I wanted him to use a downhill stretch to his advantage and floor the pace, using the hill like a slingshot. He had to get rid of Daschbach there. If he somehow stayed close, Nico needed to have enough in reserve for one more push. Nico glanced over his shoulder at Leo and did just that, dropping him—or so it seemed. With 300 meters to go, Daschbach was still within range somehow. He'd come back on Nico and matched the move.

With 15 seconds left in the race Daschbach tried one final time to catch Nico, but Nico covered the move with his own. It was a picture-perfect response. Standing against an orange fence on a hill above the final straightaway, I was blocked from seeing the last few meters. Someone relayed that Nico had won.

Relief.

Oh, thank God.

Nico won in 14:28.90, two seconds ahead of Daschbach. Strangio was third, in 14:49.10.

NICO YOUNG

In the interview after that Desert Twilight race, Leo was like, "Now I'm gonna go to California to beat Nico Young." And he's like, "It's not about beating him, it's about how much I'm gonna beat him by." And I was like, "Are you kidding me? Who says that? That is crazy. No one says that in this sport." Not gonna lie, it did scare me in the moment because I wasn't very confident in my abilities at the time. But we made a plan before that race, and Sean wanted me to just take it from the gun and wear him out. We went out extremely fast and Sean was like, "Every time you sense him coming up on you, surge again to break his spirit." The whole time, anytime I wanted to let up, I just started to surge again, and if you watch the replay, you can see it in his face every time that was happening. I would say I ran that race pretty scared, which is not the way I run races now. It's not really a good mindset, but I was, like, sixteen—I didn't know any better. It was definitely pretty scary. But coming out of that, winning and beating him, was very, very satisfying.

Sean told me later that Alberto Salazar had watched the race. The jersey I was wearing was too big, so the whole race I was grabbing and pulling it over myself to try to keep it on. Alberto watched the race and kept count of how many times that I did that. He told Sean, "He did it thirty-one times—that's six seconds! We need to get you a jersey that fits."

Just as he'd done at Woodbridge, Jace stayed within sight of Nico with the instruction to pick off as many runners as possible who had tried to match his speed, only to fall back. Jace did his job, finishing fourth in 15:03.5. And entering the second mile, it wasn't only Nico and Jace near the front for us. Our top five were in the first fifteen runners at the mile mark, Goldstein, Sahlman, and Appleford all running as a pack while still maintaining fast times. It was impressive considering that we were coming off an intense week of training. It also wasn't sustainable. Great Oak's pack moved up steadily, picking off our runners. Christopher Verdugo and Cole Sawires Yager finished eighth and ninth in identical times. Sahlman was twelfth. But then Simone (15), Abbes (18), and Mateo Joseph (20) rounded out their top five all within the first twenty places. Goldstein finished thirtieth, Lex Young thirty-first, and Appleford thirty-eighth. The result would have been hard to predict: Newbury Park's combined time of 76:10 broke the course record, but we still lost to Great Oak by 8, 57–65.

We could rationalize the loss given where the race fell in our training block, but it didn't lessen the sting. When I heard questions from reporters asking if the results concerned me, I knew where they were coming from. We'd blown out everybody at Woodbridge, only to see ourselves passed on the state-meet course. But concern? No. That was overstating it.

Seeing our guys go out hard and fade a bit didn't make me reassess our progressive training philosophy one bit. We trained through Clovis week, and that's a decision we made with the express purpose of being better at the end of the year. It didn't shake my belief about how to run the team later in the year, either. I truly believed that our formula was a winning one: go out hard because we'd trained ourselves for that in a way that I didn't believe many had, push that second mile, and finish hard.

And it didn't shake my belief that nobody, even Great Oak, could beat us when it counted. We would be better at nationals because we had a low stick in Nico. At nationals, there would be more separation, and with more people in the race Great Oak would be losing all those points. The faster the field, the better we would perform.

So, no, the loss at Clovis didn't dim my confidence. But as much as I contextualized it, the fact remained that all of us left feeling a sting. And we would have to live with that for the next five weeks, as we stopped racing.

At the October 19 Ventura County Championships, our top finishers were freshman Aaron Cantu, sophomore Zaki Blunt, and Colin Sahlman's younger brother Aaron, a freshman. At the Riverside Invitational one week later, it was Thomas McDonnell, Leo Young, and Aaron Sahlman leading our team. And November 7 at the 3-mile Marmonte League Finals, a meet our fastest five would have swept without question, we again held them out. And we swept the first five places anyway, all our athletes running faster than 16:46, led by Leo Young's win in 15:16.

What were our top runners doing all that time? Exactly what we'd planned months before as we charted what we hoped would be a national-title season, carving out a block of time for pure training. Between the Southern Section Prelims on November 15, the section finals on November 23, the state meet on November 30, and, hopefully, Nike Cross Nationals on December 7, Newbury Park would be racing four consecutive weekends. Top teams from other states didn't face nearly that arduous of a path to nationals, allowing them to be fresher when it mattered. Corner Canyon High, in Draper, Utah, had dominated en route to their state's big-school title by finishing second, third, fourth, fifth, and tenth. Their championship meet was held October 23. Utah's regular season would be over for five weeks by the time California held its state meet.

Illinois, meanwhile, held its state championships on November 9. At that meet, Josh Methner of Arlington Heights had run the 3-mile in 13:49.9 to win the individual title and cement himself as someone I was monitoring for NXN. And St. Charles East High had secured its NXN place by winning the big-school state title. By the time top runners from Illinois began turning their attention to NXN, we wouldn't even have begun the first round in California's qualifying process.

And at the Virginia state meet on November 17, two-time defending boys Nike Cross Nationals champion Loudoun Valley put its top six runners within the first eight finishers to dominate the field and earn a return trip to NXN.

Disadvantages in scheduling were why it was so important that we pause our racing in October to put together a strong training block. It takes confidence to not race for that long. People on the outside wanted to know our hardest and craziest workouts during this block, and we had some. Nico would open mile repeats with a 2:02 first 800 meters en route to a 4:18 mile, followed by miles in the 4:30s to get his body used to running with lactic acid and to allow him to feel comfortable closing out races after opening in around 4:25–4:30. People never wanted to know how seriously we took our rope-assisted stretching. People didn't ask about our recovery.

How do you get better without running? You consider all of the other factors that go into being an athlete, outside of the actual running. You learn how to sleep more hours, make better nutrition choices, and drink more water. You learn the benefits of understanding your hemoglobin levels. We heard so many accusations that we were able to do things other teams weren't because we lived in an affluent LA suburb, but it's not expensive to have sliced fruit and electrolyte drinks available for the runners after workouts, something we covered with a small fee. Tanya, assistant coach Steve Hawkins, and I weren't making a dime off the extra supplies—we just wanted to think of any factor that could make a difference. I printed out the ingredients in the drinks and showed the parents, and if the runners didn't want them or were allergic to them, they were free to say no. The combination of a banana, a scoop of peanut butter, and an electrolyte drink, called by some the "poor man's recovery," works just fine.

It's not sexy to talk about those relatively boring aspects, but maximizing our recovery and allowing our athletes' bodies to absorb and adapt to the hard training was as important as the crazy workouts. Among the goals the boys had written down at Big Bear was "Do the little things"—and they were walking the walk.

Losing at Clovis pissed our guys off, which I didn't necessarily mind. If we had won, they might have taken it for granted and not realized how close we really were to Great Oak.

Not racing for that five weeks also requires your runners to have confidence in the process, to push through while not seeing any results from their training in the moment, while feeling like their competition is gaining ground. Waiting was hard. Our athletes watched as Great Oak left Clovis victorious and kept racing, and our team started getting antsy to prove that Newbury Park was still the one to beat. Jace wanted to run the Ventura County meet. I had to tell him we weren't because his whole team had decided not to run it.

"I'll let you run if you want, but do you want to not be part of this team?" I asked. "We have a plan."

He asked to be entered. A few days later, he changed his mind. He wanted to follow the plan, one that prepared for everything we might face in Portland.

CHAPTER ELEVEN

COACHING INVOLVES KNOWING YOUR athletes' strengths and weaknesses. It's anticipating objections to training and problems on race day. It's knowing when to demand more and when to ease off. It's creating an environment in which your athletes feel so secure and motivated that they will give everything they have.

In 2019, it also meant figuring out something a bit more obscure: When did the city water the grass at Dos Vientos Community Park?

Sprinklers soaked the park by early afternoon, just in time for high school to get out and practice to begin.

Our team knew entering the 2019 cross country season that we were among a few favorites to win Nike Cross Nationals. To maximize that potential we had tried to control for as many variables as possible.

Going to elevation.

Learning to cover surges.

Training to run our preferred style.

All season, our plans had been driven by one question: What else could we do differently?

Well, how about finding a way in sunny Southern California to mimic the wet conditions of Portland in early December? Unlike in past seasons when we'd taken road trips to scout courses in Riverside and Woodward Park, we couldn't pick up and fly to Portland so easily. At first glance, Dos Vientos Community Park wasn't an obvious solution for our Portland problem. But its value was more than sentimental as the site of the 2016 team meeting where I'd made my state-title promise.

The last thing I wanted was for my athletes to endure the mental and physical uncertainty I had in college, when I'd been unprepared for a rainy cross country national championship, or when I learned about a certain course's quirk the day of the race. I was a rhythm runner, easily bothered by changing surfaces. There was a perception that California kids struggled at NXN when the Glendoveer course was at its softest after a rainstorm. I didn't buy that. It wasn't that they couldn't do it, it was more likely that they simply hadn't prepared for such conditions. Running on firm ground leads runners to expect a certain amount of rebound with every step—especially when that running is done in cushioned trainers. But there is no give wearing spikes on soggy grass. Glendoveer was a golf course, with manicured fairways, but the course cut through the rough. We had to do something about it.

I knew of high school coaches whose athletes tracked the distance of their workouts off their watches, but a GPS signal would never be accurate enough, no matter what. I always kept a measuring wheel in my car and would wheel our course for the day to know the exact distance. And at Dos Vientos, I wheeled a route past a sand volleyball court, through an open field, and weaving through the outfield of one of the park's baseball diamonds. Cross country courses are not always a smooth, flowing course like Woodbridge. They interrupt the runner with switching surfaces and turns that bottle up large packs, forcing runners to chop their steps to avoid falling. You have to be used to interruption, and this loop offered plenty. Cones marked turns as tight as ninety degrees, like those the runners would have to navigate at NXN.

When it was done, the loop at Dos Vientos measured 1,000 meters on the dot. No fooling around this time. I repeated to our runners that the grass at Dos Vientos was just like the long blades in Glendoveer's rough. That day, the mud flew and the times were crazy during our kilometer repeats. Nico averaged between 2:46 and 2:47 per kilometer—about a 4:28 mile—during repeats on grass that was far softer than what he'd run his kilometer repeats on at Pepper Tree in August. Those times, and his chances to win the biggest prize in high school cross country, were legit. No other high schooler in the country could do this. It's almost dangerous to promise that we were going to win a national title if we did everything I asked. But I never thought we wouldn't.

Nico and Jace finished one-two at the 3-mile Southern Section Prelims in Riverside on November 15. With their finishes at or near the front of every race becoming a formality, my attention often turned to our number five runner and who might play the role of final scorer for us at state and NXN. At prelims, Daniel Appleford, Thomas McDonnell, and Lex Young all crossed in the same time.

We returned to Riverside the next weekend for finals, where Nico and Jace again went one-two. Not only did Nico smash the 3-mile course record by 30 seconds, in 13:54.1, but Jace's time, 14:23.2, would also have broken the old course record. Once again, the race laid bare the contrast between Newbury Park and Great Oak. We ran our full-strength team in the Division 2 race, and Great Oak chose to rest its top runners in Division 1, knowing that even at less than full strength they could qualify for the state meet. National polls ranked the Wolfpack the nation's number one boys team, and Newbury Park number two.

It was a great day for our program as a whole. Newbury Park's girls won their first section championship, with Sam McDonnell eighth. In 2016, advancing out of the boys section finals felt like our Olympic moment, and at the state meet, we had no presence. Just three years later, winning section finals had become our baseline expectation, and at the state meet no one could miss us anymore. Out went the tarps that had held our gear at meets early on in my tenure, when there had been no forethought about creating an atmosphere that could help our runners perform their best. It made me want to do the polar opposite and have the biggest, most obnoxious tent ever. More a compound than a tent, really.

Once the gun goes off, I can't control what happens on the course, or in our runners' minds. But until that point, I tried to figure out every variable I could to create the right environment to run fast. I wanted our runners to feel they were more physically prepared and more mentally focused and relaxed than anyone else going to the start line. I also wanted other teams to arrive for meets and immediately register, *Oh, Newbury Park is here.* That's why I wanted our tent to look better than everybody else's. It was the image I wanted to portray. And it worked.

Around 4:30 in the morning on November 30, hours before the state meet began, I showed up to Woodward Park along with parent volunteers to start raising our tent, as banana yellow as our uniforms. NEWBURY PARK CROSS COUNTRY was emblazoned across the top. Illuminated by flashlights and with temperatures in the high thirties, we installed zip-up walls for privacy, hauled in heaters, and laid a rug inside. On the outside, for everyone to see, we hung a shiny green garland and miniature red-and-gold stockings on which we'd written the athletes' names. The centerpiece was our Christmas tree. Golden ornaments decorated its branches. On top sat a star, complete with a photo of Nico.

Nico, for one, couldn't help but laugh when he saw it.

NICO YOUNG

It was so over-the-top, it was hilarious. And it was so Sean: randomly silly and kind of weird. It made us realize if our coach could be like that, we could be, too. It lightened the mood and took the edge off at just the right time.

The Division 2 boys final began at 9:30 a.m. It was a cold morning, around forty-four degrees when the boys ditched their warm-ups and lined up for the start. Yes, we had national-title ambitions. But one thing hadn't changed since our first state meet together in 2016, and that was the feeling that winning a title in the toughest cross country state in the nation would be an immense achievement.

It was within our grasp right from the opening mile. Nico and Jace dashed off, daring anyone to stick with them, just as we'd trained. Nico cruised to his second consecutive state title in 14:28.5, ridiculously fast considering that, for fear of overtaxing himself one week before Nike Cross Nationals, he wasn't even trying to break German Fernandez's 2007 course record of 14:24.

Even though we tailored our taper to leave our runners freshest at nationals, not state, Nico's state-winning time at Woodward Park was 15 seconds faster than Strangio's winning time in the Division 1 final later in the day. Nico remained undefeated for the season. Jace came in second in 14:53.7, a one-two finish that would have been impossible to predict at our first practice together at Pepper Tree in 2016. I'd promised the boys a state title within four years at our first team meeting. Now we had two, because Colin Sahlman was fifth in 15:09—making him the fastest sophomore finisher not only in Division 2, but across all five divisions. Nick Goldstein, our fourth runner, finished tenth. And our all-important fifth was Daniel Appleford, in twenty-fourth.

Our top five all ran 15:37 or faster, averaging between 4:39 and 5:01 miles. Statistically speaking, no team had ever had a better day at Woodward Park; our combined team time of 75:27 broke an all-time course record held by, yes, Great Oak, since 2015.

Woodbridge, Clovis, section prelims, section finals, and state—we'd run five courses that fall, with a full-strength roster, and broken five course records. Our combined team time at the state meet was even faster than that of Great Oak, which won its sixth consecutive Division 1 title in 76:23.

As usual the state's sports governing body, CIF, produced a "power merge" to determine the fastest finishers and teams, regardless of classification. Some put a lot of weight into that theoretical result, and others don't. It showed we would have beaten Great Oak head-to-head, 67–78, and guaranteed that we would both be heading to Nike Cross Nationals as automatic qualifiers.

After the state meet, I admitted that we shouldn't take the merger results as a suggestion that we actually beat Great Oak. Had they been in the race with us that day, things could have gone differently. Had anyone forgotten October's results at Clovis, when we'd broken the average course record but still lost?

I hadn't.

When I took the stage for the Division 2 trophy ceremony, someone handed me a mic for a statement.

"We have one more goal left next week," I said. "We're not done yet."

I was so nervous the morning of Nike Cross Nationals that I threw up.

I knew we could win it. I also understood it could be very close. The showdown was not only with Great Oak but with Corner Canyon, from Utah, and Loudoun Valley, of Virginia, which had won NXN in 2017 and successfully defended its title in 2018 while scoring even fewer points to hold off Great Oak.

I was confident Nico and Jace would carry out their race plans. I was more concerned about our third, fourth, and fifth scorers.

We wouldn't have Lex Young, whose piriformis injury in November had sidelined him, raising my anxiety. The freshman had become a dependable fifth or sixth option and had shown himself to be tough against big competition, which is what really stung. The thing is, the national race is so different from a state meet, where we're used to being in front. At nationals, our midpack guys might be running around fiftieth place, and our lower scorers around ninetieth place, not used to navigating around forty other runners. Colin, Nick, and

Daniel had to be comfortable running in a large pack, but they had rarely had to contend with that during the season.

We'd planned for this day since the previous winter, and we arrived with not only our boys but our girls, who had also qualified. Yet the day began gloomily. Nearly a half inch of rain fell on Portland on December 7. And on the bus ride to Glendoveer, as Nico sat next to me, I learned I wasn't the only one with nerves.

"What does it mean if you don't sleep a lot the night before the race?" he said.

What I thought was *Oh, shit. How is his body feeling after not sleeping much?*

I tried to project calm. "Doesn't make a difference at all. You slept two nights before. That's most important."

NICO YOUNG

I woke up that day being extremely nervous for the race. I had barely slept the night before and many of the nights leading into it, and I remembered talking to Sean on the bus over and telling him that I was stressed-out and I hadn't slept well, and I was really nervous for the race. He told me that it didn't matter and that I was fitter and better than everyone else, and it just took that to kind of get my mind back on track. I felt really good in the warm-up, which also gave me a lot of confidence. I felt ready to race.

Nico and I had a strong relationship, and he trusted my counsel, but that was the one time I was a little nervous because I could tell that *he* was worried. He could not go into the race that way. Our team-title hopes rested on his scoring the fewest points possible, but I also badly wanted Nico to get his crowning moment. He had owned high school cross country that season, including breaking the national 3-mile record, and he deserved a win. College coaches told me before NXN that no one else was in Nico's league. I thought so, too, but you don't know on race day how anyone will react.

I always favored cross country over track because of the team element. Great Oak ran its way, and we had to run ours. You've got to do what's right for your athletes, and they know how to win with their style. The best teams also have to be able to weather a bad race by any of their best runners. We knew Nico and Jace could each be among the top finishers if they ran as we thought they could, but the time gap between our first and fifth runners had always been bigger than Great Oak's, and their ability to separate our runners was a huge risk. It was why I heard so many people predict before the race that we wouldn't win.

If we were to win, Colin would be key.

Results from earlier in the season at Woodbridge and Clovis indicated that he, as our likely third or fourth scorer, would be close to Great Oak's pack. I gave him explicit instructions before NXN: He had to stay tethered to the number one Great Oak runner. Under no circumstances could Colin fall behind Great Oak's pack. If our top three finished ahead of Great Oak's number one, we could beat them. But Colin would be on his own trying to fight through that traffic. It was going to test all of our nerves.

One of the rainiest days in NXN history had muddied the course and reignited the debate over whether California kids could handle it. I sat down with the kids to try to squash that line of thought. I asked them to name one team in the race that regularly ran in a half-inch downpour.

"I grew up on Long Island in New York, where the weather was terrible most of the time," I said. "We never ran in conditions like this. Nobody's used to this."

I needed the kids to know that everybody would be suffering the same. Thinking otherwise would be repeating the lie of when people go into a race thinking they would be feeling good at the two-mile mark. No, you're not. So many runners have an idealized vision that, with a mile and a quarter left, they will have enough energy to *go*. No. The truth is, you're going to feel awful, and because of that, you're going to doubt yourself and slow down. You have to switch off that instinct. If you can do that, and you've done the work, you're dangerous.

At NXN, coaches are allowed to remain with their team at the starting lineup to the last second. I asked our guys to come in for a final huddle.

"No one has trained as hard as we have and as smart as we have," I said. "When it gets tough—and if you don't think it will, you're lying to yourself—you need to put your head up and say, 'I can, I will,' and then keep repeating it.

"Nico will be out there dying. Jace will be dying. No matter where you are in the race, you guys are dying for each other, every one of you. Everybody counts. Every body is a point. You have to finish.

"Go win a national championship!"

JACE ASCHBRENNER
Coming into nationals, we knew we could win because we'd been competing with Great Oak the whole season, we'd been going back and forth, and we knew, just from looking at meets across the country, that we were the two teams to beat.

But before that race, Sean told us that this is obviously the biggest event, probably, of our high school careers, but no matter what, the race isn't bigger than us, we're bigger than the race, and we can conquer this thing, and we can be national champions. The message was "We're gonna rewrite the history books today." It sounds very matter-of-fact that we're capable of doing that, but we knew what we could do. The workouts and other races that we'd done proved it. He'd have us do these workouts and then show us that this is possible: workouts where we'd bang out three-, four-, even five-by-mile at just ridiculous paces. And at the end of it, we'd just be like, "Oh my gosh, did I just do that?"

Before NXN, I turned to the guys and said, "This is something we do day in and day out every day, and this is the culmination of all of our hard work. It would be a disservice to you guys to not have a good time. When you're out there, just remember everything you've done and everyone who supported you, and everything you've worked for."

I jogged through the mist to the course's one-mile mark, still holding the water bottle I always carried to the starting line in case anyone needed a last-minute sip. Anxiously, I waited for the sound of the gun, unable to watch the start. The first time I looked up, the race was about 1,000 meters in, and I searched the flood of bodies for our Nike-provided hot-pink singlets. I could see Nico in front, making the move we'd discussed. *Perfect*, I thought.

Nico's race plan was again to run a hard first mile. Normally, that would have meant coming through in 4:25 to 4:30, but the soggy conditions led us to project that a 4:40 mile was more likely. But more specifically, I had told Nico that if his competitors weren't pushing the pace 1,000 meters in, he would need to be the one to do it. Strangio was in front by a stride at that point, but I could tell Nico knew that the pace was too slow and that he had allowed the lead pack to get too big. The longer they hung around, the more confidence it would provide his challengers.

As a team, we often talked in code on the course. I liked to use the expression *G* to mean "gap." If I yelled, "One G," it meant our runner had a one-second gap behind him, and so on. Nico had surged at 1,000 meters. From across a Glendoveer fairway, I saw the gap build between him and the pack.

"Four G!"

Nobody was staying with Nico. They either all believed Nico would eventually die and wanted to wait him out, or they knew he wouldn't and effectively began to race for second place. I understood the skepticism, even if I didn't believe it was justified. Yes, we were a new program entering new territory and Nico looked as if he were running a different race from everyone else. But Nico had also proven before that he could take a race out this way. If anyone thought he was going to fade, they were in for a surprise.

The only unknown was Josh Methner, who had qualified out of Illinois as an individual. He was a popular pick to win NXN after he'd run 13:49 over three miles earlier in the season. As I scouted the competition, I had nothing to compare that result to because he kept winning races. I thought Methner would match Nico's surges and even prepared Nico for it to happen.

"He's going to be with you through a mile, and at the 3K mark you're going to surge so freaking hard, like you do in practice, that he won't be able to match you," I'd told Nico beforehand. "He'll have to let you go."

The surge at 3K opened an eight-second lead. Strangio, Methner, and Sprout were all staying back.

I glanced at my phone, tracking the live results as spectators tracked the hot-pink Newbury Park and maroon Temecula jerseys as they ran past. Nike's live results showed we were in first place by just 12 points at two miles. The live scoring purposefully cut off after two miles, however. For the final mile, we'd be flying blind in the team standings. It didn't help that the crowds around the course made it hard to see who was where as a huge chase pack flew by. I didn't know if Colin was sticking with the top runner from Great Oak. While looking for Colin, I missed Daniel Appleford and Nick Goldstein.

The last hill on the Glendoveer course is short but devilishly steep. One stumble, one slowdown, and everything changes. Nico scrambled up it without a problem. Unlike at Clovis, when he glanced to see how close Daschbach was, there was no need to look back. Nico was all alone down the final straightaway as he won in a course-record 14:52. As he closed in on the finish, his expression was typical Nico—calm and understated, as if this was no big deal. Crossing the finish line, as he split in two a roll of black tape held by volunteers, his celebration was similarly restrained. Nico raised both arms above his head and formed his hands into fists, punching through the raindrops.

Methner was second, Strangio fourth, Sprout seventh. No one was within 14 seconds of Nico.

That race capped what I believe to be the best cross country season ever run by a high school boy. Nico completed an unbeaten season that day with a wire-to-wire win at nationals. It remains an exclusive accomplishment other than that of Katelyn Tuohy, who would later accomplish a similar feat on the girl's side.

That legacy was something I thought about later, though. I didn't have time immediately after the race to register the insane feat Nico had pulled off, four years after I'd met him as a scrawny, tiny freshman, because his victory was the only thing that was certain over the last mile of the race.

NICO YOUNG

The biggest piece of confidence that I had going into NXN was the state meet one week earlier, when I ran 14:28. I'd run the same time in the middle of the season on the same course, at the Clovis Invitational, and then it had been extremely hard, as fast as I could go. Then, when I raced at the state meet, I thought I was being conservative and I still ran the same time. If I had known that I was four seconds off of the state-meet record or that course record, I totally think I would have gotten it because I was being very conservative in that race. It made me feel that I was in totally better shape and was validation I was ready for NXN.

When I crossed the line having won at NXN, it seemed surreal because I was so nervous, and I had the anticipation leading up for weeks and days leading into that. It solidified some belief in my ability when I won that race. Sean had told me that I was by far the fittest in that field, but I didn't believe it until that actually happened. I really did realize after that that I could do a lot of great things in this sport. I had aspirations of winning that title earlier in high school, but I didn't fully believe it was possible until I won Arcadia my junior year. Coming into my senior year, I felt, *Okay, I can beat everyone.*

I only had a partial view of the finish, blocked by bodies and umbrellas. Someone told me that Jace finished eighteenth. He was an all-American. He'd achieved his goal and kept our title hopes alive.

All that was left to do was wait.

The pack spilled over the final hill through the finish. Eight seconds separated the twentieth through thirtieth finishers, but no one from Newbury Park or Great Oak was among them.

Six seconds separated thirtieth through fortieth, and still no hot-pink jerseys, and still no maroon, either.

Suddenly, there was Colin entering the final straightaway—behind Great Oak's pack. Since his freshman season the year before, Colin had flashed a devastating kick. He was summoning it again. With 50 meters to go, he was ahead of four of Great Oak's top five—Mateo Joseph, Leandro Candray, John Worthy, and Aric Reza. In a surprise, Christopher Verdugo and Cole Sawires Yager, usually Great Oak's two fastest and most dependable runners, were nowhere to be seen. They would eventually finish 139th and 125th, respectively, yet more proof that nothing can be taken for granted in cross country.

Yet Colin was still two strides behind Great Oak's number one, Gabriel Abbes. Colin's long strides claimed ground just as a finisher in front of Abbes began to slow, momentarily blocking him. It was the tiny opening that Colin needed. Colin zoomed by on the left to pull out one of the gutsiest finishes of his life and cross in fifty-third place, 0.1 seconds ahead of Abbes.

Everybody counts! Every body is a point!

But four more Great Oak teammates finished in the next 10 seconds after Abbes, ensuring that their top five scorers all placed within the top seventy-two spots. Nick and Daniel, meanwhile, were still out on the course. Running up the last rise into the final straight-away, Nick came into view and held on to ninety-fifth, 0.1 ahead of ninety-sixth place, only 0.2 ahead of ninety-seventh, and a mere half second ahead of ninety-eighth. Daniel was right behind in one hundredth, in 16:17.8, 1.6 seconds behind Nick.

Trying to crunch the mental math, I didn't think we'd won. There was just no way.

When Jace saw me, instead of saying anything, he just shook his head. Making top three, at least, had been our expectation for months, only for a 16-minute race to upend everything that had seemed so certain. I didn't believe we'd made the podium.

We had about 30 minutes before the girls race to stew in our anxiety. While Nico was quickly ushered into a tent by Nike officials and handed a warm winner's jacket and food, I was running around to the warm-up area to give our girls team a quick talk, trying to figure out what to say to one team when I still had no idea what had happened to the other. Tanya took the girls to the starting line from there. I had to run back to hear the boys results.

A Nike representative found me. "Sean, get your team, we need you over here."

"For what?"

"You're on the podium."

"We made top three? What?"

We tracked down Nico in the tent as we were called to the stage. Utah's Corner Canyon—referred to as Draper for the day—was to our right in orange uniforms, and Great Oak to our left.

None other than Galen Rupp, Nico's favorite runner, who'd met Nico months earlier at Nike's Elite Camp, handed him his winning trophy—a statue of Nike, the winged goddess of victory. Then it was time for the team results.

Our runners had their arms over one another's shoulders, shivering in the rain. I put my right arm around Nico and stared at my feet as the public-address announcer began reading backward.

One of the teams was about to get the news we'd all worked months to hear.

"*Fourteen points separating these three squads for the NXN title . . .*"

Shoot, we might have won?

"*Our third-place trophy, with one hundred forty-two points, Draper . . .*"

Either Great Oak or Newbury Park was going to win the national championship. My first thought: *This is it.* My next: *I really should not have come up onstage with the team. If we get second, we're going to have to walk off in shame, and we're right in the center.*

Photographers jostled at the foot of the stage.

"*Just four points separating first and second . . .*"

"Oooh," reacted the crowd, watching under golf umbrellas and hoods.

After circling each other all fall, Great Oak and Newbury Park were now separated by just four points, and a few inches on the makeshift stage. Gabriel Abbes was standing as close to me on my left as Nico was on my right.

Standing behind Newbury Park and Great Oak, a race organizer raised the second-place trophy, another winged goddess, over our heads.

"*Our 2019 NXN runners-up, with 132 points . . . Temecula!*"

Screams burst from the crowd. My eyes, shut during the reading of the final score, opened wide, and I screamed, too, as my left hand shot out into a fist. Seconds earlier, we'd stood in a neat row, motionless. Now we were jumping, hugging, yelling, smiling, looking like a hot-pink mosh pit. Colin was pumping his fists. Bouncing from the news and still shivering from the cold, we jumped our way into a circle, arms around one another. My left arm was around Jace, my right around Nico. Nike officials handed out black rain jackets to our runners, CHAMPIONS written in bright green on the back. Leo Young, our sixth runner, in 109th, wrapped his older brother in a hug.

Our combined team time was 1:18.48, to Great Oak's 1:19:44. We'd won with 128 points.

JACE ASCHBRENNER

Standing on that stage just waiting to hear who won, it was like everything in our high school career had come down to this moment. Did we measure up? Or did we fall short? When they announced the runner-up, it was just this feeling of *Oh my gosh, we did it—we are national champions.* Everything that Sean said we could do, we achieved, and we conquered. It was so gratifying and just beautiful to see. Sean gave us this standard. He instilled it in us. We convinced each other of it, we put the work in, we supported each other every single day, and it all came together and it happened. And that's something you can only do with just that ruthless mindset and knowing where the top is—and knowing that you can top that.

COLIN SAHLMAN

Sean came up to us after the race and he looked a little disappointed, saying he didn't think we'd made the podium. I knew that we raced the best we could, but I was a little sad, because it was between us and Great Oak going into that race. It was a little bit of a letdown. So, we were all a little shocked when we actually did make it on the podium. And then when we found out there were only fourteen points between the three teams, I thought, *Okay, we have a shot.* When they announced four points between the first two teams, I thought this could literally go either way—Great Oak got five guys in front of our fourth guy, but we put three in front of their first, so I was thinking, *Well, which one is it?*

There was silence for a little bit—and when they announced second place, "Temecula," I just remember thinking, *No way,* and just erupted. It was super-rainy, windy, and cold, and in that moment when we knew we won, I wasn't cold anymore. The coldness went away, and it was just joy that filled my entire body.

Doug Soles found me afterward.

"We knew we were in trouble when I heard you were taking your team to altitude for a month," he said.

I still had to coach the girls race. I was sprinting to the first mile marker when I realized too late that the puddle I was about to run through was deeper than a little one. I tripped, completely submerged in freezing water, and came up shivering. Some coaches get a Gatorade bath after winning a national championship; I'd taken a fall and looked like I'd come out of a pool. My emotions were all over the place. After such a high, I had to leave so quickly that I couldn't even think about the boys anymore until the girls were done. They finished a more than respectable seventeenth.

After a long round of interviews, I took a Nike bus back to the hotel. Soaked and freezing cold, I took a shower. I thought about how if those four points had gone differently, maybe it would have dimmed the commitment that was building within our team culture.

In our hotel room, I confided in Tanya, "Do you know how bad I needed this?"

"What do you mean *you* needed this? You mean the *team* needed this?"

There was no question they deserved it. But I *needed* this because I needed a result that proved their commitment had been worth all of the trust they'd put in me. I needed them to see that accomplishing more than they had ever dreamed possible started with being willing to do things that were hard and different, like going to a monthlong training camp, and sacrificing our early mornings, and not racing for four weeks. I needed that to happen for them to have full belief, so that in the years ahead we could push to do even more. I was the high school coach whose pro mentality made me feel like an outsider from my first season; I needed this validation of my methods.

Nike hosts a huge celebratory dinner the night of the race. There, we accepted our honors for team of the year. All-American honors were handed out. I was named national coach of the year. Ever since

I'd started at Newbury Park, I'd joked with friends—okay, maybe *half* joked—that I would win an NXN title within four or five years and then leave high school coaching completely. Yet in the first hours after actually winning, I was busy trying to figure out indoor meets for the following weeks, while not wanting to *over*-race indoors like East Coast schools do; I was thinking about how to get our girls to set national records, too; I was planning to go to elevation for a month every summer.

Instead of pulling away like I'd once thought, I was consumed by going even more all in at Newbury Park.

The one thing I wasn't doing was lingering in the moment. What do you do when you get what you want? A reflexive urge told me to quickly turn the page, feeling that if I allowed myself to get stuck, I would be done and our momentum might end.

I would savor this title in retirement.

"Nico," I said. "What do you want to do next? Do you want to break four minutes in the mile? Do you want to break eight minutes in the 3,000?"

"I want to break 8 minutes."

We had our next boundary to break. We were going after the 3K national record.

"Don't run tomorrow," I told the team after dinner. "And I'll see you guys Monday."

CHAPTER TWELVE

I WAS NERVOUS.

It was late January. Gatorade had named Nico its national cross country athlete of the year. NXN was behind us. An opportunity to go for the high school indoor 3,000-meter record had materialized. But would a record?

All of this had happened because of a phone call two days after NXN. I was back home from Portland when Ray Flynn, the track and field agent, called me. I'd known Ray since my late twenties, when I was trying to scratch out a career as a postcollegiate runner and Steve Scott had introduced me to Flynn, who represented many of track and field's most accomplished athletes. We'd stayed in touch. Flynn also served as the meet director of the Millrose Games, the most prestigious indoor meet in the United States, held at the famed Armory in New York City. He'd noted both Nico's record-breaking cross country season and his commitment just before Christmas to run for Northern Arizona University, in Flagstaff.

Flynn had a question. Did Nico want to run the mile at Millrose in February?

My first thought was *Wow, we're good enough now that people care.*

My second was *Is he inviting Nico to run in the meet's signature event, the Wanamaker Mile?*

No. It would be a different mile race, also at Millrose, but the same one that Drew Hunter used in 2016 while still at Loudoun Valley to run 3:57.81 and smash the high school indoor mile record.

"Well, there's one issue," I said.

"What's that?"

"We would love to run the Millrose Games, but we don't want to do the mile. Nico wants to do the 3,000."

Problem was, the Millrose Games didn't have a 3,000 for high schoolers. So instead, Nico was offered an opportunity to run a 3,000 in late January, a few weeks earlier than the February 8 Millrose Games. That was out of the question from our perspective. He needed those extra weeks in January to rebuild his training following NXN if he was going to attempt to break Hunter's high school record of 7:59.33, also set in 2016. Hunter was still the only high schooler to ever go under 8 minutes. The American under-20 record was 7:56.31, set by Chris Derrick in 2009, but that was when Derrick was already in college.

Flynn called back a few weeks later. Was Nico still sure he didn't want the mile? Nico was resolute. During the 2020 track season, he wanted to chase records at 3,000 and 5,000 meters, not join the tiny club of prep four-minute milers.

"It's either Millrose or nothing," I said. "I'm giving him a down week and I need to get him ready. This is coming up soon for us."

Flynn had always been helpful to me, even when my own performances never warranted any special treatment, and now he was going to bat for Nico, too. He promised to get him in.

In, as in running in the Millrose Games' professional 3,000. Nico would be allowed to run unattached, meaning not representing Newbury; doing so would preserve his high school eligibility, because Millrose didn't offer a high school field.

We would definitely need those extra weeks of training now. And it was why we entered Nico in the 1,500 at a winter meet at Arcadia High School, northeast of Los Angeles, on January 25. That's where I got nervous.

Breaking Hunter's record required us to solve the same problem that had helped make Nico unbeatable during the cross country season: determining a pace that was fast enough for Nico to be comfortable with early in a race but too fast for anyone else to hang with. To us, that was 4:12 mile pace. At the Arcadia warm-up, he won easily—with Jace, who had just committed to run at the University of Colorado, traditionally a distance heavyweight, finishing second. The win wasn't important. It was that Nico had done it while running 3:52.39. When converted to 3,000 meters, that pace was just about dead-on to what he would need to run to break the record. I'd hoped to see Nico run a faster time to allow a bit more breathing room. Nico's training workload had increased as he went into the Arcadia race, and he was tired on race day. Still, I wasn't sure what that meant for his chance of breaking the record. He would be two months removed from NXN on race day at the Armory. Would that be too soon? Would he have enough fitness to achieve what only Hunter had ever done in high school history? The margin for error was slim.

Any nerves were smoothed over during his last demanding workout, ten days before the Millrose 3,000, which called for an opening mile in 4:10. He made it look impossibly smooth. Video of the workout was posted online, and I read reactions that said it was simply too fast. It made me shake my head. This wasn't the same athlete who had run 8:13.31 for 3K a year earlier. His aerobic capacity was better. He was in the kind of shape where he could run anything from 7:50 to 7:58. More important, his mindset had changed.

We arrived in a rain-soaked New York City on February 7. As always with high schoolers, we kept it fun, riding the subway and stopping at the kind of tourist-trap memorabilia stories I would have avoided growing up. The next day, Nico and Jace finished their pre-race warm-up at the Armory.

When the gun went off for the 3,000, I knew Nico was ready to roll. There was one thing about him that I never questioned—his ability to go to a place that *hurt* physically but to keep pushing. Inside the Armory, Nico gamely stayed with runners much older than him. Even after he tied up during the final lap, he finished in 7:56.96, easily ahead of Hunter's mark. Another record toppled. He was only the second high schooler to run a 3,000-meter indoors in under eight minutes. I was immensely proud. When I see an athlete reach a goal or overcome a huge barrier, it's a pretty special thing, and with Nico, it was affirming to be a part of that.

Nico had spent his senior year demolishing records in both cross country and indoor track. Naturally, we wanted to keep it rolling into the outdoor track season. All of the available evidence suggested the national high school records in the 3,200 and 2 mile were in sight. I thought he could run 8:25 for 3,200 meters, and anywhere from 8:22 to 8:25 in the 2 mile. He and I talked about how he would go to Arcadia that April and no one would be able to touch him. The goal was to be prepared to open faster than ever, with a first mile in 4:10. Everything about his training was falling into place. His tempos were strong. For his weekend long runs, Nico had begun comfortably ripping off twelve miles at 5:30 pace. He was like a college athlete who runs 13:30 for 5,000 meters, just without the high-mileage training—and what was scary was the 7:56 record he'd run at the Armory represented just the beginning of what he was capable of that spring. Nico wasn't motivated by the mile, but if he wanted to give it a try, I thought a 4:02 or 4:03 was within reach. And I was already thinking of entering him into a spring 800 meters, because he had speed, to see if he could run close to 1:50.

And then, one month later, all those plans hit the fan.

A pandemic hit. School was closed, then moved online. Meets were canceled. How, where, and even if we could practice was unclear.

I didn't want to accept that anything late in the spring track season would be canceled. I was a little resigned that high school sports in

California might not come back in time for the end of Nico and Jace's senior season; the state's shelter-in-place regulations were some of the country's most restrictive. But I was hopeful, maybe delusional, that races would still take place somewhere.

Not until April did I realize that those opportunities were gone. If we wanted to train for something, and race for something, it would be up to us to create them.

We shifted plans. We had to. Nico's goal was now to break the high school 5,000-meter record, 13:37.91. Breaking that meant big things might be in your future. Why? Just look at the guy who held it: Galen Rupp. He went on to win an Olympic silver medal in 2012 at 10,000 meters and a bronze medal in 2016 in the marathon, and he held American records at 10,000 meters, 3,000 (indoors), 5,000 (indoors), and 2 miles. Before Rupp, the high school 5,000-meter record was held by Gerry Lindgren, one of the legendary runners in American high school history. Trying to break a record in a race as long as the 5,000 isn't something you get multiple shots at; running that fast takes it out of the body of any athlete, let alone a teenager's. We'd have one chance—if we could get even that, given the regulations that shifted from state to state and month to month.

Jace, meanwhile, wanted his last race in high school to be a 3,200. I thought he could run 8:50. He and Nico were among the cornerstones that had built our program into a winner, and I owed it to them both to send them out the way they wanted. Everyone said I was crazy, that I could never put together races amid the lockdown. I looked everywhere. I would have gone to North Carolina or Florida. I would have done anything.

Getting an athlete in that kind of shape would normally be a straightforward challenge. Not in 2020, as the world grappled with a pandemic that no one knew how to deal with. Things we took for granted, like access to a track, or the ability to gather as a full team, were no longer so easy. As hospitals filled and deaths climbed, the importance of keeping Newbury Park's athletes running probably seemed trivial. This wasn't just about chasing records, though; it was about replacing the connection that was lost when COVID-19 and the rules put in place to contain it pulled everyone apart.

What bothered me at first wasn't the lack of racing but the prohibition on *practicing*. Kids didn't have anywhere to train, and by that, I mean anywhere to connect other than through their phones. Some schools weren't even allowing coaches to hold virtual meetings through Zoom. I didn't understand that. Our school district helped. They told me that they recognized that students were struggling without interaction and asked coaches to have meetings at least once a week, even if it meant creating a stupid game as the reason why.

Eventually, we were told that new rules would allow us to practice with a maximum of ten athletes at a time. I was lucky that our roster of distance runners wasn't enormous, though it was still bigger than ten. We organized days with three practices. To get everyone in, I said I would meet one group at 6:00 a.m., another at 2:30 p.m., and a final group at 6:30 p.m.

These workouts didn't happen at Newbury Park High's track, which was off-limits. Trying to figure out new places to run led to many times when I literally lay in bed all night unable to sleep. When I couldn't sleep, I figured I could at least run. I'd leave the house at 4:00 a.m., coach our first practice, come back in time to teach my economics classes, pass out after school, and then go to my second and third practices.

One night when I got up, Tanya asked me what I was doing. "You're literally going running at 3:00 a.m."

"No, I'm gonna go look for places to run. I need to find other places. I found a trail near our house and just want to check it out."

I left the house with a bunch of flashlights, running through the woods on a scouting trip. I was sleeping three hours per day. It just wasn't healthy for me. I was trying to find places where nobody would see us and nobody would care. In Ventura County, at one point camp became considered "essential," which allowed us to meet, and anytime anyone asked us who we were, we would say Mile High Running Camp. Sometimes they'd be mad, saying, "You're Newbury Park High School." Well, yes, some of these kids were. But we actually had one or two kids who weren't from the high school running with us.

Was this ever going to end? My frustration grew to the point that it led me to do some things that weren't strictly by the book.

There was a city near Newbury Park where few people seemed to abide by social-distancing restrictions. People were using the pool, playing on the baseball diamonds, hosting soccer games on the high school's football field. It seemed like a place where our top runners could gather in small groups and train. When one of my guys injured himself jumping the fence at the track, I was done with climbing it, but we still needed a place to run. But at the back of the track, in a place where hardly anyone walked, was a locked gate.

I dressed in black. I almost made a joke of it, feeling as if I were in a heist movie. I went to Home Depot and told a worker that I was looking for a big lock-cutter.

"Actually, let me tell you the truth," I said. "I'm trying to cut a link to a chain."

"It's probably not good"—he laughed at me—"but I'll help you."

"It's a pretty thick chain."

"Okay." He laughed again and pulled out a tool. "Well, this would do it."

I drove to the high school that night. I couldn't carry out the plan yet because some students were smoking weed in a car in the parking lot. I waited them out, then went to the gate after they drove off. I didn't cut the lock, but I cut a link on the lock's chain and replaced it with a carabiner so no one would know where it was except us. We could just unscrew it, take the chain off, and run our laps. No one cared. The coach at that high school knew I did it because I'd told him. We were in similar positions. He couldn't use his own track, just as I couldn't use our track at Newbury without getting in trouble.

When we would show up for workouts, I'd put the carabiner in my pocket. We were never alone; there were always members of the community using the track, jumping the fence to get access. They thought I worked at the school, assuming I'd opened up the facility.

We found other options. Not far away, a small college had what I would describe as a relaxed approach to enforcing usage rules for their track. Basically, their security guard didn't care who showed up, even though it was technically closed. Still, I was averse to having the team show up en masse. My first plan, which worked for a while, involved being unrecognizable. Wearing a new shirt, a cloth Halloween mask that covered my whole face with an image of a skull, and gloves, I jogged as if I were just some psycho wearing a costume while getting in some cardio. I was really watching our athletes and tracking their times from the track. It was terrible. I began to think people were getting suspicious, so I started hiding in some bushes a little farther away. From there, I could watch our runners from a distance as they worked out, track their splits, and then call them between intervals to chat about it. If I went on the track, I was worried people would recognize us and send pictures to the school district. I almost bought a ghillie suit, which is designed to make you look like you're part of the foliage.

Among coaches I knew that spring, responses to COVID-19 varied. Some were ambivalent, some didn't believe in it, and some were deathly afraid. I was in the camp that understood it was something—I could attest to that after losing several pounds and feeling awful after contracting a bad case of it months later—but I wasn't scared of it enough to keep me from trying to give the athletes an outlet during a time of mass isolation. The work-arounds were, admittedly, getting ridiculous. But I was doing what I'd promised the parents and athletes I'd do during our first team meeting in 2016, when I said they would not find a coach working harder than me. Trust me, I knew Newbury Park's growing fame had led many to criticize my coaching. My response was to shrug. So what? Our athletes believed in themselves more than ever; I cared about *that*.

From the time the Olympics first fascinated me as a kid, I'd been interested in people who are the best at what they do and how they did it. I found an interview with Dave Mirra, who was one of the biggest names in BMX. Asked what made him so accomplished, and when he first started progressing, Mirra said that he didn't care if he looked dumb to others. He'd grown up practicing in a crowded skate park where everyone was scared to fall for fear of looking bad. But that didn't worry Mirra because he knew that only a few weeks later he would be landing that backflip that others were scared to practice for fear of being laughed at if they failed. I had to learn not to care if people thought my coaching was too eccentric or too brash.

That doesn't mean that things never bothered me; the critiques got personal. But, bottom line, I had to ask myself if I was making decisions in the best interests of the athletes, or because of what others would think of me. If someone disliked me, so be it. If we put stock into how we were perceived, then Newbury Park's best runners would have competed ten times every cross country season, the same as just about everyone else in California; we would have taken seriously the traditional meets like the county championships and the midweek duals; and we would never have questioned whether the CIF system was actually setting runners up for success. If I let critiques guide my decisions, then I would be creating an artificial boundary.

And at Newbury Park, all of our success hinged on looking past boundaries.

At a certain point that spring, it was time to admit that the official track season wouldn't be coming back. No state championships. No national championships. We had to find our own motivation.

If a COVID-type pause had happened earlier in my time at Newbury Park, I don't know how many runners would have stuck with it, but the runners now viewed training as something they *wanted* to do. And frankly, it was a great outlet from the monotony of going to school online and being apart from one another.

We held time trials. Lex and Leo were running 4:16 to 4:17 in the mile. No one would have known when they showed up as freshman in cross country that they would be that good that quickly.

Jace and Nico wouldn't be receiving the final send-off either had imagined back in December when we'd won NXN and, around the celebration dinner that night, dreamed big about the spring ahead. They decided it made sense to give up their remaining high school eligibility. They would still run, just not technically for Newbury Park High School, which unburdened them from the regulations the school district put in place about when and where athletes and coaches could meet. Once they acknowledged they would not run for Newbury Park and didn't even want the PE credit everyone earned from being on the team, it became acceptable for me to meet with them from the school district's perspective because it became my prerogative as a teacher and private citizen, not as Newbury Park's coach. And it was ours, together, to get them one fast, final time before they went off to Colorado and NAU.

If we were looking for silver linings, it was that going to school online meant there was more time for both to run. Nico had consistently run about 60 miles per week for the previous two years, but that spring it topped out three times at 70 miles, the most he'd ever run at Newbury Park, while still taking one day off per week. Jace approached that weekly mileage as well, doing quality workouts, like three repetitions of two miles, all finished in the low nines.

They had the fitness. Now they just needed a meet to showcase it. By early May, we learned that Jace's family had a connection a two-hour drive south at Concordia University in Irvine who was willing to open the school's track for us. Five athletes wanted to run, including Jace, who would run 3,200 meters, and Nico, who would pace him.

To make a meet, and the times run at it, count, you essentially need an official from USA Track & Field, a starter, and a timer. That bare-bones setup was a good thing because Orange County was limiting our in-person gathering to fifteen people. We cut a deal with a company that provided official timekeeping and results, but only one person could come to the meet because of that limit. There were other things we had to consider that most people who go to a track meet never think about. Because the track didn't have a metal rail on the inside of lane one, we had to put cones up. (And don't even get me started about trying to get our little races insured.) A few family members were invited. Tanya would be taking video of the race on her phone, high above the track in an announcer's booth, to ensure that everything people saw on the video was official. This was Jace's last run. We didn't want it to be for naught.

Golden rays from a setting sun lit a hillside behind Concordia's track on May 23 as Jace and Nico toed the line next to Nick Goldstein, now a junior at Newbury Park, and Billy Atkinson, from Mira Costa High in Manhattan Beach, who had committed to run at Virginia. Nico jumped out at the gun, cruising at the equivalent of 8:40 pace for two miles and looking so comfortable I almost winced. Our plan called for Nico to go for the 5K record one week later in Oregon. *Dammit*, I thought, *he could break the record right now!* It was sad that a time trial inside an empty stadium was the backdrop to Jace's final race.

And yet, could there have been a more appropriate send-off? For seven laps, Nico and Jace ran far ahead of everyone else within a stride of each other, just as they had done since our first practice at Pepper Tree in 2016. At the start of the eighth and final lap, Nico stepped off, and it was up to Jace to bring it home. We all watched his black singlet, yelling our heads off. "Go Jace, go!"

I stood twenty yards from the finish line, waiting as Jace sprinted in. Before he'd even passed, I raised both my arms to celebrate. When he hit the line, there was a shriek from across the track, where friends and family were sitting. I punched the air with my left hand. I thought he could go 8:50. He ran 8:44. From what Jace told me, all of the pent-up frustration and training he'd held back since March broke free for eight laps.

"I just needed to make the most of this opportunity," he said. "It's the last race in my high school career."

JACE ASCHBRENNER
Going into the spring, we were obviously riding really high off of the national championship. Our eyes had been set on the state meet and CIF and hopefully Nico and I finishing in the top five at the state meet in the 2 mile, but that all kind of went out the window with COVID. Our work-around for it was making an independent track club and we kept having practices because we weren't affiliated with anybody, but we just kept showing up together and we just wanted to keep running and see what we could do. My sights were set on being able to get a good time for college. It was an interesting time because it was very difficult to manage how locked down people were about COVID and social distancing and not meeting up. I still wanted that one race. Nico, Sean, and I had a group chat together where we started talking about how do we make this happen? How do we get track access? How do we train? It was kind of funny because Sean and I would have back-and-forths about whether something was plausible to do.

Before the race at Concordia, we were hitting superhard workouts. Sean instilled in us that if you want to run really fast, you've got to be comfortable at your race pace and be able to be powerful throughout the entire race, so that's what our training was modeled off of. One was three by two miles in the nine-minute range. Another was five by one mile, where I remember closing in 4:35. I remember the last well because I was trying to kick down Nico, and I was close enough to where that was almost plausible. That was probably some of the best training in my life, because without school in-person we could hang out and rest. I don't think I would have been able to do it, actually, without the rest I got due to the COVID guidelines.

Those workouts told me I was capable of something really fast, sub-nine-minutes, and maybe even a little under 8:50. Nico paced me for almost exactly alternating 66- and 67-second laps, and then I was able to close in about a 63. Running 8:44 just blew all of us out of the water.

That was a moment that I wouldn't compare to NXN, because NXN was just so incredible—but it was one of those moments where I was like, *Dang, I just broke what's possible again for myself.* I always joke that I technically had the US number one time that year, because nobody ran the 2 mile, and Nico was off doing the 5K. He paced me for seven laps at 8:45 two-mile pace, and then he took three minutes rest and did another two kilometers at the same pace. He was capable of so much more that year. If he had run a 2 mile, it probably would have been sub-8:30.

After Jace finished, I asked Nico to stay loose. His pacing job had essentially been a workout, and I wanted him to run one more interval—a fast solo mile.

He did it in 4:12.

Life went on. When Newbury Park's seniors walked in a graduation ceremony on June 12, Nico and Jace were among the class's valedictorians. Their audience was a parade of cars that stretched past the high school down Reino Road.

We had one more big race to run: Nico's 5,000; it wouldn't have been the spring of 2020 if those plans didn't change constantly, too.

Lewis & Clark College, just south of downtown Portland, was our first choice to hold Nico's record attempt. Its on-campus track was dependable, having hosted professional meets for years. Then . . . the race was canceled. Oregon's COVID regulations were just as tight as California's. I tried to see whether we could use the track on Nike's corporate campus, the same place where I'd observed Schumacher and Salazar almost a decade earlier, but that was nixed, too.

Access to a track wasn't our only hurdle. Following the time trial at Concordia, Nico developed a slight hip injury and backed off his training for a week. When he said he still wanted to try to break the record, a coaching friend of mine told me about a new track at Franklin High School, tucked in a southeast Portland neighborhood, that was open to the public. Three weeks after our intended date, we showed up in Portland committed to racing on June 23.

In my eyes, we were setting up a guerrilla operation. We weren't asking for permission from school officials. We rounded up USA Track & Field officials and timers and contacted RunnerSpace, a running outlet that could broadcast events, to ask whether they would live stream the race. They would. Athletic.net, a site that tracked results around the country, sponsored the bibs. Nico never knew we were flying by the seat of our pants; we didn't want to add stress.

We didn't announce where it was because we were wary of its becoming a sequel to the Quarantine Clasico, a race held in late May at a high school outside Sacramento. Dozens had come out to watch racers who, like Nico and Jace, were mostly high school seniors trying to get in a last race by being creative. The field was organized by Strangio, who was still in high school but couldn't run due to injury. He had gotten commitments from a strong group of racers that included Daschbach and past NXN qualifiers such as Easton Allred and Cole Sprout. In a way, it was a major success: Daschbach ran 3:59.54 to become the eleventh high schooler to run a sub-four-minute mile. It also created serious fallout. The high school's longtime track coach was suspended for the following academic year for what the school district said was allowing an unauthorized competition at the facility.

We wanted to go for a record and not ruffle any administrative feathers, so we kept Nico's arrival in Portland as quiet as we could. The day before, Nico was doing what we called our standard "prerace," which was a warm-up done the day before to activate the body. People are scared to have their athletes run fast the day before a race, but I'm aggressive about prerace warm-ups because I believe you have to wake up the central nervous system. Obviously, I wouldn't schedule a full workout, but I wanted our athletes to run fast in specific, concentrated bursts that, by the end of the warm-up, were close to their race pace. At Newbury Park, where our training was built on a foundation of finding specific paces for each run, our preraces were similarly tailored for every athlete's goal pace. A prerace during cross country season is not the same as one during track; a prerace for a 3,200-meter runner was different from that of a miler; a prerace for a faster runner was different from that for a slower teammate. A prerace for a 3,200 on the track, for example, started with a three-mile warm-up, then four repeats of 400 meters, with the first two at mile pace and the second two at 3,200-meter pace, before closing with a two-mile cooldown.

Nico was doing his 5K warm-up when a teenager at Franklin High's track recognized him.

"Is that Nico Young?" he asked me.

"Yeah, I think it is," I said.

"Wait, are you Sean Brosnan?"

"Yeah." *Gulp.*

"What are you guys doing here?"

"Oh, just visiting some friends."

We had to get out of there, or someone was going to figure it out.

The problem was our record attempt had grown into a pretty big production. You couldn't miss the eight-foot-long, LED-lit timing board next to the finish line. The cameras also gave away that something was happening.

The next day, race day, Bowerman Track Club coach Jerry Schumacher came by to watch, as did professional runner Craig Engels. The kid who'd recognized us the day earlier was back, too. He'd figured it out. At least he was by himself; now, we just couldn't let word spread.

The one wild card were the protests that had been held almost daily in Portland since the murder of George Floyd in Minneapolis. I'd heard that another protest was scheduled that evening in southeast Portland, two miles west of the high school. I had no issue with what they were protesting; I just hoped it wouldn't attract any unexpected attention to Nico's last shot at the 5,000-meter record. That night, I wasn't sure if what I saw was the protest itself, or just people on their way to join it, but I looked down a road leading to the track and saw a group walking by, only a few blocks away. No one turned down the lane toward the track. *Thank God,* I thought.

Once Nico started, my concern faded. Mostly, anyway. At that point, we weren't going to stop Nico. I mean, I would have tackled anyone and been arrested before Nico would have been prevented from finishing.

In one of the track's outside lanes, a guest of honor watched from a lawn chair: Rupp. Initially, he had agreed to act as Nico's pacer. When he developed hamstring tenderness, it wasn't worth the risk. Nico's new pacers would be Logan Orndorf and Sam Truax. The 5,000 is twelve and a half laps on a track, and Truax dropped out with nine remaining and Orndorf with seven. Soloing a record attempt is extraordinarily difficult, but we had no choice. The last six laps were all on Nico's shoulders. Through 3,000 meters Nico was directly on pace, running off pure guts. Then he kept going.

He finished in 13:50.55. He didn't get the national record. But Nico's time smashed the California state record of 14:01.40, which had stood since 1986. In national high school history, he was fourth all time, faster than the legendary Prefontaine. The only names ahead of Nico were three future Olympians: Dathan Ritzenhein, Lindgren, and Rupp. Elite company. In early July, Gatorade named Nico its national athlete of the year in track and field. National athlete of the year awards have been given out for thirty-five years, and no boy had ever won two in one year. Until Nico.

NICO YOUNG

I really am grateful that Sean still got us to meet together for runs and workouts during that spring because there were so many kids during that time who didn't have any social interactions. As it went on, it was starting to be super-irritating, but there were also a lot of moments in there that were really fun. We took that as an opportunity to transition into college training a little bit, with a little bit more mileage and more volume in workouts. Throughout my high school career, Sean knew he was preparing me for college, so we were very specific, slowly increasing my mileage from my freshman year until I was a senior, never anything too crazy. Just to the point where I could come to my freshman year at Northern Arizona and be in a really good spot.

Going after that 5K record was not ideal in any way because we had dates planned for when we wanted to do it, and then we kept having to postpone. It was a month after when I thought I was at my best fitness, and I was definitely reaching the end by the point we got to that race. Still, it was cool to run that race and attempt it and still run 13:50—and to see Galen come to watch. Before Galen ran 13:37 for his record, he had run 13:50 twice, so it was a really great start that I didn't really realize in the moment, because my goal was to break his record. I think I didn't appreciate that as much as I should have.

The graduation of Nico and Jace ended one era with two state titles and one national championship. But we had improved every year, and our objective was to build on their success. That was a tall order, for sure, but I believed we could because I knew we had the talent to do it with Colin and Aaron Sahlman, Lex and Leo Young, Daniel Appleford, and others returning.

And we had the mentality. I no longer had to persuade runners to dream big because Nico's progression was all the blueprint they needed. That success gave us something that was invaluable—newfound perspective on what we thought was possible. The athletes and their families didn't even think twice about the commitment it would take; they simply thought trying to beat Nico's times was the next step. It was late June. In a few days, we would leave to spend another month training at Big Bear. In 2019, doing that took convincing. This time, the response from our runners and their parents was "Let's go!"

The idea of attempting to break national records sounds crazy at first. But when that becomes the norm, it stops seeming like that big of a deal. The 2020 cross country season was about to start, and a new crop of Newbury Park runners thought they could do it. It was the same for me. At one point, I thought, "How cool would it be to coach a team that won NXN?"

Once I got there, I wanted nothing more than to do it again.

CHAPTER THIRTEEN

FOR THE FIRST FEW days at Big Bear, we checked the forecast every day. We were keeping watch for a strong eastward breeze.

It had nothing to do with a workout.

We were going to float the length of the seven-mile lake.

In my email to parents that summer outlining everything we would need for our four weeks at altitude, I had included a new request: "Can everyone bring a raft? I found some on sale at Big 5 for fifteen dollars."

Finally, we got the conditions we needed. Parents dropped off everyone who wanted to go near the Bear Valley Dam on the lake's western end, and we started paddling—with our hands. Well, Lex and Leo and a few others brought a nice boat with oars, but the rest of us moved with the breeze and the current and paddled with our hands, staying close to the shore. Floating that far would take a while, I knew, but how long could it really take?

All day, it turned out.

A few runners called it quits when it became clear we were going to be on the lake for the equivalent of a marathon, not a 10K. Others quit when their boat popped. For the rest of us who went the whole way, it was a brutal slog that didn't end until it was almost dark and we were destroyed with fatigue. There was no way we were cooking dinner after that ordeal, so I went to Domino's and ordered what felt like a million pizzas and mounds of salad.

As the fall of 2020 approached, it was easy to feel rudderless.

The state had loosened many of its COVID restrictions in early May, but a spread of cases throughout California led the state to pull back on its reopening plans just as we arrived at Big Bear. In late July, toward the end of our stay, Tanya called me from Newbury Park to say that CIF had postponed the start of the high school sports season until December, at the earliest.

"We can't have practice," she said.

Administrators at Newbury Park High called me to ask what I was doing at Big Bear with the athletes. They could take issue all they wanted, but I told them this wasn't going to get them in trouble because it was organized entirely through Mile High Running Camp. There were athletes from other high schools staying with us at Big Bear, and Nico trained with us, too, to help his transition to Northern Arizona, at Flagstaff's elevation. We wanted to help those runners from other schools, while ensuring that Newbury Park's kids didn't miss out on the kind of opportunity that had proven invaluable in 2019.

At a demoralizing, uncertain time around the world, it was a release to be at Big Bear, around one another. What I cared about was giving all of the kids the most "normal" experience possible under extremely unusual circumstances.

Every season, we had been fighting against something. In 2016, it was pushback against my new, higher standards. In 2017, it was our own disappointment. In 2018, it was against doubts we could win our first state title; a year later, doubts about whether we could win our first national title. In 2020, it was COVID restrictions.

In Ventura County, which included our high school, I'd read that youth day camps had been deemed "essential." The athletes paid a small fee to Mile High Running Camp, and we became an official camp, welcoming athletes from other high schools to join. Giving away our program's "secrets" wasn't a concern—I realized everyone needed a place to run. Even with the exception I'd found, we were still limited that fall to meeting with ten athletes at one time. The only way to coach a whole team was to continue splitting up practices the way we had in the spring, with one practice starting at 6:00 a.m. before online school, then another one around 2:30 after my classes ended, and then another session in the evening. Without much light for the evening practice, it limited where we could run. Also, we couldn't mix the kids between groups. They were running not only in packs but in pods.

In the mornings, we were still holding supplemental training three days per week, sessions that would have been easy to scrap considering all the hurdles to holding them. But they were essential to our success. If other ambitious runners might add an extra "easy" run a few days a week to increase mileage, our philosophy centered on emphasizing speed and the strength to sustain it. But it came at a cost: I wasn't sleeping because of the schedule. I was fried. It wasn't sustainable.

I was more concerned for the kids. The training wasn't the issue: It was hard for them to watch as many states around the country went back to racing during the fall, while California hadn't.

I set a goal to make the season feel as normal as possible. I piled ankle weights, mats, and resistance bands in the back of my black Jeep and drove into the hills above Newbury Park High, to Dos Vientos Ranch Park, where we could resume the supplemental morning workouts we'd started in 2018. The park had a concrete basketball court and a grass field that wasn't quite a full 400 meters around—not big enough to truly do workouts on, but flat and soft enough for drills like plyometrics. It wasn't a problem because the runners who would do an easy jog in the mornings before school would head out to a nearby trail, then come back to the park and start their weight training on the courts. Beyond the obvious amenities, the park also offered a measure of seclusion. Even though many of the school's students and teachers lived nearby and would pass by in the morning, the park was tucked out of view from the road. We were cleared to train, but I wanted to be off the radar to avoid drawing attention. Experience had proven that just because you're allowed to do something doesn't mean that it's going to be welcomed.

Though I would try separating the athletes with cones six feet apart, these were kids who weren't seeing friends except during small chunks of the day. They didn't mean to do it, but they would start talking and inevitably inch closer. People would take pictures of us and send it to the school district. I got frustrated because I was trying to make it clear to them that I could get fired if complaints kept happening. Passersby would film us, and my defense became to film them back. A couple of times the interactions made me snap.

"I'm the coach at Newbury Park High School and I'm a teacher there, and you can call the principal and you can tell him you saw me because we're allowed to be here," I said. "I don't freaking care."

I made a choice that I wasn't going to pretend I was somebody else. I was going to fight through this because I didn't think it was unsafe to practice. The school knew how I felt. Some people didn't like that, but I didn't break any of the school or state rules. I don't know how all of the runners felt, but I wanted them to know that I was looking out for them, to find opportunities for them to have a semblance of normalcy at a time when that was hard to come by. The teams from previous years had incredible opportunities. These kids didn't deserve to have that taken away because of bad timing. The CIF wasn't going to do anything to step up and fight for the kids. I would. If I wasn't willing to lose my job, I wasn't doing a good job. Of course, I didn't actually want to lose my job coaching, but I felt that if I wasn't trying to do what was best for the kids, if I just went along with the program and the way it had always been done, then I think we would have been a good team. Not a great team.

As September neared, the actual running was one of the few things I wasn't worrying about.

Now sophomores, Lex and Leo's training had progressed to long runs up to ten miles. There was something special about the twins. I'd first seen it one year earlier in their high school debut. At that point, Lex and his brother had still never gone more than six miles on a regular run. Before the Cool Breeze Evening Invitational, I told the twins to stay with the top guys in the race, and Lex did it, running 14:42 for three miles and finishing third, behind two seniors. That wasn't generational talent on display; it was guts. He believed and went for it.

I don't think it bothered the twins that they were coming up in Nico's shadow, partly because they were running even faster than he did at the same age. That was partly due to their being more physically mature than he was as a freshman. Yet precedent also played a role. The times that Nico, Jace, and Colin had run early in high school had set the bar higher for everyone that followed. Lex's and Leo's personalities were completely different from their older brother's. Where Nico was quiet and had to be drawn out in conversation, Lex and Leo were extroverts from the day they stepped on campus, moving a million miles an hour, juggling running with school, their love of cars and cameras, and a YouTube channel that was catching on. Their L&L channel often featured behind-the-scenes footage of our practices and races.

From what I'd seen of Colin's kick and his toughness hanging with Great Oak's fastest runners at NXN, he had the ability to fill in for Nico as our low stick. Aaron was streaky but had undeniable speed. Daniel Appleford and Nick Goldstein were often overlooked, but on any other team their times would probably have made them the number one runner. And we had more talent coming.

Christian Simone from Great Oak had contacted me that summer to let me know his family was moving to Thousand Oaks and that he wanted to come to Newbury Park. The news was more of a homecoming than a surprise; before he'd transferred to Great Oak, Christian had started high school at Chaminade in West Hills, about a half hour east of Newbury Park in the San Fernando Valley. I wanted to talk with Great Oak's Doug Soles to let him know there hadn't been any sort of recruiting. But if Christian and his family were moving to the area, of course I was going to say yes to an incoming senior who had run 14:23 for three miles the previous fall.

You can't predict how a transfer will work out. Inherently, they are there to take the spot in the top seven of someone who is already established. Depending on how they handle interpersonal relationships with their new teammates and how the teammates receive them, it can either feel like a perfect fit or a challenge from the first day they show up. Christian instantly got along with our guys, particularly with Lex and Leo. He looked like a great addition—if he could stay healthy enough to keep running. The previous fall, as a junior, Christian finished fifth at Woodbridge and fifteenth at Clovis, within one second of Colin Sahlman. The talent was there. The issue was his health: Sidelined by injuries, he had never run after October. Had he competed at Nike Cross Nationals, the title might have gone Great Oak's way.

Christian joined a team with a chip on its shoulder.

Any rational look at our roster would have shown huge gaps to fill because of the graduations of Nico, the national champion, and Jace, an overqualified number two runner if there ever was one.

Yet being around our runners at Big Bear showed me that those who remained weren't seeing it as a loss, but as an opportunity. In sports, coaches love to throw around the word *culture* to describe anything that can't be quantified that explains a team's success. I'd use *mindset* instead. During our first few seasons, we had believed we could pull off state titles without any proof to suggest that we could. But that wasn't the case anymore. The confidence that Nico's and Jace's success had instilled trickled down to younger runners in the program. We had at least six boys who already knew what it took to pull off huge goals, and now that we were ranked number one, we weren't going to lose it. I told the team that it was an honor to have the target on our back. Let people talk about who might try to take that from us, and we would see how long we could be number one. I felt that because Nico was Lex and Leo's brother, and because Colin had known Nico since he was a kid, that they didn't look at Nico in awe, as if he had won accolades they couldn't.

No, they thought Newbury Park deserved to remain number one, and that it was now their time.

His talent alone told me that Colin, now a junior, could be the fastest of them all, the next low stick everyone would be trying to keep up with, not only on our team, but across the country. Though he was a junior on a team with seniors, I thought he should be our leader, too. But it became clear to me through the early fall of 2020 that Colin would have to grow into that role.

In late September of 2020, we were at a workout at Waverly Park in Thousand Oaks. That day, Lex and Leo were taking the lead from the start of each repetition. Instead of setting the pace and the tone for the workout with his example, Colin was settling, I thought. Colin is a great kid and runner, but he could get very comfortable running with his closest friends, including Daniel Appleford. That Colin wasn't up at the front, with his amount of talent, irked me.

There had been other practices like this. Nico was an effective leader because despite being quiet by nature, he realized he could lead without putting on a front and being somebody he wasn't. We never asked him to give rah-rah speeches. We asked him to set the tone during every hard workout. Our post-Nico era had begun with our top three waiting to see whether someone else would take on that responsibility. In a way, you could understand it. They were all talented runners around the same level and conscientious kids who probably felt uncomfortable imposing themselves as the clear leader. Nobody seemed to feel, *Oh, I'm so much better*, which meant nobody was ever a star in a workout. When nobody took the lead, Lex, Leo, and Colin all fed off one another. While that wasn't necessarily a bad thing, it also wouldn't push a runner like Colin to his fullest potential. Make no mistake, our runners were self-motivated. The whole framework of our team would have crumpled if they weren't, because only they could find it within themselves to push toward that red line when it's no longer easy in that second mile, or that last kilometer repeat. But it was also my job as a coach to provide that external motivation when I recognized that slack was forming. If you wait to confront it, the moment will pass.

This was that moment.

At the park, I asked Colin to speak with me away from the rest of the team.

"There's a time, Colin, that you either need to take the lead or you're never going to be the athlete that you think you could be. I get that you're a junior. But, if you don't lead this team, someone else is gonna lead it and you're missing out."

It wasn't our first discussion on the topic. A year earlier at Big Bear, when Colin was a sophomore, I asked him why Lex and Leo had been so much farther ahead. Though he was in their training group, Colin had hung back, running with other friends. We had all afternoon to be social, hanging out at the lake, jumping off the rocks. But right then, he needed to run with Lex and Leo, who were putting in the work up front.

Now I was pressure-testing Colin, and I wondered how he would respond. I'd seen others before him use moments like this as a catalyst to come through in a way they never had before. If you give someone the opportunity, I find they usually take it. If they don't take it, then they're not a gamer. This is as true in running as it is in other arenas.

When we returned to Waverly the following week for another workout, it was as though Colin had heard what I said and a light switch had gone off. He took the lead from the start. I had been around these athletes so long that I could read their mood just by watching them run. Colin's run told me, "All right, I'm the leader now."

As much as I wanted to reward the kids for their work, I also had to be real about how much the pandemic's ongoing effects had changed our expectations. Because of the summer surge in COVID cases, the CIF had announced in July that it would be too dangerous to hold a fall sports season. Sports held in the fall, which included cross country and football, wouldn't be allowed to begin until December at the earliest. Until then, we were operating under essentially offseason rules. If our principal and the county's health department gave the green light to practice and hold unofficial competitions, then we were fine to continue practicing.

We got the green light.

CHAPTER FOURTEEN

AT A MEETING AT the beginning of the fall, I told the runners and their parents our plan for the months ahead.

Because we wouldn't technically be running "in season" through CIF, we would be competing as an unaffiliated group I'd formed called Newbury Park Athletic Club. We even needed different uniforms. Our goal was to run at one regular race, followed by a national-level meet. It wouldn't be Nike Cross Nationals, which Nike had canceled in July. From talking with other coaches, though, it sounded as if too many other states were running their season in the fall for there not to emerge an NXN type of replacement.

In any other season, early October would have been not long after we raced at flat-and-fast Woodbridge—a meet I always viewed as an opportunity to show everyone interested in distance running what Newbury Park had been working on all summer.

In a year in which everything had changed, nothing about that original intention had. By the time we arrived at a golf course in Queen Creek, Arizona, for the Desert Twilight on the night of October 2, I firmly believed our new team could beat our 2019 national champions. We had a new dynamic. For three years, Newbury Park's racing style had been dangerous and consistent: Nico and Jace out front, and the rest of our top seven trickling in as fast as possible behind them. Now, thanks to Colin's, Lex's, and Leo's similar skill levels, we could run as a pack, with the difference that our pack was also fast enough to stick together while also leading a race. That was what our training had indicated, anyway, but the Twilight was our first chance to prove it. Given the uncertainty of the fall schedule, it would also be our last chance to make a statement for weeks.

Our top seven at the Twilight had been determined only days earlier. Results by Colin, Lex, Leo, Nick Goldstein, and Daniel Appleford in previous seasons ensured their spots were secure. But with Nico and Jace off to college, we had two vacant spots, and the fairest way to fill them was to see who could prevail in a race with real pressure riding on it—a preview, of sorts, of the kind of test they'd be facing on race day if they made the cut. Our runoff was held at Thousand Oaks' Waverly Park. Newcomer Christian Simone and Aaron Sahlman earned the spots.

The times Christian had run at Great Oak clearly suggested he was capable of making our top seven. I was less sure of what to expect from Aaron. Younger than Colin by a year, he had run in the same youth track club in Camarillo as Colin, Nico, Lex, and Leo had, but Aaron also loved football, and in high school he hadn't committed to running until a few months before the race-off. His raw speed was clear, his consistency less so. But to make the top seven at Newbury Park was no small feat.

Ten months after NXN, we were finally back racing. It didn't look the same. Our new top seven donned new black-and-white Nike singlets with yellow shorts, competing on a course that was new to us. We hadn't raced the Desert Twilight before for a reason: It was ninety-eight degrees when the JV race started in late afternoon, and it was still brutally hot when the varsity races went off at night. Even the starting line was different, each team lined up in a box with several feet of spacing on either side for a socially distanced start. Our mission was to prove that what hadn't changed was our claim to being the country's top team.

Fireworks lit the night sky above the course. I said my few words, then let the team huddle by itself. This was a new group learning, for the first time in a race, how to set the bar of excellence for themselves.

Our boys shot off the line, with Colin leading a big pack through the first mile in 4:38.

We were again watching out for Great Oak, which, like us, had formed a "club" to race out of state, now called South Temecula Track Club. Portable lights set up around the golf course were spread out enough that for stretches of the second mile it was difficult to pick up everyone's position, as runners turned into half-lit shadows flying around the fairways and through stands of trees. But when the light caught them, it revealed Colin in the lead and Lex one step behind, with Goldstein and Leo only two seconds back.

Ten minutes in, John Scherer, from Wisconsin, passed Colin coming off a downhill. For the next four minutes, Colin and Scherer dueled by themselves while breaking away from their pursuers, Scherer one step ahead entering the final straightaway, with fans watching three deep on either side. Colin came up on Scherer's right and pulled even. If this was a competition of closing kicks, I already knew how it would end. With less than 100 meters left, Colin created enough space to swing in front of Scherer and keep him on his back while sprinting in for a win in 14:53.

COLIN SAHLMAN

I kind of knew I was next up in a leadership role, and for me, it was a lot of pressure because naturally I feel like I'm not a super-vocal leader. But I just had to step outside my comfort zone and try and do it for the team. When we'd huddle up at meets, I would give the prerace speech and would let all the words come naturally and tried to be there for my team, even during workouts, too. It's definitely a big jump from being the one who is being motivated to doing the motivating.

The Desert Twilight was our first team race together that season. I remember we all huddled out there, and because there was no set team captain, no one knew who was going to speak, so I just spoke up. Then my teammate Daniel Appleford chimed in after me. We kind of naturally took over those roles. In the race, it was about ninety-five degrees out when we ran, and my mouth was dry and I felt spent. But I knew that season I wanted to be one of the best in the nation, and when Scherer passed me, I remember thinking, *I don't know who this kid is, I'm not going to let a random kid beat me.* He was pushing the pace and I just wanted to stick on him and not exert any extra energy, because I knew I had a strong kick, and if I was with him in the last 200 meters, I knew I could take the lead. I was so tired and wanted to let him go, but I just never did.

After that race, I knew that I was going to be hard to beat because even when I wasn't feeling the best, even when my mind was telling me, *Don't*, I still held on. It told me I was probably one of the best runners in the country, and that my mindset in the race was probably different from a lot of other high school runners'.

Colin hadn't lost a step, and neither had his teammates.

Lex was third overall in 14:56.

Leo was fifth in 15:06.

Aaron, number seven on the team just days earlier, was sixth in the whole race in 15:10.

Goldstein was ninth in 15:17.

And Christian was thirteenth in 15:22.

When individuals were filtered out of the standings, leaving only full teams, Newbury Park's 17 points were only 2 more than mathematical perfection.

AARON SAHLMAN
I didn't really take running seriously until my sophomore year because freshman year I was balancing between whether I wanted to do cross country or football, because I'd been playing football for six years. I was talking to the football coach at Newbury, too, so I would show up to some football practices, and then some cross practices and never really took it seriously until after my freshman year. I'd had multiple concussions in the past while playing football, so I was at a higher risk if I'd continued with football. I stopped after that. That's why I had to race for the top seven, because Sean didn't know if I was ready. It was very stressful because I was racing against my teammates who were juniors and seniors who had more experience, so I was a little bit nervous on how I would do. I barely snuck in at number seven. Once we hit the Desert Twilight and I got fourth on the team, then, that was a huge indication that I would be a factor for Newbury.

The Desert Twilight confirmed my suspicions that 2019 hadn't represented our program's peak, but was only a preview of a long run of success to come. And yet, when I'd met with the runners and their parents at the season's start to outline my goals for the months ahead, I didn't focus on results I wanted to see, but on the process. No one had wanted a pandemic to throw all of our lives into upheaval, yet from a running perspective it had come with a significant silver lining. In 2019, our team had benefited by taking four weeks off from racing in the middle of the season to focus on training. Now, in 2020, we were going to essentially treat the entire fall and winter like a big, uninterrupted training block.

Did we still want to dominate? Absolutely. But development was more important in the fall of 2020. I wanted to take advantage of this rare opportunity to train to focus on our runners' long-term potential.

Once, I was talking about another team with Scott Simmons, my former boss back in Charlotte, and he said something I never forgot: "They won't win."

"You don't think so?"

"They don't know how to win, Sean. Some coaches don't know how. They don't know how to get their kids ready mentally and physically for that one day."

It's one thing to have them run fast here and there. But being primed to perform on that one day, when you have one shot? That's so hard to do. Newbury Park's entire program was oriented around being ready on the day that mattered—which meant prioritizing what mattered. For me, it was being smart about how we trained and calculated about when we raced.

To me, this was training as it should be.

The guiding motivation in all sports should be focusing on the biggest possible goals and aiming to get athletes to perform in the biggest moments. In my opinion, the structure of the European club system does this well and the US system does not. The US system emphasizes who could score points at meets, an incentive that doesn't always align with the mission of how to get your athletes to be the very best they can be. That comes from years of development.

Every year, I would attend league meetings and propose doing away with dual meets. The value of having our team go against just one other team was negligible in the bigger picture of kids running their best to set them up for the future. Dual meets were customs that were important at one time but had outlived their usefulness. They continued because upending a norm is hard.

In the fall of 2020, though, we would have raced just about anywhere. When options weren't available, we dug into training.

At times, it was monotonous. Boring, even. Still, it wasn't hard to keep our runners motivated. Professionals were beginning to emerge from COVID lockdowns and race again, and we noticed they were running *fast*. Some of the times had to do with new shoes stacked high with different foams that were changing road running. But to me, the performances reinforced the belief guiding our 2020 training, which held that good training led to good racing. Physiologically, runners can't perform at their absolute peak three or four times in a single season, and I reiterated that over and over to our runners. If we trained properly, and patiently, Newbury Park's runners were going to emerge from the pandemic limbo stronger. Not just as individuals, but as a team.

The kids were focused on building their fitness, but without realizing it, they were building the connections that bond a team, too, because so often they had to be accountable to one another. I couldn't be at every run for every group. The school was being sent complaints about our team training together, and even when I protested to our administrators that the complaints were bogus and that we were complying with rules set down by the school district and the state, at times I had to back off out of caution, sending our athletes the details of their runs and hoping they carried them out.

Other teams got away with so much more because everything we did was in the spotlight: Our success had made us just so much more visible. The people who recorded us during our morning strength training at Dos Vientos Ranch Park weren't outliers. My frustration built. Once, someone spotted a totally different Newbury Park High team running a hill near the school for conditioning and complained that the cross country team was gathering. They'd seen a bunch of kids running, so it had to be us, right? No.

Months later, when COVID delays pushed the fall and winter seasons together, CIF relaxed a rule that prohibited holding practices on Sundays. I thought this was a rare good move by CIF. Tanya and I met with a handful of Newbury Park's girls for a long run on a Sunday at Satwiwa, the trailhead south of our high school that traveled south toward Malibu through Sycamore Canyon. It was a laid-back run, until I saw someone hiding behind a bathroom along the trail, their phone out taking pictures. When I took a closer look, I saw it was another high school coach from our area. The pictures got sent to the district.

You have to be freaking kidding me, I thought. Did the coach not know the rules? I had to explain to our school officials that I did, and that we were operating within them.

I was glad that Newbury Park's principal, Steve Lepire, always supported me. He told me once that it was just perception that I was pushing the envelope. I still remember the smile on his face when I walked into his office one day.

"Sean, it's Friday, and I didn't have one complaint," he said.

COLIN SAHLMAN

With success, you obviously have your fans and you have your haters, but it was definitely weird when people would show up to a workout and take pictures of us and then send it to the school. We were just high school kids trying to make the most out of a pandemic. Sean was good about taking up his entire day to go to multiple different practices just so we could have smaller groups to work out with. We were very cautious and safe about it, but it wasn't enough to satisfy people. It felt as though people were trying to bring us down. It definitely felt like it was us against the world.

Because the Youngs and the Sahlmans lived close to one another, the four of them often worked out together, sometimes driving a half hour away to find a track or a trail where they could get in their work. Other times, the runners would text one another in their group chat about when and where everyone was meeting, and they'd get their miles in without me. For so much of my first two seasons at the school, I'd been pushing the athletes, and in turn getting pushback. But winning it all in 2019 had created an intrinsic motivation that a coach alone can't put in place. If trying to navigate through the restrictions was grating, the runners' response was gratifying.

Some things hadn't changed in my five years at the school. Where some coaches would set in stone a season's worth of mileage and workouts, I only scripted a few days in advance what our practices would look like, preferring to react to how the runners were feeling. To me, that was more natural as a coach than rigidity.

Yet in many ways our program had evolved. It had taken me two years to iron out how to coach high schoolers and get them to buy in, and every runner who followed benefited. We now had systems in place. As soon as younger runners entered our program, they immediately had morning supplemental workouts and runs planned that Nico and Jace never did as freshmen and sophomores.

Our ambitions were higher, too. Nico and Jace had just wanted to make state as freshmen and sophomores; now, because of how high they had set the bar, new freshmen arrived *expecting* to make nationals. The result was that our new era, Newbury 2.0, was still following the same progressive training philosophy, a slow build that peaked around some of our most important early-season meets, but the new kids were able to handle more advanced workloads as freshmen and sophomores than Nico and Jace were doing at the same age. Where Nico had run twice a day about two times per week, his brothers were already doubling three days per week. The 30/40 workout made famous by Prefontaine—alternating between 200 meters done in 30 seconds and 40 seconds, teaching your body to change pace when it hurts—which Nico was doing as a junior, was being pulled off by his brothers as sophomores.

The rising tide lifted everybody. Whereas Nico had led almost every workout, we now had four guys who could almost always run together. Colin was usually the lead guy in workouts, but some days he wouldn't feel good, which taught the rest a lot about competing. One day Aaron was good. Then it would be Lex and Leo.

LEX YOUNG

Nico went off to NAU before our sophomore year, and while it would have been awesome to train with him for another year, we stayed in continuous contact. Nico was really insightful about all the things that you do outside of practice; things like nutrition, hydration, rest, recovery, all of that. His guidance almost felt like a secret power.

COVID, obviously, put a wrench into things. Without any races on the calendar our focus turned entirely to the process. It was like a really long training block focused on improvement, without regard to the actual quantitative number that you'd get when you finished a race.

I think this differed from a lot of our competitors, who stopped training as intensely given all the COVID restrictions, while we managed to keep stacking those bricks. And if there was a secret to our success, it was that simple: consistent training; just showing up is paramount. Undoubtedly, doing that uninterrupted training for a year set the table for our rise junior year.

We couldn't wait to get back to racing. And at Big Bear, Sean had us write out our goals. The key to that exercise that summer, and maybe this was partly a legacy of COVID, was that our goals were more process- than outcome-oriented. We weren't focused on specific things, like winning states or running a specific time. It was more about how we were going to do it, like every single person doing our weight training together.

And it was things like that that allowed us to get in a better mental space, because we weren't just like, "I want the glory. I want the attention." It was more about what can we do to push ourselves there?

That collective, team-first mindset helped us as we got into the fall and had a really fit group up front with Colin, Aaron, Leo, and me. It's natural that there would be some competitiveness between us, but I always felt that the workouts were more collaborative than competitive; in workouts we understood that we were at such a similar fitness that if one was going to do it, we all should be doing it. So we wouldn't take off in a workout with the purpose of dropping the others. It was more that one of us would pick up the pace with the purpose of bringing us all through at a faster pace. We're gonna work together, split up the pacing, and, if someone is feeling good, just ride behind them and just hurt like hell until the workout is over. It was all about capitalizing on our individual strengths to benefit the entire group.

Typically, I excelled in the longer, more rhythmic tempo-style workouts, while Leo was especially good at maintaining a fast pace on shorter intervals (800 meters to a mile) during the middle portions of the workouts. When the end of the tunnel seemed far, we could usually count on Leo to keep us going. And when it came time to close out a workout, we could almost always count on Aaron to hammer the end. And Colin, he was our leader. No matter the challenge he was there for us to look to and always held us accountable.

That teamwork translated to races. We didn't know who would lead us from one race to the next. But because we were so accountable to one another and working so closely together, we knew we would get results. Had we been just as fit but at four separate high schools, I don't think we could have had the same results, but as it was, training as one, we knew if one of us was doing it, the others could, too. And as we started to attack races as a group right at the front, we started to appreciate how beneficial and self-perpetuating this style of training really was.

The hardest part of changing our team culture had been the first push. But once Ethan Duffy, Nico, and Jace did that, it felt like we were a snowball growing as it rolled downhill, gathering speed. Had we been forced in 2016, 2017, or even 2018 to go through a prolonged block of training like this, I'm not sure what the commitment level from the team would have been. But this team, having seen what was achievable, found the motivation to keep going despite shifting rules and a high school sports calendar that often changed. Distance training calls for *hard days* and *easy days*. Usually, the definitions are tied to what pace you're running. The fall of 2020 was mostly hard days, for reasons that often had little to do with running.

For all of the reasons why I felt Nike Cross Nationals wasn't perfect—too many obligations that pulled runners in too many directions—it was indisputable that within high school cross country, it had become the agreed-upon national championship site.

That fall, Nike had introduced a virtual competition format, but it wasn't the same as a real meet, and without NXN, the best teams in the country splintered off. Some were going to a meet in Texas. Some were going to the RunningLane Cross Country Championships in Huntsville, Alabama. In Terre Haute, Indiana, a third option was the XC Town Meet of Champions, held November 15 by the National Scholastic Athletics Foundation on the same course that hosts NCAA cross country championships. XC Town intrigued me because, for one, the organizers said they would pay to fly our team out. I had also always wanted our runners to compete on the Terre Haute course, one of the country's most famous. It was a good course, and by mid-November the conditions would probably be brutally cold. I had always wanted to prove that California kids could run courses perceived as "real" cross country—through mud, thick grass, and hills.

Ultimately, though, we would go to whichever meet could promise us the best competition, so that we, number one in many rankings ever since Desert Twilight, could prove we were the best. Once I heard that Jesuit High School, a team from suburban Portland that was ranked just below us, was going to Indiana, so were we.

Terre Haute in mid-November was, indeed, freezing cold. On race day, gusts of wind tipped over Porta Potties and kept us from putting up our team tent. Conditions were the opposite of our last race, in Arizona. The outcome was not. In the "boys open" division, our B team won with 83 points, led by Thomas McDonnell. Then, in the "championship" division, it was a rout. Christian Simone was sixth overall in 15:24.2 to lead three from Newbury Park in the top thirteen, followed by Lex in ninth and Leo in thirteenth. All seven finished under 16:06. Our top two were in front of Jesuit's number one, and nearly our entire top five were faster than their third-best runner. Jesuit, which ran as Stumptown Running Track Club, scored 97 points to finish second—65 points behind us.

It was hard to work up much emotion over the victory because it wasn't a unified national championship. We broke for Thanksgiving the next week, and then we had one last meet to go in our "season." Sound Running, a meet promoter in LA, had found a way to put on a night of 5K competitions about an hour south of Los Angeles at JSerra High School, in San Juan Capistrano. It was going to feature high-level pros like Matthew Centrowitz, the 2016 Rio Olympics gold medalist in the 1,500 meters, but also a section just for high schoolers. We were excited; this was as close to home as we would compete that fall.

Or so we thought.

Two days before the December 5 race, the meet promoter's founder sent me an email that started with an apology. That wasn't a good sign. The meet wasn't canceled—only the high school section, he said, and it wasn't his choice. A record number of new COVID cases had just been announced in counties across Southern California. The leadership of the high school hosting the meet had gotten second thoughts about hosting teenagers amid the continued COVID precautions.

I was mad. But what could we do? We didn't want to waste our runners' fitness. I was sending out mass emails and texting coaches when I remembered the Desert Twilight. Arizona, as a state, was open. Through distance-running circles I had known Ellie Hardt, a former high school coach who helped manage facilities in the Queen Creek school district, the city southeast of Phoenix where the Desert Twilight had been held. When I contacted her on Thursday, December 3, I outlined our hope to find a place to stage a meet ourselves.

Ellie surprised me, giving us our choice of tracks within the district to use as soon as that weekend. We chose a new school, Eastmark High. Even better? We could "rent" it for free. It was 2:00 p.m.

Thursday, and I was about to see whether I could stage a meet on two days' notice.

Sometimes you have to do something so crazy . . .

I called the athletes. I called their parents. We're going to Arizona, I told them. Who wants to go? Todd McDonnell, the father of Thomas and Sam, our top girls runner, was in. The Youngs were in.

I was trying to coordinate how we would get to Arizona, where we would stay, how to hire an official timer and get the word out to other schools, while finishing my schedule of remote classes for the day. I threw clothes into a suitcase.

Tanya rented a van through Mile High Running Camp. We couldn't meet at Newbury Park High, so I told anyone who wanted in that we'd pick them up at Pepper Tree to drive the seven hours to our meet that currently had no name. One of the people I'd alerted to our last-minute plan was Kevin Selby, an announcer for FloTrack, an outlet that covered and broadcast meets. I'd known Kevin since I was a postcollegiate runner living in California's Bay Area.

"You have to name it *something*," Kevin said.

I hadn't thought that far. Because of the heat, we were going to race at twilight. I remembered that I'd always liked the name of a surf shop on Long Island, near where I grew up, that was called Sundown. It would be the Sundown 5K.

I couldn't find an available timer based in Arizona, so I hired one from California. To get our times official, I had to make it worth their time, which meant that I covered the costs of their drive, their hotels, and their fees. I was losing money on this meet already—the only thing that was saving me was the money I'd set aside from my summertime high-altitude running camps.

By Thursday evening, as our fourteen-passenger van was driving east to Queen Creek, we still didn't have a place to stay—until Lynne Young, the mother of Lex, Leo, and Nico, texted us the listing of an Airbnb she'd found mid-drive. It was a mansion, and available right now. Families split the cost with us. We arrived at two thirty in the morning. The next day, the students logged into their remote classes and I taught mine from our rented mansion, and then we went to the track for our prerace.

Because of the announcement I'd made, interest poured in from runners from high schools like Great Oak, in California's Bay Area, and in Arizona. Displeased messages from my school district also arrived. Our athletic director had heard about the race, too.

I was told I couldn't be at the meet.

"The one that I'm at, in Arizona, right now?" I said.

I wasn't asking for permission. My money from my business was behind the meet. It was an "open" race, with no direct affiliation to Newbury Park High. The runners all had a choice whether they wanted to join. When the conversation ended, the district asked me to at least not make a big deal of it. But of course it became a big deal because we were Newbury Park, and wherever we went, we drew attention: Our athletes inevitably ran national-caliber times.

On the same December weekend when we would have been competing at NXN, we hosted our one-race Sundown 5K. Colin won in 14:27.03, just barely ahead of Lex. Lex was disappointed. He had wanted to break the California sophomore state record and had come up short. But being a great teammate, he came back to the track half an hour after his race had ended to pace Sam McDonnell as she raced her own 5K.

As Lex and Sam ran, an assistant timer called me over to look at a camera screen. One of the kids who had been lapped by Colin and Lex during the boys 5K had been mistaken for Lex. When the timers looked back at the footage, they realized their mistake and changed his time to the accurate one.

I sprinted over to Lex, who was still acting as Sam's rabbit.

"You broke the state record!" I screamed at Lex. "They messed up!" All of a sudden, he perked up, going harder. He was so excited that he pulled Sam to a time of 17:04.

Lex's time of 14:27.11 was indeed a California sophomore record and the third-fastest time ever run by a sophomore nationally. Six months after Nico had broken California's state 5K record on an empty track in Portland, one of his younger brothers was joining him in the record book. It was an amazing feat, one that we didn't at first even realize had happened.

The meet would have been a success if it had only been Colin's and Lex's performances. But Christian ran 14:46, Nick Goldstein 14:47, and Leo 14:49. After the meet, I read a story that said no high school had ever produced two sub-15 runners in a track 5K in the same race—let alone five.

The trip wasn't just productive, it was fun. A willingness to take something that seemed crazy and make it real? *This* is what I wanted to create for our runners. Since our 2019 title, I had seen or heard so many comments, whether typed online anonymously or said to me in person, that were critical of our big, outlandish team tents with lights and rugs, and our willingness to push boundaries, because people saw a coach trying to draw attention to himself.

The critics and comments had missed the point completely.

Creating the tents and the opportunities like the Sundown 5K had been in service of making an experience that was bigger and better than simply showing up and running. The same had been done for me by my grandfather, who was willing to drive across state lines to help me get a workout in, and by Damon Martin, whose pump-up speeches ramped up the intensity of an Adams State workout. It was what I'd observed from top coaches.

Distance running is a punishing, often lonely sport. If you're going to put in all that work, why not make it memorable? Why not make it feel like something that is bigger than yourself? I'll admit that I demanded a lot from our athletes—like the flexibility to get a call at 2:00 p.m. on a Thursday and be ready to go out of state within a few hours. Our training philosophy wasn't any different. I demanded workouts that pushed them to "go to the well," my saying for giving me all they had. All fall, through weeks of workouts, they'd done that.

From the outside, people believed Newbury Park's team was full of rich kids who had shown up to campus already stocked with all the talent in the world. That just wasn't the case. You can't buy your way to a national or state record. You have to earn it.

The trip had triggered something. On the drive home, I wanted to find ways to keep rewarding our runners while continuing to lower their times. The hope was that leaving 2020, there would be more opportunities the following year. When they opened, I wanted Newbury Park to be ready.

I called Ellie to thank her for the use of the track.

"I have an idea," I said. "What if we came back?"

CHAPTER FIFTEEN

HOW MANY HIGH SCHOOL distance-running coaches receive hate mail?

Well, I did.

It started the previous summer, in 2020. A YouTube channel that was dedicated to distance running was interviewing Newbury Park's runners and coaches as part of a series about our 2019 championship season, and the duel with Great Oak. During my interview, I tried to explain the mindset shift that underpinned our program's sudden success.

"4:20's not fast for a high school mile," I said. "It's just not fast. And if they believe that, they're going to start thinking—it's a state of mind."

With that, our program probably set yet another record—fastest time between a coach saying something and it becoming a trending topic on running message boards.

Coaches sent me critical direct messages on social media. Parents of athletes I'd never met sent me horrified emails.

The most outspoken critics were fixated on my choice of a time, 4:20, assuming I was taking shots at kids who couldn't reach it. But the time could have been *any* time. It was simply an example that served my larger point.

Stop setting artificial limits.

"How dare you say that?" most messages started. "That's insulting to people who don't have the ability to run faster."

"Let me ask you: Is 4:20 fast for a high school mile?" I'd respond. "If it is, you just answered your question."

If you have the mindset that 4:20 is fast, then you're never going to run any faster. A phrase I've always found powerful is *your wish is my command.* To me, it articulates the idea that the belief you have in your head will directly translate to the outcome. When I was growing up, when I had shrugged off my grandfather's suggestion of following my uncle into stockbroking, saying it wasn't my thing, he told me the only reason I would not be successful selling stocks was if I told myself that.

It had nothing to do with running. It also had everything to do with running. I didn't want runners believing that certain times were "fast," because it would act like a cap on their potential, where if they reached it, they might become satisfied. Listen, I know not every kid can run a mile in sub-4:20, or sub-4:10, or the holy grail of sub-four, but improvement for any runner, regardless of skill, is rooted in believing they *can* run faster. Had we believed a California state title represented the pinnacle of our success at Newbury Park, we would never have aimed for a national title. If I, as a coach, had allowed Nico to think the ceiling was running sub-15 in cross country as a junior, then he would never have run 14:28 on the same course just one year later.

NICO YOUNG

I have a water bottle with Sean's 4:20's NOT FAST stickers on it, and people always ask about it. I always explain that the time could have been any time and 4:20 itself is irrelevant. It's just the standard that you set is how you determine what is "fast." To run that 3K that I did indoors, Sean had told me that I could run 7:50. That's crazy for a high schooler to run, but I thought, *Okay, let's do it.* It's important to have enough courage to put that kind of goal out there.

By then, I was used to criticism.

That our expectations were too demanding. Our focus on quality, year-round speed work led our mileage to rarely creep above 60 per week, and even those weeks were outliers done by only a few. I had no hesitation to scrap my training plan for the day if I could tell during practice that a runner just didn't have it, mentally or physically. When some runners felt their bodies couldn't handle a morning *and* an afternoon run, we changed course and gave them a single, longer run to approximate the miles.

That our workouts were too hard. The trade-off of lower mileage was that the whole point of a workout was to go hard. If you expect to break four minutes in a mile, and you're not running 100s in 13 seconds year-round, or 200s in 27 seconds year-round, what do you think? That you're just going to start in March? The proof was that we were making the best runners in the country by developing our speed all year. And our training was tailored so that we weren't asking runners who couldn't sustain that speed to live up to the standards of our fastest.

That our runners were doping. To suggest that is not only wrong but insulting to both the runners and their parents. We would all be in jail if we did that. Faceless online avatars would try to explain away our success by suggesting our runners were taking drugs after workouts, when they were really eating watermelon slices.

That it had to be the shoes. Nike set off a boom in running-shoe technology in 2016 when it released its Nike Vaporfly 4%. The 4% in its name stemmed from studies suggesting that the shoe's carbon plate, wedged between new, bouncier foams, could improve running performance by a small percentage. Within a few years, as other companies tried catching up by placing thick slabs of foam under superlight fabric uppers, records in road running and on the track were getting demolished. Teenagers watch what works for pros, and immediately "supershoes" began showing up in cross country meets. Once, later in 2021, I asked our runners to run in them while going over the brutal hills of Mt. San Antonio College, east of LA, because I hate that course, and I wanted to save their legs for the state meet the following week. But otherwise, we never ran in those shoes.

That out-of-district transfers were bringing ringers to Newbury Park. There were more than fourteen thousand transfers across the state in 2021. To suggest Newbury Park was some outlier always rang to me like a hollow criticism, serving to mask what critics seemed to be truly implying—that I was somehow recruiting, which isn't acceptable or allowed in high school athletics. Families transfer their students or stay within their district for any number of reasons. As a track coach I was friends with once told me, "Sean, if you build it, they will come." He was right. But why they came was never something I was involved in. I never recruited anyone for running.

That, between the Youngs and the Sahlmans, we'd hit the genetic lottery. Obviously, natural speed can't be ignored. But you can't do much with it without work ethic, and Newbury Park was proving that the drive to succeed could be implanted in anyone who was committed. How else to explain Nick Goldstein and

Daniel Appleford and others who could have been the number one runner on nearly any other team in the country? Or that our girls, including Sam McDonnell, were becoming national class in their own right?

The criticism was good and bad. People were paying unprecedented attention to a team of high school distance runners. Our running records—together with my willingness to talk openly about our not being satisfied until we ran even faster—arguably pissed some people off and turned many more into fans. The records inarguably made the spotlight on us bigger and hotter. But I always told the parents that the runners were learning a valuable lesson in dealing with pressure to perform. Adding thousands of followers on social media, as Lex, Leo, and Colin had, was a testament to their achievements—something usually reserved for the top high school football or basketball players.

To their credit, the kids handled it well. And even though I always knew they would earn fame if we reached our goals, I found it weird that as our national profile blew up, strangers began to know who *I* was, too. I couldn't prepare our athletes for fame because I hadn't been through it before myself. As a runner, I'd spent a lot of time around popular pros, but as someone who was always on the fringes, it was hard to know what it was like to be in their trainers. I didn't mind the attention, but I found it odd all the same. I focused on making it all about the kids.

Shoe Dog, the memoir by Nike cofounder Phil Knight, was released before my first fall as Newbury Park's cross country coach, and I devoured it. What stuck with me was Knight's warning to innovators and rebels that "the better they get, the bigger the bull's-eye." I understood that criticism would come with the territory as we changed expectations for how fast US teenagers could run. It's easy to say that, but harder not to be bothered when people insult you personally. It got to me at times, and I know the Youngs and the Sahlmans felt that, too, at times. I took pride in fighting for our team, though.

Another *Shoe Dog* line applied. Knight referenced something General Douglas MacArthur had said: "You are remembered for the rules you break."

And so, just before Valentine's Day of 2021, we set off again for the Arizona desert.

The first Sundown meet in December had been such a rush that I immediately wanted to host more.

Queen Creek became Newbury Park East, as the Sundown Track Series was born, with my running camp acting as the operator. In late December, California had canceled the state cross country championships it had scheduled for late March. The abbreviated, pushed-back "official" cross country season in the state wasn't going to happen at all.

There was no reason to wait around in California for others to create opportunities. We needed to make our own.

Our first meet back in Queen Creek, on February 13, hosted four races: a boys and a girls mile and a boys and a girls 3,200 meters. Sam McDonnell ran 4:55 in the mile, just ahead of a promising freshman from Ventura named Sadie Engelhardt. In the boys mile, Colin dropped his personal best to 4:09.86.

On February 27, more than 130 runners showed up at Eastmark High for another boys and another girls mile—4:17 for Lex—and a 3,200, in which Colin ran 8:47.05 and Nick Goldstein ran 9:00.

A month to the day later, we threw our biggest bash, with more than two hundred athletes at Queen Creek High for eight races. The meets had become so popular I had to cap our entries, turning athletes away. We split our miles and 3,200s into regular and "championship" heats. Lex dipped under the nine-minute barrier in the 3,200 for the first time, going 8:57.23, with Daniel Appleford clocking 9:04.03. In the mile, Colin lowered his personal best, again, to 4:04.86. It stood as the fastest time by a high schooler in the country until June. In the mile, Sam took seven seconds off her time from just six weeks earlier.

Nearly one year into an incredibly difficult pandemic, the trips felt like getaways where stress evaporated—*whoosh*. We made Sundown Series T-shirts. Every weekend, we rented mansions with tennis courts and basketball courts on the cheap because the pandemic had cratered demand. One had a ballroom. One had a library, which doubled as my bedroom. One had a front door that I swear was twenty feet tall. One had a pool surrounded by fake boulders. You would think we were paying outlandish sums to rent them when each family was contributing not much more than $100. We were in our own bubble. Everyone tested for COVID before we left and during our stays and followed masking rules. From my bedroom, I would teach my business classes, and the runners would take their online courses by Zoom in their own rooms. After a class, I'd jump off the rocks into the pool, then dry off and go teach my next class. They were some of our most memorable times at Newbury Park. I wanted our runners, still largely separated from friends, to have the best experience they'd ever had. I felt like I was ready to move to Arizona, like I was on vacation—our getaway. At one meet, a parent of an athlete from another school approached me and said her daughter had been isolated and depressed since the pandemic began and that the meets were all she wanted to talk about because they had given her something to look forward to. I wanted anyone who didn't love that we were spending so much time out of state together—including our own high school—to know that.

But we couldn't stay in Arizona forever. The Sundown Series had been an opportunity to stay sharp. Back home, we finally had a chance to shine.

I hated when strangers would take videos of our practices, knowing that the audience would be school and district officials, and that I would have to explain how we were not, in fact, breaking their protocols.

But not all cameras were discouraged. When running-focused YouTube channels asked if they could film a workout, I allowed it, knowing that the audience would be big and that the work would speak for itself, no explanation needed.

In late April, one such channel visited Newbury Park High's track—which we now were allowed to use—before sunrise to capture our last intense workout before the Arcadia Invitational the following week. Because different shoe brands hosted their own "national championships" for track in June, it had become impossible to find one place where the country's best high schoolers on the track could be determined once and for all. Arcadia wasn't a perfect solution, but for races like the 3,200 meters, it was one of the better options.

We started with rope stretching, two miles of easy running, drills, and strides to activate the body. Then the kids would alternate between slower and increasingly faster 400s, with a 100-meter jog for rest in between. For a four-flat miler, we start at mile place, with one lap in 60 seconds, the next in 70; one lap in 58, the next in 70; one lap in 56, the next in 70; a final lap in 54, followed by another 70. It's a great workout because you have to be patient; if you run too fast in the early reps, you will pay the price later. I first learned of this workout while living in Beaverton, when I joined Alan Webb for a session.

I believed we could get five runners under nine minutes in the 3,200, but I also doubted that any other runner would try to take the lead early and push a fast pace, which meant it would be up to Colin or Lex to take the lead as if it were one of our workouts at Pepper Tree. Colin had suffered a minor injury a week earlier, but he had looked good during the tune-up workout.

Newbury Park had come a long way from the 2016 team that didn't even have matching warm-ups. A few months earlier, a contact I'd met at Nike when Nico attended the company's camp for elite runners in 2019 called me to ask whether our program needed uniforms.

"Is this what happens when you're good?" I asked.

It was, and I was quite happy about it. Though the school had a contract with Under Armour, we'd quickly switched to blank Nike singlets we customized ourselves during the pandemic, when we had to rebrand as an unaffiliated club. I took the Nike offer to the high school's leadership and put it in the simplest terms. We could get thousands of dollars' worth of Nike's elite kit for free or continue to pay for Under Armour to replace worn-out uniforms we didn't want anymore.

From that day on, we were outfitted head to toe in Nike. When we showed up at Arcadia on the night of April 8 and every meet that followed, heads turned when our runners left our team tent in matching all-black warm-ups. I would get upset if we weren't wearing our new gear, outlining to our runners, "Guys, this is our image." It was the same reason I wanted our tents to look bigger and better every year. This was about portraying an image of a unified team confident before the gun even sounded that it would run fast. I was confident it could have a mental effect on our competitors. And it kind of worked.

After Aaron Sahlman won Arcadia's mile in 4:14.07, four of our runners went under nine minutes in the 3,200. I couldn't stop smiling. Our race plan was effectively the same as in cross country because it played to our strengths: Lay down a hard first mile and then follow with three hard, successive laps to burn off anyone else who was still hanging around the lead pack. It had the intended effect. For the final three laps everyone drifted off the pace that Colin and Lex had set. Colin had just a bit more left in the final 50 meters to win in 8:43.42, his finishing kick giving him just a stride on Lex in 8:43.71, a state sophomore-class record. They embraced after they crossed. The third-place finisher didn't cross for eight more seconds. In the previous ten years of high school track, only seven boys in the United States had run faster than Colin, a group that included future record holders, future NCAA and US champions and Olympians. Leo (8:55.82) and Daniel Appleford (8:56.77) were next under the nine-minute barrier.

In the stands, I pumped my fists, ecstatic. I knew right then that we were going to be way better than our 2019 team. It was as though our sophomores and juniors had stepped up to senior-level times. Frankly, I don't know if we could have done it without COVID because the flexible scheduling gave us the bandwidth to train properly.

Arcadia was our last true opportunity to race against the best.

In late April the CIF announced that although it would hold a Southern Section championship for track later in the spring, it was canceling the state track meet. To say it made little sense to me is being kind. It was a nightmare. And when reporters called to ask my opinion, I told them so.

"It's about the kids. They need times to be recruited," I told the *Los Angeles Times*. "It's disappointing, but I think CIF has let us down."

That quote got me an earful from CIF officials, but I meant it.

We'd already booked a trip to Nashville to run unattached at the Music City Track Carnival during the first weekend of June, and we were turning our focus toward its ESPN audience, not a high school sectional final. The carnival was an open meet with sections for professionals, as well as high schoolers. In the mile, Sam McDonnell ran 4:43, a personal best and the eighth-fastest time in the country. Then we got more evidence that we could be faster than in 2019: In the boys high school mile, Colin won in 4:05.79 to lead four runners from Newbury Park under 4:10, with Leo following in 4:07.66, Lex in 4:08.76, and Aaron Sahlman in 4:09.30.

As popular as the team had gotten, it felt as though now the buzz was really taking off. Then again, we had an indication of that before we even got to Nashville. During a layover in Las Vegas a stranger called out at me from across a hallway at the gate:

"4:20's not fast!"

CHAPTER SIXTEEN

SINCE MY HEART ATTACK, running had gotten harder. There was simply no way I could keep up with our runners anymore. But I needed to keep an eye on them and their splits during workouts, which was why one of my pandemic purchases was an electric scooter.

I had two requirements while scooter shopping: It had to fold, so it could be stored in my Jeep, and it had to go at least 25 mph. Fifteen mph equates to a four-minute-mile pace. That wasn't fast enough to get in front of our kids anymore.

I was seeing it firsthand during the summer of 2021 at Big Bear, when we returned for another month of elevation training. Our runs had become more difficult. One day, our fastest boys crushed a four-mile tempo at 5:05 pace. Years earlier, when we'd first run Skyline Drive on the southern rim overlooking the lake, its inclines were so steep that I treated it as a regular run. Entering the 2021 cross country season, however, Skyline Drive became a place for twelve-mile runs, with fartleks alternating fast and slow where the guys would average under a six-minute-mile pace. That is one tough run.

Across the lake to the north in Holcomb Valley, we'd found a fire road whose hard-packed soil two miles in became covered by a layer of loose sand for a half mile. When the kids hit the sand, I yelled at them to remember their running form, each step *quick, quick, quick*. I'd roll up next to them on my scooter in the middle of runs and stop them sometimes if I saw their form getting sloppy, arms down. They hated the sand. I loved it because the best time to think about your form is when you're on a regular run. Habits form by your being fully engaged at all times. I liked the term *training run* because even if the runs weren't being done at our most grueling paces, there was still a point to them. We were training for something.

As always at Big Bear, we walked the line between fun and focus. Billy Cvecko, a YouTube personality who was popular among runners, drove up in his motor home to film videos with our team. For video, he played a game to see if I could guess the athletes' answers to a questionnaire. Asked if I had a favorite runner on the team, everyone answered Lex.

I burst out laughing when I heard the consensus. "Lex! Why do you think I like Lex the most?"

"Anytime we want to do something, like go to the rocks or do something at camp, and we need your permission, we would have Lex ask you," they said.

The runners would go to the rocks, our usual spot for swimming and jumping, and then would want to go back and swim some more only hours later. Lex would ask, and I'd shrug my shoulders and agree.

"Is that why he always asked me everything?" I said. "I just thought he was the outgoing one."

It was true that Lex was very outgoing. We always talked a lot about running and things that had nothing to do with running, such as his art. Every athlete is different. Aaron liked to keep to himself and play video games. Colin, Daniel Appleford, and Zaki Blunt formed a close pack. And during dinners at the rental house, inevitably I would be on one end of the table next to Lex and Leo, chatting well after others had left. None of it meant I cared about one runner more than another.

At times, the team would start messing around too much, and I'd have to call a meeting before practice the next morning, around seven thirty.

"This is a championship team," I said. "I'm dead serious. What are we doing? Everyone here just expects to win. There's no *expect*. You know how much work we have to do if you want to be the greatest team ever and rewrite the record books."

I had to be demanding because our elite runners had gotten so fast that few in the country, if anyone, could push them anymore, to the point that we couldn't rely on competitors bringing out the best in us. We had to be accountable to ourselves. But rarely did I feel the need to intervene. The group was competitive but close.

AARON SAHLMAN

The reason why we were good was partly because we were naturally talented and worked for it, but it was a lot of team culture, as well. We tried to set a date to at least hang out once or twice a week and just have fun, go to dinner, just maybe talk and chill at a park. We'd hang out in a small plaza about a mile from the high school. Sometimes we'd talk about school, sometimes we'd talk about what was happening in our lives, and sometimes we'd talk about the race tactics that Sean had assigned us and discuss how we could tweak them a little bit to fit our needs. Then we'd introduce that to Sean and see what he thought. Hanging out like that was honestly beneficial to know your teammates, know who you're racing with, and get to know them on a very personal level. You can look at each other during a race and know what to do without even talking.

That ability to handle whatever was thrown at us was about to be tested.

One week into our monthlong stay at Big Bear, Daniel Appleford approached me after a team dinner. His face had a pained expression. His stomach wasn't feeling well, he said. Daniel was often getting sick, which made me unsure of the severity—until he came to me again, later that night, and said that the pain was now not just noticeable, but excruciating, and he needed to go to an urgent care clinic.

In a remote mountain town of five thousand, there are few options for immediate health care at night. I put Daniel in one of the cars we'd brought from Newbury Park, left the rest of the team with our assistant coach, Steve Hawkins, and drove to Bear Valley Community Hospital, on the lake's south side. Before I left, I warned Steve I might not be at practice the next morning.

At the hospital, Daniel asked me to stay with him as doctors ran tests. By the way he looked at me, I could tell he was scared. So was I. As we waited, I was thinking that I was sitting next to a high school junior healthy enough to average high-four-minute miles. What could this possibly be? A virus? An ulcer? I called his parents, who immediately began driving the two-plus hours east to see him.

Through the long night, we sat next to each other. There was talk of surgery, then a discussion of a helicopter airlifting Daniel to a larger hospital with more resources. I think we both wanted to keep our minds off those possibilities. Instead of thinking about the uncertainty of what was going on inside Daniel, we passed the hours talking about what was ahead of him—colleges, studying to become an engineer, running, anything a teenager talks about. But when you're in a hospital, you can only avoid the topic of health for so long.

"Daniel, it's just a bump in the road," I said. "Honestly, there are so many worse things that could happen. I know you don't think it now, but I believe it."

It was still well before dawn when we were told Daniel indeed required more advanced help. Technicians loaded Daniel into an ambulance and drove him down the mountain, into San Bernardino, where his parents were already at another hospital, waiting.

I waved goodbye and went back to our rental. As I pulled into our rental house's driveway, a crew from a running media outlet that had arranged to film that day's workout was waiting. I'd forgotten about it after the events of the previous night. Poker-face time.

"Hey, what's up?" I said. I played it off as though I'd just come back from getting coffee. I jumped in the shower, changed, and went up the hill with the rest of the team for the workout. Usually, our workouts are high energy. This one was downcast. Privately with the team, I shared what I knew, which, frankly, was not much. Intuitively, I think we all believed that Daniel would ultimately be okay, but that didn't diminish how frightened everyone was by seeing one of their friends taken to not one hospital, but two.

When we had a chance to talk to Daniel, we told him we just wanted him to focus on getting healthy. Running is a great thing, but his health was more important, which is why we wrote him off as a member of our season's top seven right then. It may have seemed cold, but we wanted it to be clear, to him and everyone else, that his future was more important to us than his contributions to our season. The pressure was on for someone to step up in Daniel's place.

Here we go, Aaron Cantu. He had always performed well in workouts and was trying to put it together in a race. We need you, too, Hector Martinez, whose form always made him look like a natural.

DANIEL APPLEFORD

When I went to Big Bear that summer, the biggest thing on my mind was where I would go to college. I had wanted to commit during my junior year, but COVID had pushed back visiting campuses until my senior year, and by that July I had no idea where I wanted to go, other than it had to be a good school for both running and engineering.

My concerns quickly changed. After lunch one day about one week into camp, my stomach began to feel uneasy. At first, I thought nothing of it because I'd never felt something like that before. When the pain near my stomach got worse, I felt it was something that would go away the next day. By nine that night, I realized this was pretty bad. There was no way I could sleep like this. "Can you take me to urgent care?" I texted Sean. "I need to get this checked out." We left our house in the team van. It was the last time I would see my friends again for weeks.

At the hospital, doctors put me through a CAT scan. They gave me morphine. I threw up a couple times. I was very freaked-out by a pregnant mother who was in labor near my bed. As doctors ran through a possible diagnosis, Sean and I had about five hours to talk. We were trying to figure it out, too: Did I have an allergy, or a case of bad food poisoning? We then turned to our team, our chemistry, my teammates and their potential. We talked about friends of mine like Zaki Blunt and Colin. It was around three a.m. when I was told I had a very rare case: superior mesenteric artery syndrome. "Very rare" is not what you want to hear. Two arteries had essentially fallen onto an upper portion of my small intestine, squeezing the intestine, and not letting anything pass through. I was told I needed surgery. It scared me. The diagnosis was rare enough that the hospital in Big Bear wasn't equipped to treat it, but not urgent enough to fly me down to a larger hospital in San Bernardino. I said goodbye to Sean and, with a tube running down one nostril into my stomach to prevent stomach acid from backing up, rode in the back of an ambulance an hour down the mountain. It was a hazy ride, dazed from lack of sleep, but one of the firefighters riding next to me said he was a runner, too.

My parents were waiting when my ambulance pulled into the hospital in San Bernardino. That was when it hit me that *Oh, there is something major going on in my body that needs fixing.* I was confused when, in San Bernardino, doctors asked whether I was anorexic. Hearing I was not, the doctors seemed surprised, saying that many who had my condition were. The timeline for fixing that condition felt shockingly long. Only days earlier I had been in Big Bear finishing brutal tempos and long runs at altitude; now, one doctor was standing by my bedside suggesting to me that I probably shouldn't run for a year. I tried coming to terms with the idea I wouldn't really run again until college. *This season's over.* The tube in my nose was so uncomfortable that I often accidentally tugged on it, out of instinct, requiring nurses to take out the entire tube and put a new one in. If that wasn't hard enough of a transition to get used to, I was sharing a hospital room with a young boy who screamed every few hours from the pain of his own condition. It was a reminder every minute of every day of the extent of my unexpected detour from the summer I expected to have. It was shocking.

Surgery was recommended, but could be avoided if I could regain enough fat around my intestine to push away the arteries compressing it and allow stomach fluid to pass through like normal. To do that, an IV was inserted in my forearm and I was fed through it, but after two weeks I was only maintaining weight, not gaining it like doctors wanted, partly because my metabolism was too fast; I was too much of a runner, essentially. It forced doctors to think of a different way to add weight.

At first, an idea was floated to surgically insert a tube through my shoulder to access a larger bloodstream to "feed" me faster. What they settled on, instead, was feeding me through an additional feeding tube that ran through my other nostril. For the next three days, I had one tube in each nostril, plus my IV. But soon, my recovery started going in the right direction. I was always thinking about my recovery and getting back to running; I could only watch so much of the Tokyo Olympics on my room's TV. Not wanting to be bedridden for weeks, I began walking around the hospital for ten to fifteen minutes at a time, pushing a cart that held my IV. When other doctors saw me, it felt like they were wondering whether I should be out of my room. I was back doubling—one walk in the morning and another at night.

The additional feeding tube was working. I wasn't in nearly as much pain. Instead of staying in the hospital an additional month as I was told, I was released within the week of my second feeding tube being inserted. When I was discharged, I had been in a hospital for three weeks and stuck in a bed for most of it. I was told by a doctor, "No running for two to three months." I didn't want to stop running but also didn't want to not follow what the doctor had said.

Panicking would have gone against what I had long told our team—that if you can't win without your number one, if you can't win when someone has a bad day, then you don't deserve to win. It's almost impossible to have a perfect season, one that avoids injuries, illnesses, family problems, school issues, suspensions, or whatever the heck happens.

Still, I knew Daniel's illness worried his teammates in multiple ways—chiefly in their affection for a teammate, but also their ambitions for the season. One runner told me the hole in our lineup made him nervous. I understood the feeling. Daniel was a star in his role as our super number five. It didn't dim my confidence that we had the potential to break the national record for average 5K time, but it certainly made it harder.

In interviews, we were direct about our goals to break every record and change history. I'm sure some people listened to or read those interviews and saw a coach popping off, but our confidence was rooted in real substance. From the earliest days of COVID training through tempos and mile repeats at altitude, we had proven that our four fastest boys might just be the four fastest in the entire country.

Even without knowing whether Daniel would be an option over the next three months, I left Big Bear believing that our high school team could beat most college teams and could qualify for the NCAA Division I championships. We didn't see anybody that could match our combination of top-end speed and down-roster depth.

COLIN SAHLMAN

We would do a combination of mile repeats and threshold all the time. We would do tempo work at least once a week where we would run four miles straight—so one mile longer than the race—at 4:50-to-five-minute pace. That just got us stronger, and we were able to know that we could go longer than the race distance at a pretty decent pace. Then Sean would incorporate speed with mile repeats, probably at around 4:25, 4:30, so that we would know what that pace felt like, for four or five reps—again, one or two reps longer than a 3-mile race, so that when we're feeling tired in the middle of a race, it really helps. When we'd get through the first mile of a race in around 4:25, we knew, *Oh, we've done this in a workout. We can, we can do it again, right?*

The clock projected to be our hardest competition. Dathan Ritzenhein's 5,000-meter high school cross country record of 14:10 had stood since 2000. But again, that time wasn't the end-all. We wanted to go as fast as possible, regardless of precedent. We had the talent. DyeStat, the longtime media outlet covering high school running, ranked our boys at the top of their preseason poll, ahead of Colorado's Mountain Vista, Utah's Corner Canyon, and Oregon's Jesuit. Our girls, meanwhile, were ranked eleventh, and second in California to Buchanan. In their individual top-hundred rankings, our entire boys top five was ranked in the top forty, with Colin second, Lex fifth, Leo sixteenth, Aaron thirty-first, and Daniel fortieth.

I thought those rankings undersold our capabilities. When our season opened September 9 at a 3-mile Marmonte League meet at Pepper Tree, our core four of Lex, Leo, Aaron, and Colin crossed the line in 14:25, with Hector Martinez next in 14:43, in a race we treated like a glorified tempo workout. Our roster was so deep that Zaki Blunt, a senior, won the junior varsity race in 15:23—by nearly two minutes.

Normally, I considered league meets more of an obligation than an opportunity. As soon as the kids crossed the line, our coaches kept them running straight into a cooldown to get in a few more miles. At this season opener, however, there was more at play. Earlier in September, Colin had turned his ankle while running off-path, an injury that swelled so much he didn't run for more than a week, returning just before the league meet. That low-key race, then, became a key gauge. Colin wanted to be ready for Woodbridge, nine days later. I wouldn't taper our weekly mileage because of Woodbridge, but I did view it, once again, as our team's coming-out party—its flat course and evening setting the perfect place to show everyone what we, inside Newbury Park, had believed for months, that our current roster was far superior to our 2019 national title team. Two years earlier, Nico had run the national 3-mile record in 13:39.7 and blown away the field while doing it.

Running under the lights on the night of September 18, I believed Leo, Lex, Colin, and Aaron could all run faster.

CHAPTER SEVENTEEN

SUNSET WAS STILL A few hours away on the night of September 18 when I poked my head out of Newbury Park's team tent and glanced at the commotion outside. The first of Woodbridge's fifty-two races that evening would be starting soon, and thousands of kids were milling around Norco's SilverLakes Sports Complex. Yet from what I could tell, most of them were standing outside our tent.

Our exploits had made us used to the spotlight. But the size of the crowd tonight was unlike any before. One parent tried counting and got to nearly three hundred before stopping.

I think some people expected me to walk back my comment that "4:20's not fast."

Instead, I'd trademarked it.

As a joke, I commissioned stickers with the saying. I posted on social media that the first 150 who stopped by would get a free sticker. And just like that, a line hundreds of kids long formed by our team tent. They wanted me to either sign their sticker or get a picture. They asked if the runners were around for pictures, too.

The high school that had shown up here just five years earlier with no one paying us a second thought was now attracting literal crowds, and for far more than a sticker promotion. It was unusual to have an individual runner as fast as our number one, but to have multiple runners at that caliber was something that drew fascination. Fans—even competitors—of the Panthers wanted pictures with our boys, before they'd even stepped to the line. Colin told me that he'd been stopped so often that he'd resorted to putting up his hood while waiting in line before races for the bathroom. Yes, other runners were coming up to our guys even when they were waiting for the bathroom. Being around Lex and Leo, with the reach of their YouTube channel, was like being around celebrities. Race-day preparation now included not only creating strategies for how and when to move in a race, but before it. "Find us after!" became our go-to response for fans who wanted time with us. I'll be honest, though, it was exciting to have that much buzz surround our runners and their accomplishments.

After I ran out of stickers, I went back into the tent to focus with the team. Woodbridge always delivers a fast race, and I expected another. Yet, I also understood that on this night, we would be dealing with two unknowns: Colin's ankle, and the unexpected return of Daniel.

I had had zero expectation that Daniel would be ready to race this early.

For weeks that summer, we didn't know when Daniel would run again, period. Though the rest of his teammates returned home from Big Bear in late July, Daniel didn't leave the hospital until early August. As we trained, measuring progress in seconds and kilometers, he waited in San Bernardino, his recovery marked by the weight he gained under doctor's orders and the steps he took while circling the hospital. His hospitalization stretched on so long that it did something I never thought possible, which was to make a teenage boy bored with playing video games.

In those early days, learning that Daniel was expected to eventually return to full health calmed the worst fears we'd felt at Big Bear, when he'd been rushed off to hospitals and answers were few. He'd call Colin and the guys and check in. We chatted most days, and my message was that we only needed him by late November—*if* he was even up for it.

Released and returned home, Daniel dropped by practices just to observe and watch his friends. His good spirits lifted ours. After that long mostly in a hospital bed, just walking around our practices counted as a milestone.

We told him to take it slow. All the while, we wondered whether he could regain his form by December.

Doctors had asked him to gain about twenty pounds and kept him from running for five weeks, which meant that before we could even think of resuming Daniel's training, we had to rebuild his fitness from scratch. Being off his feet for that long had led to muscle atrophy and thrown a wrench into his aerobic engine. I didn't have any concerns that running would worsen his condition, but I *was* worried that he would injure himself as his miles increased. While everyone else on our roster was focused on how fast they could go and how hard they could push, with Daniel, the mission was a slow build.

Typically, like the rest of our varsity boys team, Daniel would run between 50 and 60 miles each week. He started back at half that mileage. When he began jogging in late August, it was under doctor's orders to run two miles, maximum. Daniel never made an excuse about his condition. His commitment to being part of our top seven never broke, even if I could sense some hesitation from him about how much his fitness had changed.

What convinced me he was ready for Woodbridge was a low-key workout he'd done a few days before we left for Norco, where he looked as if he was ready to ramp up his workload. His recovery was a microcosm of our training philosophy of quality over quantity. He didn't have to run a ton of miles every week, but I still needed him to run hard, even if that meant advising him to take every other repetition off during some workouts.

His parents suggested to me before Woodbridge that Daniel

should race. I agreed. Daniel was reluctant because he wasn't comfortable with the amount of fitness he had lost.

"I'm going to run you at Woodbridge," I said.

"I don't want to."

"Race with the B team. Just have fun, and see if you can break 15 minutes. That would normally be a tempo for you. It'll be a little bit harder now, but, Daniel, we don't need you until the end of November, early December. That's the only time we need you by. You're on a different trajectory."

He agreed to do it.

At 9:14 p.m., a lower-division boys race took off with Daniel inside its field of 229. I bounced between worry and optimism, nervous about whether it was right to have him aim to break 15 minutes. All of that second-guessing stopped after he took the lead at one point. Less than two months after leaving the hospital, Daniel ran 14:53.9. I'd seen fear in his expression at Big Bear; here, I saw determination during his run, and happiness afterward. The run seemed to embolden him, or at least to calm his nerves. I knew then he was going to be a factor for us later that season.

DANIEL APPLEFORD

While I was away, I'd kept in touch daily with my teammates about their running while being able to do none myself. By text, they kept me in the loop about their fartleks on Skyline, and how altitude camp was going. It seemed like our team chemistry was still there.

When I left the hospital in early August, hearing my doctor recommend not running for several months, I didn't want to take a chance. Even my daily walks felt weird, like I was regaining control over my body. But after two weeks of walking, and five weeks after I'd first been taken to the hospital, I began slowly incorporating jogs...then walk-run fartleks...then real miles. With our team, Sean emphasized focusing on the day-to-day, and I viewed my recovery as no different than our team thought about training. You have to worry about how you're feeling that day, and the work you have planned for it, not what you'll be doing three weeks from now. Compartmentalizing my recovery into a day-to-day focus was how I got through it. Early on, it meant making sure I could run one mile farther, and then the same the next day, and the day after, and the day after. Self-belief was at the core of why our team got better, and why I did, too. The doctor may have downplayed how quickly I could run again, but I believed I could get back to being myself as a runner, back to being with my teammates and back to helping the team.

My usual mileage would have been about eight miles a day, and I got up to that fairly quickly. The important thing was watching my weight. If my weight went down at all, I had to back off. I wasn't about to risk another extended hospital stay. Every day, I drank cartons and cartons of protein-rich drinks my doctor prescribed.

In early September, about a month after being discharged from the hospital and two weeks before the race at Woodbridge, I had my first "speed" workout since Big Bear. We were running 800-meter intervals around Pepper Tree. I don't think Sean wanted me to push it too hard, and while I settled into finishing reps in sub-2:20, the top group of my teammates was well ahead of me. I thought I would stop after two or three repetitions. Instead, I did double that. It gave me a lot of confidence. I never thought I would be able to do that type of speed so early in my recovery.

Woodbridge was always a staple and always had a crazy atmosphere. My race made me more hungry. Racing is such a unique feeling, and when you have just an "okay" race, it makes you feel how much better you could have been. It invigorated me. I wanted it more.

Finally, just before 10:00 p.m., our top seven of Colin, Leo, Lex, Aaron Sahlman, Hector, Aaron Cantu, and Zaki finished their strides and toed the line alongside 215 other runners. A mile and a half in, Colin, Lex, Leo, and Aaron Sahlman were bunched together at the front along with a runner from Texas and another from Clovis, a good 10 seconds clear of the field. Our pack covered the first mile in 4:32. There was still no separation among our four at two miles, and only the Texan was still close, though the gap was widening. With half a mile left, Leo and Aaron had pulled ahead by a few strides on Colin and Lex when Leo took off in a way that I could hardly believe. There were still 400 meters to go when I heard a coronation already starting over the loudspeaker from Rich Gonzalez, the meet director at Arcadia, who was serving as Woodbridge's public-address announcer.

"At the start of the week the commissioner of CIF asked, 'Just how good is Newbury Park?'

"I simply told him this is the greatest team this nation has ever seen. And we are seeing that on full display tonight!"

Leo was now all alone. His last 400 was about 60 seconds. I had never seen anyone do that. And he didn't even appear to be hurting, smiling and spreading his arms wide in his final strides before the finish, barely breathing hard as someone handed him a blue ribbon in the finish-line chute. His expression lit up when he heard Gonzalez scream that Leo had just run 13:38.1 to break his older brother's high school record for 3 miles by 1.6 seconds. Aaron pumped his fist when he crossed the line in second in 13:42.3, showing just how great he could be when the stars aligned. Next was Lex in 13:44.4. Colin was fourth in 13.48.0. Exactly one minute after Leo's victory, Hector finished as our fifth. Our top seven had all finished in less than 15:13. This wasn't two fast families, it was a program where *everyone* had bought into the idea that faster was always possible.

It wasn't hyperbole to say our runners had just put on an unprecedented performance. Our overall team time of 69:30.9 smashed the previous national record that we had ourselves set in 2019—by nearly two minutes. Our new group had averaged 13:54 for 3 miles—20 seconds per runner faster than our fastest average from our national title team.

Many teams had run fast in Woodbridge's history. But among the top ten fastest boys team performances there, we owned the first, second, and seventh spots—the last from 2018. And we'd produced the number one mark on this night despite that two of our expected top five—Colin and Daniel—were either not healthy or not in the race at all. Everyone was better than in 2019. Our fastest time was now better. Our JV guys were better. The gap between our winning score and second place—25 to 190, for Great Oak—was so massive that we might have won even if we'd held out two, or maybe three, of our top five finishers. Our girls had won their own team title, led by Sam McDonnell, who finished third in the most competitive girls race in 15:54.

I was proud our kids had handled the pressure of our own making. We liked to publicize our record attempts because I felt it created excitement around the country and raised the stakes for us to live up to our words. We certainly had. It was as though our runners didn't know any better. Ever since Nico's breakout in 2018, kids in the program had become used to attention. As our goals grew, so did our comfort with being the target.

The results were validating. That didn't mean the day was perfect.

One glance at Colin afterward told me he was extremely upset. Number one at most races, he had just finished behind three teammates, including his younger brother. Everyone told me it must be easy having all this talent, when it was actually very difficult. Jace was second fiddle to Nico for most of his racing career and had to learn to handle that. Consider the Youngs—you could set a national high school record and not even be the best runner in your family.

It felt like a moment that I couldn't let pass without saying something. I pulled Colin aside: "Walk with me."

Amid the pandemonium near the finish, we got away from everyone else for a few seconds.

"Do you realize what you just ran?" I said. "You literally got no workouts in the last two weeks. You're the fifth-fastest person ever in the three-mile, but that's because all of your teammates are ahead of you. You'll be fine. You'll be leading this pack in a week."

Pushed earlier in the season to be a more consistent leader, Colin had responded impressively; the look in his eyes after finishing fourth made me curious how he would respond now.

I *did* think Colin had the chance to be the fastest that season, given how hard it was to outkick him when he was healthy. But when it came to our team dynamics, race day was a meritocracy. During hard workouts with multiple reps, our top four often alternated who led the pace to spread out that burden. I was fine with that. Big races were different. My philosophy was that we were a team until two miles, and then for the last mile, it became every man for himself.

COLIN SAHLMAN

I was two miles away from the high school when I'd rolled my ankle in early September, and I got back to campus by alternating between walking and limping all the way back, barely being able to walk, holding on to fences whenever I could to take pressure off my foot, which was swollen when I got home. I didn't run for about eight days. I think that's where my mindset kind of differs from other people's is that even though I had that setback, I still was going into that race believing that *I'm going to win*. I left it about 10 seconds short of what I wanted to run, and I was so upset with myself.

Sean was just reassuring me. "Hey, you were out for a week, you ran amazing; you shouldn't be disappointed in yourself at all." I don't like to make excuses. What I felt was that it didn't matter if that was true. I had still wanted to win and I fell short of that, and I think for the rest of the season, that fueled an attitude that, selfishly, I was like, *I'm not going to get beat by my teammates again*. I raced every race afterward a little smarter and maybe wouldn't take the lead until the last mile, when I would push it at last. I remember after that race thinking to myself, *I'm never getting beat again.*

AARON SAHLMAN
I talked to him after the race in private on the way back home after we got dropped off at the high school. I just told him, it was one race. Forget about it. Use it as your motivation. In workouts there had been no competition at all just because we didn't see a point in it. The reason why some teams are decent but never good is you see them at workouts, they all just want to beat each other. If you saw any of our workouts, you'd see me leading one rep, you'd see Colin leading one rep, Lex and Leo leading one rep—we needed to hit a time, and that will build our stamina, build our speed, more and more throughout the year, and we don't have to worry about "Oh, I want to beat you in practice." What do you get from that? There's no officials, the only time is off your watch. That's it. But once it came to races, I know my junior year and senior year, we would take turns in California races, like I would lead the first mile, Lex and Leo would lead, like, a portion of the second mile, and then Colin would take it. We'd just go off of who feels the best is who's going to lead it for a little bit, and then once you hit that second mile, it's a free-for-all. It was, whoever has the most will win.

In late September, I stared blankly out the window of a Las Vegas hotel room at the Strip below.

Normally, I love Vegas, and only a week before, our times at Newbury Park made me feel like we were on top of the world. But as soon as I'd gotten off the phone with Rich Gonzalez, the festive mood I'd had for my Vegas weekend celebrating the wedding of a friend had, figuratively, gone out the window.

Gonzalez had called to share awful news: For a second consecutive year, Nike had canceled Nike Cross Nationals in December over COVID concerns.

Dammit. It was true that in cross country, the ultimate competition is between you and the clock, and that a defining run can come as easily early in the season as at the end. But this team, these boys, wanted to leave no doubt about their place in history by lining up against the best in the country and seeing how large a gap Newbury Park's runners could put between them and everybody else. We needed a unified championship race to do that. And now we didn't have one.

I was pissed—until I realized I didn't have time to be. What was done was done. We had to forget about Nike's national showcase simply because we had to do everything we could to build another.

I texted our guys, wanting them to hear the news from me and not from a post on social media. I got Lex and Leo on the phone. They were not happy. We were still going to have a national championship, I told them, spinning it as though the replacement would be even better. The truth was that I didn't know what that would look like. But I could let the world know that Newbury Park was in the market for a single meet, not a split one like the previous season, when some went to Indiana, and others to Alabama.

I got on Twitter and found more people like me, scrambling to create an alternative national championship.

"Things are happening," I wrote to a coach from North Carolina. "Info should be out in a day or two. We all need to be on the same page and go to the same meet to make a true National Championship."

"Great news!" he wrote back. "We are all on the same team and agree 100 percent."

Within five minutes of posting I got a text from somebody from RunningLane, the race in Alabama: "Sean, hi, could you jump on a call?"

Newbury Park's success created a cachet we could use. Running-

Lane was willing to change its date if we would commit. It had to be the original weekend of NXN to avoid conflicts with California's state meet. Done. We were in. I went back into sales mode, as if I were back hocking sunglasses and shoes as I called and messaged coaches from Utah, Colorado, California, and all over, selling the idea that this would be an even better national championship than NXN if we all committed. I was even more motivated than before to put on the biggest show cross country had ever seen, something we couldn't have done on a soggy, slower Portland course in early December.

I wanted to pivot quickly from the disappointment of hearing about the cancelation of NXN, too, because I didn't want to waste our team's momentum. We could go one of two ways: dwelling on what could have been, or channeling our frustration into something more productive.

We chose the latter. On October 9, with Colin healthy again, our boys shredded Woodward Park's course record for 5 kilometers at the Clovis Invitational, our annual preview of the state-meet course. We were still taking midseason trips to Clovis to practice at Woodward Park, but by now, our runners knew the course as well as they knew Pepper Tree. Yet in all our time running at Woodward Park over the years, we'd never run it as well as we did on this day. Colin, Leo, Lex, and Aaron finished first through fourth and ran by themselves for the last mile.

Newbury Park had by then moved back up to CIF's division for the largest-enrollment schools, Division 1, but even there, we were unchallenged. If this was a state-meet preview, it forecast a landslide.

First place: Newbury Park, 19 points.

Second place: Great Oak, 154.

On this day, two years after our 2019 team had averaged 15:06 for 5,000 meters to set the course record, Newbury Park's new era of boys had just averaged 14:45. It was also a national high school record, crushing the 15:00 average set in 2020 by American Fork of Utah.

Colin had vowed never to lose again after Woodbridge, and at Clovis he made that clear as he pulled away from the Youngs and Aaron with a half mile to go and never slowed down. With Daniel still not ready to go full speed—finishing in 15:18—we needed Hector Martinez to step up. Did he ever, finishing twelfth overall in 15:16 while battling knee injuries. Based on the effortlessness of his form, I thought Hector could be really good. He had transferred from nearby Oaks Christian after his freshman year, and while he was supertalented, he dealt with a lot of injuries. It was a reminder that this wasn't a two-family phenomenon. So was Sam McDonnell's first-place finish in the girls race.

Winning never got boring, and to do so at Clovis felt especially good. Stopped first by Great Oak and then a pandemic, Newbury Park had never won the prestigious invitational—until now.

Even though our times were faster than ever, our core training hadn't changed since 2019. The difference was everything surrounding our training. Our belief that we could challenge history's fastest high school times was now a given. And our recovery had become a habit. *Focusing on all the little things equals a big difference.*

Visualizing success was one element we had added. I knew Tim Bayley, a former professional runner and sports psychologist who had worked with championship-caliber medalists and with big companies. I couldn't afford to pay for individual sessions with all of our athletes, but we arranged group sessions on Zoom, always letting parents know that no one was obligated but that we would have a session for anyone interested. I wanted the runners to see the benefits of visualizing success. Bayley helped teach them affirmations. A lot of it was straightforward, such as "control what you can control." It's not voodoo, just having the right mindset—the ability to relax while competing. At times I would tell the athletes, particularly our girls team, that, at the end of the day, your friends will love you, your family will love you, and all we were doing was just running. Understanding that perspective would make it easier to find the courage to put everything out there because what happens if you make a big move and it doesn't work? Nothing happens. So, let's go for it if there's nothing to lose. I wanted to get it in their heads that running is not life-or-death. If you start thinking like that, you start getting nervous.

Our goal was to take that nothing-to-lose belief and apply it. I demanded a willingness from our runners to keep pushing. It wasn't a perfect process—it wouldn't have been with mature professionals, let alone teenagers. I'd spent enough time around our athletes that at a certain point my intuition alerted me that something was holding them back. I always saw it as my responsibility to draw an effort out of them that they might not be able to themselves. For all of our record-breaking success, I wasn't satisfied with some of our workout splits that fall. When I'd ask for mile repeats in 4:28, they weren't committing to it.

It was why on November 10, less than three weeks away from the state meet and less than one month before RunningLane, I built a workout around a lie.

CHAPTER EIGHTEEN

TWO YEARS EARLIER, AT Pepper Tree, I had purposely marked a kilometer repeat workout a few meters short to make our times look absurdly fast for the camera crew documenting the day. Our runners had been in on that plan.

Not so this time; on this day I had designed a workout that I hoped would help our guys understand that they had more in them than they previously thought. We would run three-mile intervals with fast 400s in between, and an extra 400 at the end for four miles of work . . . or so they thought.

When our team showed up at Conejo Creek South Park in Thousand Oaks, a fifteen-minute drive east from our campus, it was an earlier start to practice than usual because of our school's early-dismissal schedule on Wednesdays, which was better for what I wanted. Sprinklers doused the park in the mornings, and the earlier we ran, the soggier its thick grass was. The conditions weren't as slow as in Dos Vientos Community Park, the site that had reliably mimicked NXN for us. But Conejo Creek had thick grass, along with something that Dos Vientos didn't but that RunningLane's course, home of our de facto national championship, would: a hilly stretch. That incline, along with the wet grass, made running fast a challenge. Our workout called for three loops of the park, plus 100 meters, to equal 1 mile. I measured the distance with my wheel and knew exactly where the mile mark was, but I told our boys it was actually a few meters farther.

The workout began. Every time our boys went up the incline, I could see them struggle with the soft grass underfoot, which is what I wanted. Just like on the sandy fire roads we ran at Big Bear, our guys would have to nail their form here, their steps *quick-quick-quick*. I called out the times after each mile. When the first was in the low 4:40s, the boys were surprised, bordering on annoyed, to be working that hard and running times that, for us, were too slow for our targets. I feigned frustration. As the workout went on for two more reps, our times improved considerably.

It was then that I revealed my little secret. The true mile mark was about five seconds before what I'd told them. I laid out my reasoning. I wanted to prove to them that they could absolutely run 4:28 miles in cross country. This was my way of convincing them. When everyone expects you not just to run fast but to demolish records, that is a challenge you have to overcome well before the actual race day.

"Nobody in the country does what you just did in these conditions," I told them. It might have bordered on crazy, a plan that could just as easily have backfired. But I believed in my athletes, and in the end it was a breakthrough.

AARON SAHLMAN

We were doing mile repeats and two-kilometer repeats that year close to 4:20 for five or six of them. When me, Lex, Leo, and my brother were able to do that, we were all just looking at each other like, "Okay, we are fit and we should be able to win a national title—and maybe do even something more."

That meant not limiting ourselves to a certain time.

> We always knew the course records and wanted to break those, but we felt, "I want to see how far under the course record I can get. I'm gonna make my body hurt for it."

I had to figure out what would unlock their best. To do that, I'd often say, "Put a hard rep in right now." Take a basic workout of ten by 400 with a minute rest. If I wanted the runners to hit their mile pace on the seventh repetition, I would tell our runners that I did not care about rep eight, nine, or ten; I did not care if they even walked the reps after this one; right here, throw down the time we need. But a funny thing always happened. They *didn't* walk the next reps. Freed of thinking about the totality of all the work still ahead of them, and just focusing on the next effort, they went harder and dug deeper. Because unlocking what they're capable of is a mind game.

I'd seen it at work for the first time at Nike's track, watching Alberto Salazar walking up to an athlete between reps of a hard workout and saying, "Think about what's happening *now*, how you feel *now*." I started saying it to my athletes as they got deeper into a workout: Be present and aware of how your body feels *now*, in this moment, because in a race, you will reach a moment where you feel the same. It should make you feel strong, and confident, because you will know how to get through that pain. You've done it before—right *now*, in training. You are about to run your best interval. Right *now*.

LEO YOUNG

Through my time at Newbury Park there were definitely workouts that we did that opened up our mindset as to what we believed was possible. The best example of that in the fall of 2021 was a workout we did in early November, just before the state meet. That was our last, huge well effort, as Sean would call them. Before workouts like these Sean would say, "Yeah, we're going to the well today," and when he said that, we knew we'd be digging deep and just hoping to make it out alive. We didn't know if we would or not, but we seemed to make it out alive a lot, which is, I think, a big part of what expanded our belief of what we were capable of.

This particular workout was really, really intense. It was even tougher because we had to shift days. We were supposed to do it one day, and then, due to the fields full of people playing soccer, we scrapped it, went for a six-mile run, and hit it the following day. That delay just built up the anticipation and nerves for what we were gonna do.

I remember the next day being quite warm, and Sean reiterating that this was one of those days that he wanted us to really go for it. We were doing three by a mile followed by 400s in about 65 seconds. He wanted us at 4:30 for the first mile, and this was at a park in town with some deep grass, soggy water spots, little up-and-down hills, and sharp turns, which all made it tough to run really fast. On this course, we knew we'd have to push wherever we got the chance.

So Lex, Colin, Aaron, and I got after it on the first one. We were going really, really hard, and the split came out to 4:40, which was really, really frustrating. I mean, it wasn't uncommon to run my first rep and feel kind of crappy. I feel like I often felt terrible on my first more often than I felt good, and I would usually feel a little bit better throughout the workout. But to plan on going out in the low 4:30s and hit 4:40 was just kind of insane. We were all thinking, *What the heck is wrong with us today?* We suspected that maybe the mile was long, but Sean was adamant, "No, it's perfectly accurate. You guys need to pull it together. You can't expect to go out in 4:40 at the state meet. You might as well not even race!"

And he was right. We were going for these big times, and a big part of our program was training to go out really, really hard. We were so frustrated that we went out in 4:40 when we were supposed to go out so much quicker that we went into the next mile full of adrenaline, determination, and focus.

But first we had to run a 400. That one and the following ones more or less took care of themselves between 64 and 66 seconds.

We hit that second mile full of intention. I mean, we were just destroying it, and it was like 4:32, which we were all happier with. Sean was like, "Okay, perfect! This is good. Keep it right there." It was exactly what we needed. But he needed us to carry that momentum through, because that's kind of what our racing strategy was all about.

We did our next 400 in 65 or so. Fine. And then we had the final mile. We were tired, really tired, at this point with two hard miles under our belt and one more to come, but at the same time, it was the last rep. We knew we had the end in sight, so we just went after it. I remember Lex, Aaron, Colin, and I just building off each other, which was really the key to success for us. We went out really, really aggressively, just pushing with absolutely everything whenever we had the chance.

We hit that last one in 4:31, and we felt really good about that. But, at the same time, I was like, *Man, I was working harder than the times reflected, right?*

We finished that last 400 and saw Sean kind of laughing. He was like, "Guys, I measured the course like 5 seconds slow." That way we would push harder, you know? So our first rep was actually a 4:36, the second was 4:28, and the last was really a 4:27. That still means that that first mile was slower than we wanted it to be, but the frustration and determination to go faster that we drew from that meant that we started hitting those second and third reps at paces that we would have been happy with even if they were accurate miles.

Being able to do those in under 4:30, it definitely expanded our mindset and our belief of what we were capable of. And the focus that we put into just getting through each rep, and doing it, translated so much to the mindset we would carry into races, where we were like, "You know what? We're gonna go out as fast as we possibly can, because it's a 5K, and we know we can survive, and we know we can come back." It was absolutely just the preparation that we needed to expand our mindset and be ready for such performances.

This day, this instance, wasn't an isolated occurrence. There were other times like that, and that was absolutely the cornerstone idea of our program, which was all about expanding our belief so that we didn't limit ourselves.

November. In every cross country season, this month was the proverbial third and final mile, when teams, athletes, and coaches either stay strong or fall apart, unable to maintain their early pace. High school sports were more or less back to their pre-pandemic norms in California by 2021, which was overwhelmingly good, but annoying nonetheless. Our Marmonte League championship would be up first, on November 4, against teams from neighboring cities, such as Westlake and Thousand Oaks. The preliminary round of the Southern Sectional Finals would follow on November 13, and the finals after that on November 20. Then came the two dates our season built toward: The California state meet at Woodward Park on November 27, and one week later, on December 4, the RunningLane championships we'd thrown our support behind, in Huntsville.

As someone who saw diminishing returns from racing often, I wasn't thrilled with the prospect of doing so for five consecutive weeks. Then again, we were insulated by our speed. Our team was so fast, and so dominant, that unlike in my first years at Newbury Park when even qualifying for the state meet took everything we had, we could now afford to take our foot off the gas slightly during some of the qualifiers, to conserve energy. It was purely survive-and-advance until November 27. Our training wouldn't begin to taper until a couple of weeks before RunningLane.

No other team in the state would be held to the standards we would be this month—which was to say, anything less than winning our program's third boys state championship, and probably breaking some records along the way, would be considered a disappointment. That wasn't unfair; it was our expectation, too. But I just wanted our teams to get to RunningLane in Alabama healthy.

Our five-week push began perfectly.

Quite literally.

At the 3-mile Marmonte League championships, Colin, Lex, Leo, and Aaron all finished in a pack in 15:06, within four-tenths of a second of one another. Four seconds later, Daniel finished in fifth overall. By the time the race's next-fastest finisher crossed, 32 seconds later, our top five were already off on their cooldown. The eighth-place finisher, Hector Martinez, was our sixth runner.

I was no longer surprised that Daniel had moved back into his role as our fifth runner. By late October, he'd reached full mileage and was running tempos at a lower heart rate, close to where he had been before Big Bear.

Even if our perfect score at the league final was something we utterly expected, it happens rarely enough in the sport that headlines about our league title drew even more attention during CIF prelims, which were held at Mt. SAC. Our principal and athletic director had attended a few CIF races, and when they showed up, they would tell me they couldn't believe the swarms of people around our tent and that our runners were being asked for pictures on their way to the bathroom and the starting line. I remember our principal and athletic director describing us as celebrities.

They weren't wrong—seventy thousand people had watched Lex and Leo's YouTube recap of our Clovis team-time record from the previous month.

CHAPTER NINETEEN

IF I HAD BEEN impressed by one thing since our program's new era had begun, after Nico and Jace's graduation, it was how our new runners had performed when it mattered while under a microscope that no other high schools and few, if any, college teams even dealt with.

Our runners had a unique ability to block out distractions, even when my own ire was raised.

Like it was for Southern Section Prelims and Finals.

Until this season, those prelims and finals—which determined who made state and who didn't—had always been held in Riverside. In 2021, both races shifted to Mt. SAC. Ask anyone who knows even a little about cross country about the most famous courses in the United States, and names like Van Cortlandt Park in New York and Woodward Park will pop up. So will Mt. SAC—and I have no idea why. It starts outside the school's track and field stadium in a narrow street and for the next three miles goes up and down hills. The first mile is two loops around a hill; the second mile climbs higher up switchbacks; the third mile goes up Reservoir Hill, then Poop Out Hill, before bottoming out on flat land at the finish. In between those hills are downhill stretches with steep pitches. All that and it's still only 2.93 miles, short of the standard full 3 miles or 5,000 meters, which equates to 3.1 miles.

Old-school coaches loved to argue that courses like Mt. SAC were "real, rough cross country." Listen: I get your "grit" mentality, but in the bigger picture, running the uphills and quad-burning downhills at Mt. SAC destroyed runners' legs, and CIF's decision to put runners through that grinder for two consecutive weekends, on the eve of their seasons' biggest meets could unfairly hurt their performances when it mattered most. I liked the people who worked at Mt. SAC, but I thought the course and its hills sucked. I just wanted to find a way to make it safe for the kids. Which was why months before the meets, I'd emailed the CIF to ask whether a new starting line could be used.

The National Federation of State High School Associations is a governing body that sets national standards for high school sports. Its rule book makes clear that in cross country the starting line must contain boxes, six feet wide, for each team to line up their runners; think of chalk-striped lines, six feet apart. At Mt. SAC, where the starting line was hemmed in by the width of a forty-foot-wide street, team boxes were only about thirty inches wide, which forced teams to line up in single file. Coaches were instructed that athletes could not pass for the first 200 meters because of the bottleneck start.

This wasn't a race we needed to win, only to finish high enough in the team race to advance to the Division 1 finals. Even with a single-file start, our runners cruised at prelims, when six of our top seven all finished in a pack in 15:50, 40 seconds behind the winner. Our only exception was Dev Doshi, a promising sophomore who ran 15:34 to take third. We weren't unscathed, though; Lex had tweaked his hamstring.

A week later, we returned to Mt. SAC after limiting Lex in practice. Same course, same starting line. Same frustration that runners' interests weren't being considered. At 8:00 a.m., before the first of the day's ten races, I tried, in vain, to file an official protest over the starting line. Two race officials at the table wouldn't even hear me out.

What I wanted was nothing radical. When Mt. SAC hosts 5,000-meter cross country races, including the regionals of the Foot Locker championships, its starting line begins in a more wide-open location. One course was 2.93 miles, the other 3.1, with very different starting lines. Why?

Only a half hour later, the Division 3 boys race was less than a minute in when a group of boys got tangled near the start and fell hard on the pavement. Race officials called back all of the runners for a restart. One runner who had been tangled up rolled over, putting his head between his knees in obvious pain as runners surrounded him to see what had happened. He had broken his collarbone. He went on to watch his teammates race while surrounded by paramedics.

Hadn't this been exactly what I was repeatedly trying to warn officials about? It was unsafe. Unfortunately, and unnecessarily, an athlete had to suffer the consequences of inaction. I had pushed back before. I had been stubborn as an athlete and could be the same when it came to sticking up for my athletes.

During my first weeks coaching at Newbury Park, back in the spring of 2016, one of our girls was moved from one heat to another at the county track championships with little warning. I told the official that I didn't care why she had been moved, only that he couldn't do that once the heat sheets were printed, and that she was already warming up with the intention of running at a certain time. A late change wasn't fair to her. I pressed the issue until the coach in charge literally threw up his hands and restored her place. When Colin was a freshman and was disqualified from a prestigious mile race over a false start, I presented a video showing it hadn't been Colin who had jumped. Race officials wouldn't even watch it. I wanted to be heard out anyway because I thought that not enough coaches were willing to make themselves heard, even when many told me privately that they, too, disliked the rules I was trying to change. Well, why was it so hard to get others to publicly back me when it came time to talk with local and state officials?

If people wanted to label me as abrasive for my persistence, that didn't bother me. More frustrating was how decision-makers—whether at a one-off meet or at the state level—seemed focused on the messenger instead of my message: Decisions, at all levels, should be oriented around putting athletes in positions to succeed, period.

The crash in the early race raised my concern for Lex, who had cross-trained since tweaking his hamstring the previous week on the course. I thought he would be fine, but I told him to take it easy. My race instructions to our whole team were to take the first mile out fast to scare everyone off and then lay back.

Newbury Park's runners made it off the line that day at Southern Section Finals safely. Then they did something no other team had done in CIF history.

One-two-three-four-five-six. All Newbury Park. Perfection, again—with the sixth overall runner also our own, for good measure.

Our top five covered the first half mile in 2:08 and first mile in 4:35.

Of the first eight runners to pass the two-mile mark, as the constant ups and downs on the hills took their toll on the pack, seven were wearing Newbury Park's black and yellow. They were so far ahead that the rest of the race looked like a training run. At one point, more than two miles in, Colin even turned and looked behind him to see the gap behind our pack.

"Oh, my, get out your cameras!" the public-address announcer boomed to the crowd in the final minute. "This may be the greatest cross country race ever run in the history of the Southern Section, certainly, maybe in the country to dominate a field like this!"

I was chasing them down the hill to the finish as they crossed in 14:52. The crazy thing is, they weren't even pushing themselves as hard as they could go. Colin, Lex, Aaron, and Leo all finished casually as a pack. Seven seconds behind, Daniel finished in fifth and Dev Doshi in sixth. Our entire top seven finished in the top twelve.

We left with two Division 1 titles: Our girls also won their section title. Sam McDonnell, who had recently committed to run at the University of Alabama, won the individual title in 16:50. Those weren't the only races that day that I tracked—and celebrated. At the NCAA championships in Florida, Nico had averaged 4:39 miles to finish eleventh overall as a freshman and help Northern Arizona win the men's Division I championship. And in the Division II women's race, Fiona Hawkins—the daughter of our assistant, Steve Hawkins, who had graduated from Newbury Park the previous June—had finished thirty-fourth overall to help Adams State win its own NCAA title.

You could deny my protest, but no one could deny our runners.

CHAPTER TWENTY

THE DAY BEFORE EVERY state meet is like a land rush. Teams stake their pop-up tents into the grounds around Woodward Park, marking their home base for the weekend.

It's a flashy, disorienting scene—team colors as far as you can see.

These tents are where prerace nerves either begin or end, where music is played to either amp up or relax. They aren't where a state race is won or lost, though. With their nylon covers and metal legs, pop-up tents can be flashy. On the cool, blue-sky morning of November 27, our all-yellow tent reached nearly ten feet tall and thirty feet wide, with a garland, stockings, an inflatable candy cane, and a Christmas tree near its front door.

But pop-up tents don't come with a foundation. That has to be laid months earlier. Ours was as solid as the mountains surrounding Big Bear. We all knew it. This day was about making a claim as the greatest team in the history of California distance running. Perfection in the Marmonte League and at section finals did little for me. State was different, though. I really wanted our boys to pull it off on this stage.

Before the race, just before our boys left Newbury Park's yellow tent for the starting line, I pulled Colin aside. "Come with me."

I often pulled our runners aside individually to share my observations or advice. I wanted only Colin to hear these instructions.

"When you get to the top of the hill at two miles, you go hard down that hill, and when you get to the bottom, keep pushing to the next kilometer mark."

Lex and Leo could have hung on with Colin. So why was I telling this to Colin? With the exception of Woodbridge, when he'd run on an injured ankle, he had proven he was our fittest runner. He had done things in workouts that had surpassed even my high standards. He was our senior and deserved to know how his best attributes could be used in this race. You could debate which of our Newbury Park runners would win if we held a dream race with each at their high school peak—Nico in 2019–20 versus Colin in 2021–22 versus Lex and Leo and Aaron in 2022–23. But in this season, on this day, I felt Colin would be the only one who could make that aggressive a move at that juncture in the race and still hold on. Everyone else on the team knew I wanted them to surge at the next kilometer mark. If Colin surged before that mark, the others would think he was superior that day.

The boys race was the second to last of the day, not starting until 12:30 p.m. Knowing the gap between our team's potential and everyone else in the race calmed the nerves that pop up before every race, but we stayed near our tent nonetheless, trying to keep a low profile until the Division 1 girls race at 11:00 a.m. Newbury Park was leading in the team-score race after one mile, and so was Sam, who came through in 5:20, one second ahead of Anna McNatt, from Sacramento. By the second mile, both Sam and the Newbury team had fallen behind by a fraction. Our boys stood along the barriers, cheering, as Sam entered the final straightaway in the lead, a state title less than 100 meters away, when McNatt kicked past. Sam finished second in 17:08. Our girls team did as well, with a team average of 18:06. It was the second-fastest average of any team in any division that day.

It was the boys' turn.

Among runners, there is a famous video from the 2007 California state meet of German Fernandez's course-record run. As soon as he crossed the finish line in 14:24, he fell to the grass and lay on his back, exhausted. He could have stayed there for a while if he wanted; the runner-up was nearly a minute and a half behind, after all. As I became a high school coach and learned the rhythms of the California schedule, the video struck me as a memorable—and cautionary— moment, because in the weeks that followed his record, Fernandez, fatigued, didn't run well at national-level championship meets. Effort like that is incredibly taxing and even more incredibly difficult to reproduce so soon. It was on my mind in the days leading up to state as I told our boys that if they ran so hard at state that they needed to collapse at the finish line, they would be in trouble, because they would have screwed our chances at being ready for RunningLane.

We knew we would win state. But we wanted to *crush* Running-Lane.

State, then, required a balance. As much as we owed it to ourselves to not take away from RunningLane, we felt we also owed it to fans not to repeat how we'd casually won Southern Section Finals the week before by separating with a hard first mile, then relaxing. Did we want to flex a little bit? Yes.

When we went to dinner the night before the state meet in Fresno, half the restaurant must have been runners. And when we walked to our table, I could see heads turning to look at us passing, hearing whispers of "Newbury Park."

The next day, the boys surrounded me one final time at the starting line.

"Something big is going to happen," I told them. "You're going to shock everyone."

I didn't think they realized how fast they were because it had become so normal for us to dominate. The team's success depended on pushing ourselves. With five guys who could push one another, our depth made all the difference and made each meet a game of "Who's going to win?" Even for me it was really, really difficult to predict.

By now, our race strategy was well established. But we stuck with it for a reason: It worked. Colin, Lex, Leo, and Aaron ran the first mile, in that order, all in 4:32. The gap between our four and the next-fastest chaser was one second. Watching the live scoring on my phone, we had 16 points.

When our four came through the next timed marker at 2.1 miles between 10:01 and 10:02, the gap was 10 seconds. It was like watching our mile-repeat workout at Conejo Creek South earlier in the month, our boys jockeying for position with no one else around.

Colin won with his almost peerless kick in 14:26.5, the second-fastest time in Woodward Park's history, only two seconds off Fernandez's record. Leo was next in 14:28. Lex was third in 14:30. Aaron came through in 14:46, and then the wait began. Nine seconds passed before the next finisher, from Davis. Then an individual qualifier who wouldn't factor into team scores took sixth. Down the chute, in a run that no one would have predicted even six weeks earlier, sprinted Daniel. His 15:11 was good for fifth on our team, and seventh overall. The last of the race's finishers wouldn't pass through for another four minutes, but our team score was already easy to tabulate. We had already won with 16 points.

Let's rewrite the record books. We'd done that. Again.

Our team had averaged 14:43, shaving two seconds off our own national record for 5,000 meters, which we'd set a month earlier at the Clovis Invitational. For more than three decades, Woodward Park had hosted thousands of runners from arguably the fastest cross country state in the country. Yet in just one day, Colin had run the second-fastest time in course history, Leo the third-fastest, and Lex the fifth-fastest. Incredibly, Nico's time of 14:28.5 from the 2019 state meet now ranked fourth.

Despite competing against the largest schools in the state with the country's biggest population, one high school had nearly outrun everybody. It was the lowest total team score in Division 1 boys history, beating the 23 scored by Thousand Oaks in 1993, and also a state-meet record for any division, in either gender, lower even than the 18 scored by San Francisco University High's girls in 1997.

No, this wasn't perfection. And yet it was still unlike anything ever before seen at a California state meet, with all of its history of producing national team champions.

That afternoon, as was customary, CIF merged the day's results from all five division races to produce a hypothetical all-state outcome, regardless of school size. Against 117 other high schools and 986 runners, Newbury Park would still have run so fast that our boys would have finished first, second, third, fourth, eleventh, fourteenth, and forty-sixth overall, for a team total of just 21 points. No other team in the merger would have finished with less than 294 points. I later heard Rich Gonzalez describe it as "the greatest performance in high school cross country history."

I was happy we'd won, happy we'd set team-score records, happy that Daniel placed as high as he did. He had flown under the radar in college recruiting, and I wanted him to get the attention he had earned. Daniel's comeback was a reminder of how seasons never go to plan, and of how winning requires being so good you can overcome the inevitable setback. All of the kids were deserving of the title and the recognition.

Nonetheless, I was conflicted. Happiness didn't equal satisfaction. I was bummed that we had just barely missed a perfect score. I knew we were never going to have that opportunity back. It was on my mind because late that season, I'd started to believe I would only coach in high school one more year. I knew I wasn't coming back.

CHAPTER TWENTY-ONE

THE THING PEOPLE DON'T tell you about doing the extraordinary is how much of the process looks ordinary.

We approached the days before RunningLane like a typical championship week. In running, training in the final days before the biggest race usually tapers down to a lower volume than usual, built on the idea of keeping runners fresh on the big day. Our six days between state and RunningLane walked the balance between tapering while not de-training, working to keep our guys fresh but still strong. Sunday featured slow miles to keep them active with little stress. A few days later, on grass, one fast mile was followed by as much rest as they needed to fully recover, and a pair of 800s in about 2:12, with a three-mile cooldown. Morning runs had ended.

Running cross country for a certain time was never something I wanted runners fixated on, worried it would put an artificial cap on their potential on any given race day. However, the intensity of our workouts in the months and weeks leading into RunningLane had sparked the natural discussion among our team about whether breaking Dathan Ritzenhein's national record of 14:10 was possible.

On a great day, with good weather, firm ground, and competitors who would actually help us push the pace, I believed our entire top four might go sub-14.

At our program's first national championship in 2018, our runners had gone through the weekend with wide-eyed amazement at the surreality of actually being there. A year later when we returned to Portland, I saw a steely seriousness. As soon as we arrived in Alabama on December 2, a Thursday, two days before the race, I saw unbridled confidence. That night, I looked outside our Airbnb in Huntsville and saw our team sitting outside together, looking up at the stars. Through the windows, I could hear them talking about what could happen Saturday morning.

The RunningLane Championships were not Nike Cross Nationals. For one, the John Hunt Park course, which often hosted NCAA regional meets, was hillier than we'd expected and had thicker grass than Portland's Glendoveer course, which I thought could slow times. Temperatures were unseasonably warm, in the high sixties, as we familiarized ourselves with the course on Friday with our typical day-before warm-up of running each mile of the course progressively faster, followed by hard, 100-meter strides to prepare their bodies to go fast.

The logistics were also different. There were no mandatory meetings to attend, guest speakers to listen to, or hotels to stay in. This was good and bad. I could set our own schedule; very good. To our guys who were used to the pomp and big production value Nike put into NXN, and who remembered the dogfight it took to win our team title in 2019, however, I had to reinforce that they couldn't let their guard down just because this was a newer meet we were heavily favored to win; tricky. A different kind of national championship required a different kind of strategy. I felt we were running against ourselves as a team, and that no one would challenge us. At the end of our premeet warm-up Friday afternoon, I pointed out a pond along the course inside John Hunt Park.

"If we can get four of you guys in the top five, I'll swim in that," I said.

It was a serious bet: I'm terrified of snakes—and that pond looked like one that would be filled with them.

COLIN SAHLMAN

The day before, when we showed up for our premeet, I was superexcited because when we would walk past our competition, they would just stare at us. There was a look of fear in their faces. We were just smiling knowing we were the ones to beat and that everyone was scared of us. The course itself was not as flat as we'd expected—some dips here, one hill just before two miles. It wasn't anything crazy, but more of a challenge than I thought it was going to be. Still, walking around the course that day gave us huge confidence going into the race because we knew that we were already in our competitors' heads before the race started.

A different kind of race also called for a different objective from what we'd had before. We aimed to break records, period. To have four guys run under Ritzenhein's 14:10, they would have to trust our training, which had conditioned them to run up front and control the race if others wouldn't. Doing the math, I believed they had to run the first mile in 4:25. It was nothing we hadn't prepared to do. It was as if I were back in the front of the room at Dos Vientos Community Center, setting ambitious goals. Four runners from one team should not be able to outrun the rest of the country. And yet, on the right day, I knew it was achievable.

That belief was tested, though, when I woke Saturday morning and saw a small amount of rain had moved in overnight. The boys championship race was scheduled to go off at 9:30 a.m., the last of eight races held on the course that morning. The seven previous races would undoubtedly mash any spots that had collected moisture into speed-sucking mud.

We moved through the final hours before the starting gun with practiced repetition. Parents helped build the two pop-up tents Tanya and I had bought the night before, zip-tying them together and zipping up the walls for privacy. The boys and the girls, who were also racing at RunningLane, warmed up with two miles, the last quicker than the first. Our team gently deflected selfie requests. *Come find us afterward!* In the tent, the kids spent their final minutes listening to music. I ditched my black Newbury Park jacket in the tent. I wore running shoes and shorts because I had to run today, too—sprinting between the points on the course where I needed to be.

Walking toward the starting line with our team, I felt excitement but not nerves. Before COVID, a national championship marked the summation of a season. But here, now, was a moment we had built toward since our title celebration in the drenching rain in Portland in 2019, our last true competition against a credible national field. Following NXN's cancelation, our best-case scenario had come true—all of the best boys teams in the country had signed up to race at RunningLane to turn it into a legitimate national title meet. Everybody, it seemed, wanted to take a stab at us.

There was Cheyenne Mountain of Colorado Springs, which had been billed as our toughest competitor. There was Jesuit of Portland, which had become one of the fastest teams to come out of a state that regularly produced strong contenders. There was Zane Bergen of Niwot, the Colorado state champ who trained in the altitude near Boulder, Colorado, and Michigan's Riley Hough, whose unbeaten season was all the more impressive after he broke one of Ritzenhein's course records. I hadn't discussed any of the other competitors with our team, though. I didn't see the point. If we ran the way we were capable of, we could—should—be all alone, one-two-three, at least, with four in the top five.

Speakers around the course blaring electronic music paused briefly for an announcement. *The race is starting in five minutes.* The thumping bass resumed.

Fans surrounded us on our walk from the tent to the line, cameras out and voices loud, and I wasn't going to let any more distractions creep in, right before the race. I pulled our runners out into the field about 30 meters in front of our assigned box on the starting line.

Standing in grass turned brown by the first cold of the season, we huddled one last time. We were past the point of motivational speeches.

My last words were instructional: "If you guys want to win this the way we want to win it, we need to go out the first mile in 4:25."

It wasn't how I typically delivered prerace instructions. I never emphasized time. But my gut told me that several of our guys had a chance to go under 14 minutes flat—maybe even four under 14:10.

"There should be no hesitation," I said. "We've done workouts that geared us toward this."

I looked at Daniel, Hector, and Dev Doshi and reminded them of their instructions to be in the top forty or top fifty after one mile in around 4:40 and to work their way up. Just as Jace was a master at staying patient early in races and then picking off the runners who had exhausted themselves trying to match Nico's pace, I wanted Daniel, Hector, and Dev to be ready to move up in the final mile.

Other teams were lining up.

"Let's go make history today," I said.

I like to watch runners in the moments before the gun is raised. Body language reveals confidence, doubt, or readiness—or all three—that athletes won't divulge in their words. Ours threw their extra clothes and water bottles aside and lined up. They looked ready, which was my cue to get going. I ran down the course's opening straightaway, past the first mile marker, toward where the runners would pass at two kilometers. It is such an important part of any 3-mile or 5K race because everyone gets to the mile fast only to inevitably slow down. We had trained not to slow there but to speed up, to push through to two kilometers. It had its benefits logistically, too. Mile markers draw crowds hoping to hear splits over the loudspeakers. If

I stood alongside them, there was no way our athletes could hear me or my instructions.

Long runs in Holcomb Valley. Oxygen-sucking runs at Skyline. Mile repeats at Conejo Creek. Everything had built toward competing our best against the nation's best. I laughed as I ran by the pond I had promised to jump in if we finished with four in the top five. *I might be swimming in that later.*

I listened for the gun and looked away from the start.

I am a coach who believes in the science of running. However, I also can't help believing in superstition. I never watch after the gun goes off, out of fear that bad luck will lead to runners tangling and falling.

Bang. The volume rose.

Hearing the race, I thought positive thoughts for a couple of minutes until it was time to look up.

COLIN SAHLMAN

Our first quarter mile had to have been insane. I don't know what it was, but I just remember it being an all-out sprint at the start and that it was hard, right away.

We weren't dressed in our usual gold and black. Just as at NXN, RunningLane's organizers had created custom uniforms for each team, and if you wanted to find Newbury Park, you had to look for a checkerboard singlet in shades of blue. The problem was, other teams were in similar hues and patterns. Finding Lex, Leo, Colin, and Aaron wasn't hard though: Two minutes in, all were at the front, just where they needed to be, legs churning on a slight downhill. But there were hundreds in this field, and I struggled to locate Hector, Daniel, and Dev in the pack behind them.

The leaders approached the first mile. I needed to see if they had found their rhythm after sprinting nearly the first 400 to get in front of the field. I had to hear that split. I needed that split near 4:25. What I heard instead was a conversation an adult standing next to me was trying to start. He called himself a Newbury Park superfan. I wasn't going to shoo him away, but I was also a little busy at the moment.

"*4:31 through the lead,*" said the announcer over the speakers ringing the course.

The announcer had undersold it: The first mile split was actually 4:29, four seconds off our goal. That doesn't sound like a lot, but typically, you expect the first mile to be the fastest. In cross country, "negative splits"—running the second half of a race faster than the first—are the exception.

I knew rain had created soft patches of grass overnight, but I didn't understand why our runners weren't going harder. Good runners such as Hough, Bergen, and Gary Martin of Pennsylvania were still hanging around. Only later did I realize that the muddy patches were softer than I'd anticipated.

And only after the race did I realize the leaders had run the first mile in 4:29. Operating off incomplete data, a coaching decision-tree started in my head. I had two ways of thinking about this. Do I just let them race, or do we stick to the plan and still go for this record? A 4:31 first mile is still right around a low 14-minute 5K. It was fast enough to win, but right on the edge for making history. The leaders were still close to the necessary pace to break Ritzenhein's record and destroy the team 5K average record. But they would have to push hard through two kilometers to do that.

As the leaders approached where I stood, I caught my first glimpse of Daniel, in the larger pack behind the front. *Yes!* Our top five were in good shape, in terms of scoring. In terms of time, we had work to do. In cross country, I wanted to pick my spots of when to be vocal and when to give instruction. But as our top four passed in the lead, I let them have it, yelling as loud as I could in a voice as deep as I could go.

"We need to get going! Now!"

Lex looked at me. Colin was staring dead ahead. Leo kept his head down, pushing. But it was Aaron who heard what I had yelled and bolted ahead by a stride, as if saying with his surge that he was going to push the pace since no one else would. I wasn't entirely surprised. Traditionally stronger in the 800 and the mile, Aaron was capable of quick bursts. Plus, he was coming off the best training block I had ever seen from him.

AARON SAHLMAN
I'm a little bit stronger in the beginning and I tend to die out in the end, so that season I usually took our team out through a blazing pace to kill anyone's legs who tried to stick with us, which worked in our California meets. Once it came to RunningLane, I heard Sean yell at me that if we wanted to run fast, we were too slow. At that point I just decided, *All right, here we go*, and then kind of went for a little sprint of about 10 meters, just to push the pace a little bit, and then kept it close to 4:40 pace throughout the next mile.

COLIN SAHLMAN
I remember thinking, *Wow, Aaron is having a really great day, and if he keeps this up, he's gonna be really hard to beat.*

As soon as I spotted our seventh man, Dev Doshi, pass by, I took off running across the field by myself. My attention was split. I was trying to spot the short but steep hill that led into the two-mile marker. I needed to locate a place to stand by the downhill with about 1,000 meters left. I had to spot the four-wheeler that drove ahead of the leaders and sift through singlets in orange and white to find our blue. Aaron was still in front, with Colin and Lex and Leo right behind. For all of my concern at the first mile, it hit me for the first time that our boys might still run sub-14.

But what we needed was to stay in rhythm and to shake the few who were still in the race—Bergen and Hough. I intercepted our lead group again along the course, 12 minutes in, on purpose. I wanted them to see me at 12 minutes knowing there were roughly two minutes of hard running left. From their training, I believed with everything I had that no one else had done in workouts what Newbury Park's boys had. If they could just go . . . if they could just push it . . . if they could just hold on . . . if they could just trust and believe . . . they could drop everyone, and every record.

Yet no one was making a move, even though everyone was capable of it, an inaction that was maddening. Bergen was moving up on Colin's left shoulder until they were level at the very front. One of my cardinal rules of racing is that you must have a sense of patience when you decide to *go*, to tap into your finishing kick. Kick too early and you die before the finish line. Going too late is the stuff regret is made of. Bergen was trying to move early against some of the best kickers in the country. Lex looked bouncy and strong, sizing up who was still left.

"You need to drop these guys—*now!*" I yelled, my voice going hoarse. "Drop them!" Lex definitely heard me. I felt like I could see the wheels turning in his head. I couldn't read Colin and Leo—until they moved. Boy, did Colin, Lex, and Leo drop them. It was instant, as if they were deep into a kilometer-repeat workout at Pepper Tree and I had just told them to think about *now*—to put a hard repetition in right *now*.

I moved, too, cutting across a field. Below me, down a slight hill, I could see the raucous finishing atmosphere awaiting runners at the end. Organizers had placed the finish between a pair of little rises in the grass that created natural stadium seating. On either side of the final straightaway, what appeared to be fans standing two dozen deep lined the hills, held back from the course by railings. That concentration of people left a spot empty along the course with about 400 meters to go. It was my last-ditch spot to stand and deliver one final instruction ahead of what I hoped would be one last move by our top guys.

After putting in all that work to get the race's pace back on track for a record attempt, Aaron was now fading. He had sacrificed his own ambitions for the day to set up the success of his teammates, who were flying a few seconds ahead of him toward the finish. Bergen was known for having a kick, but I didn't believe it was stronger than Lex's, Leo's, or Colin's. They were ahead with 90 seconds to go. The race would be won by someone from Newbury Park—but which of the three?

In our program's history, we had already shown we could produce a national champion, an outlier individual talent. During this season, we'd sought a different kind of domination on a national stage. This is what we had envisioned—four from Newbury Park in the top seven.

Running right toward where I stood, Leo went to try to take the lead, but Colin matched his move. They were each running 4:18 or close to it for their last mile. They passed under an inflatable yellow arch with BEAT YESTERDAY written on it, our marking for around 200 meters to go in an all-out sprint. Colin probably had the better kick, but timing would decide this.

COLIN SAHLMAN

I wasn't the favorite going into the race. Almost all media platforms were choosing Riley Hough because he was undefeated all year, winning all fourteen of his races. But to me, that meant he'd already run way too much and that I would be fresher. With about a half a mile to go, I glanced over and saw Zane Bergen. I wasn't expecting to see him with us. Spit was coming out of his mouth and he looked dead. I was hurting, but seeing him like that, I thought, *Well, he's hanging on, but based off of the look, I don't think he's going to be here much longer.* I knew I would beat him. I didn't know if I could beat Lex and Leo.

While running premeet, I'd taken note that a giant yellow inflatable arch over the course marked the last 200 meters or so. Passing it, I knew it was literally an all-out sprint to the finish. With no one in front of me, it hit me that *Dang, I can really win this!* Then, Leo got right up to my shoulder, and I could see his face. He really wanted it, and I was a little nervous because he looked strong. About the last 50 meters, my legs felt dead, superlactic, with nothing left. *If anyone comes up on me right now, I can't respond,* I thought. *If Leo has another gear, he's going to win.*

They ran away from me down to the finish; I saw Colin cranking, and Lex and Leo fighting to hold on, then Colin pulling away. Down the hill they charged into the gully filled with fans, the volume football-stadium loud. Colin played his kick well. When Leo tried again to take the lead in the final straightaway, Colin was gone. I turned to the runners passing by me up the hill and saw Aaron and yelled at him to keep catching the dying runners ahead of him. Lex, Leo, and Colin crossed the line, and I had no idea what time they had just clocked. All I knew was a roar had risen up from the crowd down the hill and that we had gone one-two-three.

Daniel went by next. I'd lost count of the runners ahead of him, but estimated he was in the forties. I'd lost track of Hector, but saw Dev not far behind Daniel and then knew the team championship was ours without even needing to look at the standings.

What I still didn't know was our times.

I ran toward the finish line, where such a crush of people had gathered that I couldn't get through.

What were the times?

The field was now pouring in through the finish line, but I wasn't watching anymore, desperately attempting to get to our guys.

What were the times?!

Around me, people were holding up their phones. Some who saw me tried to take pictures.

A stranger locked eyes with me. "Hey, Coach! I got you."

He walked into the crowd and, like the parting of the waters, told me to follow. We reached the railing separating the crowd from the finish line. He yelled at me to get in there. I smiled and jumped the fence into the athlete area. As a rule, finish lines are chaos, even at small meets; at a national championship, the scene is only magnified, with dozens of runners staggering to stay on their feet, handfuls more on the ground, exhausted, their chests rising and falling, and others being interviewed with cameras pressed into their faces seconds after running as hard as their bodies allowed. The air was electric.

I saw a scoreboard and finally saw the times.

The times!

In the history of US prep cross country, nobody had covered 5,000 meters faster than Colin's 14:03.29. It was amazing to watch him pull away in the final 300, closing his last quarter mile in about 60 seconds, on grass. It was insane. And I swear, when I saw him at the line, he told me he felt good, that he could have gone faster. Aaron won that for his brother, knowing that pushing the pace after the first mile was going to screw up Aaron's own chances in the end, even as it paved the way for Colin's success.

COLIN SAHLMAN

Sean had pulled me aside before the race and told me there was no reason why I couldn't break Ritzenhein's record, or even go sub-14. It felt like it was impossible to do, though. Even at the end, I had no idea whether I'd come close or not because at the finish line the scoreboard was flipped away from the runners, toward the cameras. When I found out I ran 14:03.29, it was an insane moment where it registered that *Holy—Sean's prerace instincts had been right.*

The race would have been five seconds slower if Aaron hadn't pushed after the first mile like he had. He even told me after the race, "I did that for you guys, just to try and kill everyone else around us." I thought that was selfless of him knowing that he wasn't the favorite, but that he was still going to take it like that and make other people hurt.

We were mobbed at the finish line—cameras everywhere, everyone asking for photos and autographs. I was still recovering at the finish line when I heard a guy who looked like he was my age yelling my name as he leaned over a railing. "Colin, Colin!" he said, reaching out. He handed me a Chick-fil-A gift card.

We had a champion and a record holder. But we also wanted to cement our place as the fastest team in history by displaying our depth. Leo was now number two all-time, in 14:05.07. Lex was third all-time in 14:05.49. Even Bergen slipped under Ritzenhein's record by running 14:09.91—and Hough was right with him in 14:10.56. Aaron was sixth in 14:14.38, picking off a runner in the final 200. Daniel Appleford, our trusty number five, ran 14:44.92 for forty-second. If you couldn't break 15 minutes, you wouldn't have made our top seven, with Hector Martinez (14:52.72) and Dev Doshi (14:59.51) rounding out our team.

Our top five had averaged 14:14 per runner—only four seconds slower, on average, than the national record that had stood for twenty-one years. Just as we'd expected since Big Bear the previous summer, the clock was our toughest competition. In the team race, our 28 points were 110 fewer than second-place Cheyenne Mountain's. By way of comparison, the lowest boys team score in Nike Cross Nationals history was 77.

I was incredibly happy for the guys. I was overcome not with relief, but excitement. Knowing the debacle Daniel had gone through with his health, through five weeks of not running, just to get back to this point—it was incredible. Sitting in the hospital in Big Bear, I'd thought he was done for the season. I think he did, too.

It was now late morning, and a mist was falling over John Hunt

Park. I love warm weather, the kind we get in Newbury Park almost every day. But the cold, the mist, the true cross country conditions, brought me back to NXN in 2019, and the Nico-and-Jace-led team that set the bar so high and went after goals that nobody thought they could achieve. And they did. And so had the next generation that followed them. I was proud of these athletes, who had created something so special on this day that it may never be replicated in high school cross country.

We were interviewed for what felt like hours. Usually, I'm extremely strict about our athletes' cooldowns, making sure they finish them before ever doing interviews. But on this day, I shrugged. They'd get their slow couple miles in later. What these guys deserved was to soak in the moment they had created.

To get back to our team tent, we had to cross through a field filled with outstretched arms, all holding phones, all yelling, "Newbury Park!" Is this what a rock star feels like? Pictures were autographed. Shoes were autographed. Someone shoved a child's doll toward the boys, and—sure, why not?—everyone autographed that, too. Huntsville was famous for its space industry, and surrounded by that many people, hearing the noise, seeing three under 14:10, it felt as if we were riding a rocket headed toward the uncharted. People told me they'd driven from Georgia, from Florida, from hundreds of miles, just to watch the race. In the crowd, I saw Stephen Pifer, a friend and former Nike professional, who'd traveled with his son to watch us. Newbury Park's athletic director texted congratulations. An older man in a Newbury Park letterman's jacket waded through the crowd toward us, saying he was an alumnus from the 1970s.

"Get in here!" I told him. We put him at the front of the line for a picture.

Michael Crouch, the runner I'd coached at Queens who had inspired me with how hard he was willing to push himself for his goals, had driven out to watch the race, and I saw his eyes widen. It felt like I'd come full circle, enjoying the moment with someone who had been there at the first stop of my coaching odyssey. The crowd was deeper than at any other race I had ever attended.

"What the hell's going on?" Michael said, laughing, in awe of the mob gathered around our squad.

The previous year and a half of COVID had knocked so many people out emotionally and physically, which was why this moment felt so different from any other. Instead of that period hurting us, it had made us better. We had fought through, kept training, kept the kids busy, and kept their minds on setting national records. We learned how to train without racing. We learned how to focus on all the little things even more. We learned how to raise our personal standards and expectations.

We finally herded the team back into our tent. Fans were still outside, as if waiting for an encore. The crowd was yelling because of what they had just witnessed, but the people outside our proverbial tent had never seen so many things that had led to this moment.

Only we had seen Hector and Dev step up when Daniel went down. Only we had seen Colin take a stronger leadership role. Only we had seen how our top four shared the burden of the hardest workouts, holding one another accountable. Only we had seen the work that put our girls program on a similar trajectory, with Sam McDonnell finishing sixth at RunningLane, and the team finishing in the top ten. That camaraderie and sense of purpose is what makes a team.

I was all energy, the moment still surreal to me because I hadn't fully comprehended our team average of 14:14. But my gut told me what further analysis would reveal: We were the best high school cross country team . . . ever.

DANIEL APPLEFORD

People look at high schoolers and think, "They're not going to run fast, right?" Newbury Park definitely pushed back on that expectation, showing you could train a certain way to gain more fitness and push that barrier of what is possible. Now, high schoolers are running so fast. I do think we had our role in that. People wanted to be that Newbury Park team and wanted to have that same kind of culture.

The boys cooled down and we found a restaurant for lunch, the same one where the runner-up team from Colorado was also eating. They played shuffleboard while Lex and Leo filmed a video for their YouTube channel. People started showing me a tweet from Ritzenhein, the now-former record holder:

"Wiped from the record boards! Slowly fading into obscurity . . . Really impressive racing from these high school boys! Newbury Park with crazy depth. And of course my Niwot neighbor Zane Bergen and MI champion Riley Hough all 14:10 or faster."

It was a classy move from running royalty.

To think, six years earlier I had been in a community center, making promises I didn't know that I could keep to parents and athletes who didn't know me. Ethan Duffy's buy-in gave me credibility, and making state in 2016 only reinforced it. When I'd questioned my own decision to coach high schoolers in 2017, it was Nico's grit during his pool workouts and Jace's dogged belief in what we were building that gave me the conviction that I had to stay with these kids. Then Nico won a title and normalized the pursuit of excellence among his teammates. The bar went higher. Because of their precedent, every runner who followed them into our program arrived with a default belief in their limitless capacity and a culture of consistent work.

I thought of how proud I was of how much the kids, their parents, and everyone around the program had achieved and sacrificed. None of this had happened in a vacuum. My grandpa was right. *Peaks and valleys. Progress isn't linear.* I took it in—a decade carving my own path through running's wilderness. Six testing, thrilling, all-in high school seasons. Fourteen unbelievable minutes.

That night, the team and I wound down with buckets of balls and plates of food at Topgolf, a multilevel driving range, in Huntsville. A wariness tugged at my mind. We were the best team that ever was. Yet I didn't want to celebrate too much. To me, it only deepened my hunger. What was next? *Game on,* I thought. There aren't five minutes that go by that I'm not thinking about training, or getting faster, and averaging 14:14 had my mind racing. Full throttle.

I thought about whether we should repeat our Sundown Series in Arizona. Whether we could get our elite boys entered into pro meets. I knew Colin, unlike Nico, was a miler at heart. Where could we get him and the rest of our guys an opportunity indoors to break four minutes? I pulled out my phone and texted Ray Flynn.

My mind was still running.

I don't know if high school cross country will ever see one team average 14:14 again. But if it happens, and our record is broken, maybe people will say that a 14:14 average is just not fast—it's just not. And it will be because of Newbury Park.

EPILOGUE

Even at nearly 10:00 p.m., a summer heat wave radiated inside a sold-out Stade de France on August 2, 2024.

I sat next to Tanya in section X4 overlooking the finish line in the stadium's second deck, watching the opening night of track and field at the Olympics. We were only a short train ride north of central Paris, but it felt like a million miles from my first Newbury Park High School practice at Pepper Tree eight years earlier.

Below us on a purple track, carried by the rhythmic clapping of nearly eighty thousand fans, Nico clicked off lap after lap. He was no longer wearing the black and gold of Newbury Park, where he had first emerged, nor the yellow and navy of Northern Arizona, where he had become a two-time NCAA champion, nor the black of his new professional sponsor, Adidas. He was in red, white, and blue, competing in his first Olympics for the United States.

I'd watched Nico prove he was the best in California and among US high schoolers from up close. Four months earlier, when he had proven himself the best among collegians, too, I had cheered from the stands at an indoor facility in Boston. When he ran the Olympic Trials, there was no way I wasn't going to be watching live in Eugene,

Oregon. The Olympics have always held a special power over me. Watching them on a grainy television counts as one of my earliest memories. I often categorized Newbury Park's biggest achievements by using the phrase "Olympic moment." But this was a real Olympic moment: in France, watching as Nico held his own with the world's best distance runners, traveling 6.2 miles at a faster speed than he'd clocked during even his hardest high school mile repeats.

In front of us, we were watching the legacy of Newbury Park grow. Again.

Nearly three years earlier in Alabama, I'd contacted Ray Flynn after RunningLane because I wanted Colin's national title to act like a springboard into a big indoor performance. On February 8, 2022, with a lane assignment courtesy of Flynn, Colin toed the line at the Armory and beat a field that included professionals while running 3:58.81, his first sub-four and the third-fastest indoor mile ever by a high schooler.

It was like adding gas to an already raging blaze. One month later, back at the Armory for an attempt at the high school four-by-mile relay record with Lex, Leo, Aaron, and Colin, meet organizers anticipated such a crowd for our much-publicized run that they assigned us security and a private greenroom underneath the track. Then the boys went out and smashed the record by 30 seconds, running 16:29. Aaron led off in 4:11, Leo ran 4:06, Lex ran 4:07, and Colin finished in 4:03. Afterward, when I tried to say hello to my mom, who was watching in the stands, I had to wade through autograph seekers to reach her.

In May of 2022, Colin closed his high school career under one of the biggest spotlights in world track and field, running in the Bowerman Mile at the Prefontaine Classic at famous Hayward Field in Eugene. Colin clocked a 3:56.24, the third-fastest mile in prep history behind only Alan Webb and Jim Ryun.

Colin graduated and joined Nico at Northern Arizona, and that fall, the Lumberjacks won the NCAA cross country championship. In April 2024, Colin lowered his personal best to 3:33.96 in the 1,500 meters—the second-fastest time in NCAA history. Later that spring he advanced to the semifinals of the 1,500 at the US Olympic Track & Field Trials.

Before graduating with Colin in 2022, Daniel Appleford ran 8:58.4 to take second at California's state track and field championships in the 3,200. He committed to Colorado School of Mines. Just as he said he would, he is studying to become an engineer.

As a freshman at Adams State in 2022, Fiona Hawkins, who represented Ireland internationally, ran 16:07.55 to break the Irish under-20 national record in the 5,000.

I hadn't sought to leave Newbury Park in 2022. I wanted to see out Lex, Leo, and Aaron's senior season and push our girls toward a state title I believed was imminent. But that summer, UCLA offered to make me its assistant coach in charge of distances, and I accepted the job. After I left, Tanya became Newbury Park's head coach for the season and guided the Panther boys to another cross country national championship, this time at Nike Cross Nationals. As a senior, Aaron didn't run as he had at RunningLane, by taking the pace out hard only to fall off. In Portland, wearing the same spikes Colin had worn en route to his historic race in Huntsville, Aaron hung back patiently, waited as the leaders fell off the pace, and then surged up the final Glendoveer hill in the last 400 meters to win the national title in 14:44.5. The time was seven seconds faster than the previous NXN course record—held by Nico. On the biggest stage in the sport, and in his final high school race, Aaron had just won his first cross country race as a high schooler. He now attends Northern Arizona University.

In late January 2023, almost two months after finishing eleventh overall at NXN and helping Newbury to the team title, Leo came from behind to beat a field of collegians and win the US under-20 cross country title. One month later, Leo finished as the fastest American at the under-20 world cross country championships in Australia, helping the US team medal at the event for the first time since 1982. That spring, before graduating and running for Stanford alongside Lex, Leo ran the seventh-fastest 1,500 meters in high school history, at 3:39.39.

In 2022, as a high school junior, Lex ran the second-fastest 5,000 in US prep history, a race that was a warm-up to a record-setting senior season. He won the 2022 CIF cross country individual title, helped Newbury Park win an NXN title, ran the number two high school time indoors at 3,000 meters, and then set his sights on the national 5,000-meter record. On May 26, 2023, Lex made his attempt at a meet in Los Angeles. The record didn't belong to Galen Rupp anymore. Only eighteen days earlier, Connor Burns, a star from Missouri, had run 13:37.30 to take 0.61 seconds off Rupp's eighteen-year-old standard. Weeks before Burns claimed it as his own, I had told Lex that breaking the record would require him to run the final two laps in 2:02. Everything about Lex's training that spring had been reverse engineered to put him in position to close fast and break that record.

Boom: 13:34.96. Another record. He and Leo went off to Stanford. Their YouTube channel remains a must-watch.

Little that Nico accomplished has surprised me. Still, what he did in 2024 could only be described as stunning. In the winter, he ran 12:57.14 to establish an NCAA indoor record for 5,000 meters and become, at twenty-one, the youngest American to run sub-13, and the first collegian to ever do it.

He was just getting started: Two months later, in March, Nico won NCAA indoor titles at both 3,000 and 5,000 meters, and in May, he broke the NCAA record for 10,000 meters by running 26:52.72 on a cool, windless night back home in Southern California. It was the fastest 10,000-meter debut in US history. After turning professional with Adidas, he placed third in the 10,000 meters at the US Olympic Trials to qualify for his first Olympic team.

Then, in France, Nico gutted out the race, staying with the lead group of about ten until the final 800 meters. He finished twelfth, in 26:58.11. I wasn't surprised. This was the same runner who, as a sophomore in high school, threw caution to the wind at CIF prelims at Trabuco Hills High School by putting himself in a position to blow up, but who stayed with the lead pack. Now everyone could see his toughness, on the world's biggest stage.

NICO YOUNG

On the day of a race, I try to do as little as possible. It's important to me to have time for myself to manage my anticipation. I tried to treat the morning of August 2, the day of the Olympic 10,000-meter final, no differently, spending the hours alone in my room inside the Olympic athletes' village, keeping my emotions low.

Anything was possible, I thought. Out of my luggage, I grabbed a rope of purple-and-white thread I'd been given by my high school coach as a sophomore and stretched, using the same routine I'd learned as a Newbury Park freshman.

Months earlier, when my season began, I had a hard time believing that, at only twenty-two, I would be in a position to make an Olympic team; representing the US in Los Angeles, in 2028, seemed more realistic. To be in France, then, looking at the Team USA jersey I would wear later that night inside Stade de France gave me excitement rather than nerves or fear. This was a dream I'd had since high school. More importantly, this was a dream I'd been repeatedly told was possible since high school.

I didn't even know that professional running existed when I showed up for my first Newbury Park practice at Pepper Tree as a freshman, let alone that it would be my future. I'm not sure I ever would have believed had it not been for Sean. As I began completing more difficult workouts, he began telling me that a moment like August 2 wasn't some far-off dream, saying, "You're someone who can make teams." When you're that young and you're running nine minutes in the 2 mile, it's hard to imagine improving enough to make a national team. It's one thing to be told that you can get there, but not something you can really comprehend. The leap from being an elite high school runner to world class was enormous; just making the team for 10K would require me to run my high school 2-mile PR back-to-back-to-back.

But when Sean said those things, it came off as credible, not crazy. He had spent time around pro runners and Olympic medalists and understood that world. To have him educate me on the possibilities of running on world stages and what it would take to reach them, and for him to believe such things were within my reach before I had enough evidence to ever believe it myself, instilled the confidence that got me to maximize my talent and to want those things for myself. When he told me I could run times that at first seemed outlandish, only for it to become reality, my trust in his predictions grew even more.

By the time I left Newbury Park I believed I could make national teams so much that it influenced my decision to go to Northern Arizona and run for Mike Smith, because I wanted to go for a pro career, and I thought NAU gave me the best opportunity. I believed it enough to commit my life to running.

My time with Sean at Newbury Park created a mindset of continuous confidence that I belonged, no matter the race. And Sean was the first one to believe in me and tell me that I could do it. Ever since, I've carried that mindset and my purple stretching rope with me as a connection to the time of my life that first made reaching Paris possible.

On the morning of the final, Sean sent me a text message, just as he'd done before every big race of my career.

"Hey Nico,

"Big day. It's so amazing to watch you compete in the Olympics tonight. It's a big deal, but just another race. This is just the beginning of your big pro career. I'm sure Mike has a plan so run tough and do your thing!!"

It was meaningful to get that, and I sent him a text back to let him know I'd seen his message.

That afternoon, I left the athletes' village with Grant Fisher. At the track we met Woody Kincaid, our fellow American in the 10,000, and began warming up. Before walking out to the track for the final inside

Stade de France, I peeked out of the door while standing underneath the stadium and I saw nearly eighty thousand fans and heard a crowd that was louder than anything I had ever heard. Anticipating a fast race, I told myself just to hang on to the front as long as possible. I felt like I had nothing to lose. When it was over, I was proud of how I'd competed. Once, being at this level would have felt surreal. But now, I believed I belonged. I had made a team; I guess Sean knew all along that this would happen.

Over the years, I have heard the debate about where Newbury Park's 2021 cross country season stacks up in history. I've heard comparisons to teams like Washington's Mead High from 1993, or York of Illinois from 1999. With respect to those teams, I don't believe there is any comparison. There have always been fast high schoolers, and runners with times even faster than ours. But what made Newbury Park unique was how our speed went beyond one outlier athlete. Newbury Park's boys *averaged* 14:14. We *averaged* 14:44 at Woodward Park. Those times would win state almost every single year, and we had five who could run it. Imagine having one basketball team with multiple scorers who ranked among the best in prep history. Across all of high school sports, I don't know if there has ever been a single team that has reached the magnitude of ours, one that can boast having so many athletes rank so high in their sport's history. Success was contagious. When you see seven runners break 15 minutes, it sparks the thought, *Why not me?*

Times in high school cross country and track and field have gotten increasingly faster in recent years. It's natural to wonder why. I believe Newbury Park was a big part of it. We broke those barriers. New shoe technology is a factor. But then again, Nico didn't have those shoes. What Nico developed—what we all developed—was the confidence that we could always go a little faster. And everything flowed from that belief.

ABOUT THE AUTHORS

Sean Brosnan is a two-time national high school coach of the year who built the Newbury Park High School distance squads into an award-winning national powerhouse. In addition to national championships, he led Newbury Park to boys state championships in 2018, 2019, and 2021 and a girls title in 2019. A native of Long Island, Brosnan broke into coaching as a volunteer at Queens University of Charlotte, where he helped coach athletes who won multiple NCAA individual titles. Brosnan lives in Big Bear, California, where he coaches a professional running team.

Chris Lear is the bestselling author of *Running with the Buffaloes* and *Sub 4:00: Alan Webb and the Quest for the Fastest Mile*. At Princeton University, Lear was a two-time cross-country captain and earned All-Ivy, All-East, and All-American honors on the track.

Andrew Greif is a sports reporter at NBC News whose award-winning work has also appeared in the *Los Angeles Times*, *GQ*, and *Runner's World*. Raised near Coos Bay, Oregon, the hometown of Steve Prefontaine, Greif competed on the track team at the University of Oregon.